CAMOUFLAGE UNIFORMS
OF THE SOVIET UNION AND RUSSIA

1937-TO THE PRESENT

Dennis Desmond

Schiffer Military History
Atglen, PA

ACKNOWLEDGMENTS

It was only after I started to write this book that I truly realized no book is ever written alone; most books are the result of the efforts of many. Books result from the combined knowledge and experiences of others, a willingness by others to share these experiences, and the subsequent author's summation of this information into a worthwhile format. This is what makes books possible. So too with this work.

Although many of the uniforms described here came from my own collection, I borrowed several for study and photographic purposes. Yuri Altschuler, Beryl Barnett, Joe Caliri, and Bob Hanes assisted me considerably by providing examples of World War II and Soviet army camouflage; Rich Masunari, Frank Mrakovcic and David Keeley allowed me to borrow their loved ones (uniforms and headgear) for seemingly weeks on end for photography; and Joe and Ray Parga, Matt Talarovic, and Ted Welch who loaned me several examples of uniforms and equipment so I could complete this project.

Also, I wish to thank Chris Smith for helping me with the information on the Soviet Desert/PMK Pattern and for providing photographs, Alan Wise who provided equipment and advised me on the ins and outs of the publishing world, Dennis Salakhov who gave me invaluable insight into the workings of the special services, and also Brad Jacobs for his assistance with many of the full-length uniform photographs. To Rich Choppa, Kenny Johnson and Mark Mikulski who modeled many of the uniforms and sacrificed much of their personal time and effort, I would like to express a special thanks. Kathy Curthoys, who kindly consented to edit previous articles on the KGB and MVD, was instrumental in the initial editing of this manuscript. There are also several sources who provided valuable information but who, alas, must remain anonymous.

Lastly, I wish to thank my wife, Rita, who put up with numerous militaria shows, uniforms stacked in corners awaiting photography, and those long, strenuous trips to Russia looking for uniforms and source material. Her patience and understanding allowed me to finish this work and to accomplish a very important goal.

Dennis Desmond
January 1, 1997
Alexandria, Virginia

To my wife, Rita, who helped me understand Thomas Jefferson's words:
"Whenever you do a thing, though it can never be known but to yourself, ask yourself how would you act were all the world looking at you, and act accordingly."

Book Design by Robert Biondi and Dennis B. Desmond.

Library of Congress Catalog Number: 97-80200.

Printed in China.
ISBN: 0-7643-0462-3

We are interested in hearing from authors with book ideas on related topics.

Published by Schiffer Publishing Ltd.
4880 Lower Valley Road
Atglen, PA 19310
Phone: (610) 593-1777
FAX: (610) 593-2002
E-mail: Schifferbk@aol.com.
Please write for a free catalog.
This book may be purchased from the publisher.
Please include $3.95 postage.
Try your bookstore first.

CONTENTS

PREFACE

My main purpose in writing this book was to assist the militaria collector and Russophile with the identification of Soviet and Russian camouflage uniforms. To accomplish this, I attempted to create a simple, easy to use picture guide to the myriad of camouflage uniforms of the Soviet Union and Russia.

In order to make identification easier, I described each uniform based on its use by specific military and security (special service) units. Furthermore, my goal here is to provide an accurate guide to camouflage uniforms of the former Soviet Union (FSU) and Russia which will help interested collectors and dealers with uniform identification. My intent is to help not only new collectors who are just beginning their collections, but also established collectors and dealers who have been buying and selling uniforms for years without fully understanding what they're seeing.

Lastly, I wish to provide a comprehensive reference book for intelligence agencies (in an unclassified format) and to assist them with the identification of many of the uniforms they're likely to see both in an historical and contemporary context, especially as contacts with Russian and Commonwealth soldiers increase. Only time and your continued use of this book will tell me if I have succeeded in any of these goals.

When I began collecting militaria more than ten years ago, I was dismayed to discover that some of the items I had purchased were either misidentified or fakes. Disillusioned, I was determined to learn as much as possible about the items I collected and become more informed. I soon discovered that there existed few reference books that described Soviet militaria. While there were those that described badges and medals, only one or two dealt with uniforms. Although the paucity of books dealing with badges and awards improved somewhat over recent years with the release of new references, and a virtual flood of Russian language reference material, there still exists a void in the modern uniform field which sorely needs to be filled.

During recent years several authors have attempted to describe the inner workings of the armed forces of the Soviet Union and now, Russia. Noted authors such as Harriet F. Scott and Amy Knight provided great insight into the politics of the Soviet and Russian military and special services. Notably lacking in these works, however, is basic information concerning the uniforms and equipment of specific units of the military and special services.

Of the few uniform books currently in print, most are obsolete, contain numerous errors, or are subject to the same hearsay and uncertainty that was common in Cold War publications. Even the Defense Intelligence Agency, which continuously strives to remain current on issues of East Bloc weapons and equipment development, was horribly behind with its 1991 publication *Uniforms of the Armed Forces of Eastern European Countries.*[1] Such out-of-date (and frequently incorrect) information negatively impacts the militaria hobby and creates unnecessary obstacles to the growth of its popularity.

It is safe to say camouflage uniforms are generally sold without the benefit of proper identification, or worse, are misidentified. Generally this is the result of a lack of knowledge on the part of the original seller who is unfamiliar with his products, retail dealers who either don't know what it is they are selling or attempt to misrepresent their products for the sake of a greater profit margin, and buyers who lack the necessary accurate information about the uniforms they eventually end up with.

This lack of authoritative information often forces collectors and dealers to accept information which is, at best, misleading. In Russia, former soldiers and quick-buck artists frequently assign names and uses to uniforms which are clearly wrong and often impossible; after all, it is much easier to sell a uniform if it belongs to *spetsnaz*[2] or elite forces as opposed to "Ivan the truck mechanic." As a result, uniforms have acquired nicknames and attributes far out of proportion to their actual uses.

On a recent trip to Russia, a "businessman"[3] in St. Petersburg explained how he had berets made which he sold to tourists as naval *spetsnaz* berets of the Leningrad military district. The berets could be distinguished from authentic berets only in that they lacked linings or factory marks indicative of factory-produced berets. The seller simply attached a red flash and airborne insignia to promote the fantasy. This businessman also admitted that he obtained his information from a hobby magazine that circulated in Russia. Even a little information in the hands of unscrupulous dealers can be harmful to the uninformed collector.

This scarcity of accurate information translates to a poorly informed group of collectors and sellers-people who spend millions of dollars yearly to pursue their hobbies and businesses. Only accurate information will assist these individuals in the pursuit of their vocation or avocation.

Of course, not all of this misinformation is intentional. During numerous conversations with members of the Soviet army (SA) and special services (*spetssluzhba* – SS), I found a lack of knowledge about uniform identification and development to be relatively widespread. This was due in large part to a lack of openness in professional journals of the Soviet military. What little information was present was usually shrouded in secrecy and suppositions or inaccurately described by disinterested and uninformed journalists.

Only recently have Russian professional journals such as *Krasnaia zvezda* and *Voennii mysl'* begun to address some of the more detailed questions concerning the development and fielding of uniforms and equipment, especially among the lesser known elite and special service units. This change in policy contributed significantly to the information which appears in this book; moreover, the new policy will undoubtedly lead to a better understanding within military and special services circles of the introduction and use of their camouflage uniforms.

Granted, with the breakup of the Soviet Union and the proliferation of new countries, it has become more difficult to keep track of the latest changes in the armies of the FSU or their uniforms. Nevertheless, I have attempted to provide my best estimate of the patterns currently in use by many republics of the FSU and their associated insignia (a more detailed work on camouflage uniforms of former Soviet republics is planned for the future).

As will be seen, reliable information from primary and secondary sources, although scarce, is available if one simply takes the time to do the research. Furthermore, reasonable conclusions about the history, development and implementation of camouflage uniforms can be made from existing Soviet primary sources through diligent research and deductive reasoning. The end result of this hard work is a detailed and informative guide to Soviet and Russian camouflage uniforms, which will lead ultimately, I hope, to a more informed, better equipped, collecting public.

Notes on Translation and Transliteration

I have chosen the Library of Congress system for transliteration of Russian names and sources. Where an accepted transliteration already exists, because of popularity or historical practice (Yeltsin instead of El'tsin), I have used the more familiar term. The translation of Russian words and phrases is another matter.

During my work as a translator and throughout most of my language training, I have noticed many authors make numerous errors in translation due to their incomplete understanding of intent and function. While I have based most translations on commonly accepted military terms, some of the military terminology is my own and may conflict with those of other researchers. I first looked at purpose, and then function, within the context of Russian to English translation. For example, миротворческие сили is rendered as "peacemakers" rather than "peacekeepers" which is more closely in line with the purpose of these forces and their function. In order to provide a common frame of reference among Russian and American collectors, I have provided a glossary for some of the more commonly seen terms for uniforms and equipment with their transliteration and translation.

Period Covered/Limitations

Uniforms shown in this book were produced from 1937 through 1997. Information concerning dates of issue, uniform names and specific units were gleaned from numerous primary and secondary sources. Open source materials such as television broadcasts and published materials from Russia and the FSU make up the bulk of the sources, while correspondence with members of the army and special services also served to resolve many unanswered questions. Still, some information remains unavailable as of this writing. Therefore, where published information was lacking or knowledgeable persons were unable to satisfactorily answer my questions, I took a stand based on best evidence. My "educated guesses" may or may not be proven correct as time passes.

Where years of issue are uncertain or the uniform examples I used lacked markings, I chose to use the year photographs or descriptions of the uniforms first appeared in print as a basis for determining their issue date. Many references show uniforms in use which were certainly issued several years prior. In this case, I extrapolated the date of issue based on information in the text and references to well-known military and government leaders and their dates of service.

This method provided a good basis for determining the approximate year of issue of several uniforms.

While I have endeavored to be as comprehensive as possible in my treatment of the subject, I must admit that I have omitted some uniform variations. Although I was able to locate the majority of the uniforms in private collections, many others remained elusive or unavailable and therefore were not included in this book. Also, the sheer numbers of styles, shades and individual variations made it impractical to include all of the variants at this time.

On the other hand, there were some uniforms, rumored to exist or attributed to the Soviet Union or Russia, which could not be verified, and therefore were not included in this book. If further evidence comes to light at a later time that they should in fact be added, I will certainly include them in a revised edition.

Notes on Illustrations

In order to portray an authentic view of the uniforms, where possible, I have shown actual members of the military and/or special services wearing the various patterns and cuts of Soviet and Russian camouflage. If actual photos were not available, I used models to demonstrate the proper appearance of the uniforms as they have been seen on Russian television news (*Novosti, ITA*), in professional journals (*Voenniy Vestnik, Na boevom postu, Orientir, Militsiia*), and in popular publications. Many of the configurations and comments are based on personal observations from trips to the Soviet Union, Russia and Eastern Europe.

When configuring uniforms for photos, accuracy and authenticity were of utmost consideration. Only authentic equipment and unit-specific items were placed in photos. Patches, badges and headgear associated with particular units and uniforms are shown in the appropriate positions based on their official identification in the rules for uniform wear published by the Ministry of Defense and Ministry of Internal Affairs.

Of course, all of this becomes moot when one considers the typical conscript or volunteer in the military or special services. On more than one occasion, I have observed combat troops and inductees wearing tennis shoes instead of boots, no headgear, and strange combinations of U.S. and Russian web gear and insignia. Keeping this in mind, the photos provided should serve as guides to what should be rather than the literal truth of what is.

Descriptions and terms are also based on the 1988 uniform regulations of the Soviet army[4] and 1978 uniform regulations of the *militsiia*.[5] Where no published descriptions or numerical designators exist, I have used my own system of identification and affiliation. This will, I hope, establish a standard for future descriptions and designations.

Is it Russian or...?

One area which caused a great amount of consternation was determining the origins of certain uniforms. My guidelines for designating unlabeled uniforms were fairly simple. I assigned names to uniforms based on three criteria: first, the country or republic in which it was manufactured; second, the year in which it was manufactured; and third, the most common user of the uniform. These considerations were especially important for Baltic and Ukrainian uniforms.

For instance, after the fall of the Soviet Union, former Soviet republic defense ministries began to sell off large numbers of Soviet uniforms. These uniforms were generally offered as "such and such republic" uniforms, often for prices higher than the more common Soviet uniforms would command. Upon inspection of these "republic" uniforms, I found that they were produced in state factories under Soviet control and are dated long before the republic sought independence. In these cases, the reason for their identification as Soviet uniforms is fairly obvious.

If the uniforms were manufactured within the boundaries of the FSU prior to 1991, they can be considered to have been Soviet-produced.[6] After 1991, they would be termed republic, that is, post-Soviet. Where several factories are located in different republics and are producing the same uniform, I have chosen to designate them by their primary user. Hence, the new streaked pattern (see page 125) is designated as the "VSR pattern" (standing for *Vooruzhennye sili Rossii* – Armed Forces of Russia). If there is no specific unit associated with the pattern and the point of production is uncertain, I have chosen to designate the uniform by its most common reference in print (Moldovan – Russian manufacture, and Georgian – Ukrainian manufacture). Still, local users may also have their own slang names which, due to their popularity, have been adopted as standard (such as the PFO tiger uniforms).

While I will undoubtedly generate some heated discussion and arguments with these criteria, I felt it necessary to establish a system whereby there could be some consistent labeling of uniforms for collectors. This will, I hope, considerably reduce the confusion among producers and collectors worldwide.

Another area of confusion involves the production of civilian versions of military uniforms. Civilian production, research and development, foreign sales, and a proliferation of private enterprises producing commercial uniforms for retail sale have made it virtually impossible to keep up with the ever-growing diversity of camouflage uniforms and equipment. To offset this, I have differentiated between civilian issue and military issue items.

Several companies now produce and sell civilian versions of camouflage field uniforms. Like their Western counterparts, civilian-manufactured uniforms are frequently of better quality and fit. As a result, numerous service personnel have chosen to purchase these civilian-produced uniforms and wear them in lieu of their service issue (mainly the more highly paid officers of the special services). In this respect, there is little difference between the civilian issue and its state-sponsored official issue. Where applicable, I have noted those civilian-manufactured uniforms worn by security and paramilitary units and those that are produced on contract for military use.

Uniform Production and Variations

As this book goes to press, both privatized factories and those still under the control of the Russian government are manufacturing new camouflage uniforms at a surprisingly rapid rate. Civilian variations of military uniforms and strictly civilian patterns (such as a copy of the All-Season, All-Terrain or ASAT™ uniform) have become quite common in the last three years. Uniforms produced in these factories are sold not only to combatants in various regions of the FSU, but to the public as well. This marks a significant change in consumer goods production in that the military industrial complex (VPK) now supports the consumer market through the retail sales of civilian versions of military uniforms.

In addition to private manufacture, another important facet of uniform production has been the practice of contract production, especially with recent uniforms for the Ministry of Internal Affairs (MVD). The Central Equipment Directorate of the Ministry of Defense of the Russian Federation (TsVU MO RF) is responsible for all procurement and production of military uniforms in Russia. Its chief as of July 1993, General Lieutenant Mikhail Khrenov, is responsible for implementation of fielding and issue policies of the Russian Ministry of Defense.[7] Faced with severe economic problems, budget shortfalls, and a lack of raw materials, the TsVU has had to adjust its ordering and production procedures. As a result, some local commanders have been authorized to adopt equipment and new camouflage patterns on a trial basis; occasionally, commanders without authorization are doing the same. Often these uniforms come from privatized or foreign sources.

Presently numerous Russian law enforcement agencies are equipping their forces with uniforms and equipment from abroad. Recently, a joint German -Russian firm (KOS) completed a deal to provide the St. Petersburg *militsiia* with boots, Kevlar™ helmets, ballistic nylon/Kevlar™ vests and other items to combat organized crime. Such importation of uniform components from Europe and the United States to improve *militsiia* crime fighting capabilities has created strange mixtures of Russian/foreign composite uniforms in many cities (see *SMK* versions).

Aside from the sheer numbers of uniform types, there also exists the challenge of identifying production variations among various factories; color variations are most evident in the woodland and two-tone camouflage uniforms.

According to Russian military personnel, uniforms that are produced throughout Russia often show variations in color, fabric texture, button styles and quality. This is due to a combination of poor quality control and numerous factories producing the same uniforms on contract. The range of color variation is so great in some instances, many collectors (and dealers) have been fooled into believing they are actually different uniforms. Conversely, where specific production variations are intentional (such as the pink, blue-green, and oxblood woodland patterns) I have so noted.

Lastly, I assume all responsibility for errors in identification, especially where little is known about the actual employment or use of the described uniforms. Due to the highly secretive nature of the military and police forces of the Stalin, Krushchev, and Brezhnev periods, the reluctance of military and special service agencies to share information, and the variability of unit requirements and regulations, errors of omission or commission are bound to occur. Still, I feel comfortable that this book represents the best information currently available in an unclassified format. With these ground rules in mind, let's jump into the matter at hand; that is, camouflage.

ENDNOTES PREFACE

[1] Washington D.C.: Government Printing Office, 1991.

[2] Troops of special-purpose "*voiska spetsial'nogo naznacheniia.*" Any soldier in the armed forces or special services assigned to special duties, usually of a combat nature. These forces typically have an elite status and therefore, their uniform items are far more desirable among collectors. The term *spetsnaz* itself actually means very little in light of the large numbers of troops so designated.

[3] "Businessman" generally means an entrepreneur in Russia, often members of the mafia, who deals illegally in uniforms and badges. In order to operate they pay bribes to the *militsiia* and major mafia groups who run the markets.

[4] *Pravila nosheniia voyennoi formy odezhdy* (Correct wear of the military duty uniform), Moscow, 1989.

[5] *Pravila nosheniia formy odezhdy militsii* (Correct wear of the duty uniform of the *militsiia*), Moscow, 1978.

[6] Although the Baltics declared their independence in 1990, the disintegration of the Soviet Union did not occur until late 1991. Even then, Soviet property was still largely in the hands of the Russian Federation and had to be disposed of or sold to private enterprises.

[7] Ivan Ivaniuk, "*O novoi voennoi forme bez slovesnogo kamufliazha*" (About the New Military Uniform without the Verbal Camouflage), *Krasnaia zvezda*, 27 July 1993, p. 2.

1

INTRODUCTION

"All war is based on deception..."
– Sun Tsu, *The Art of War,* 500 BC

The awesome power of the Soviet armed forces, their ill-fated involvement in Afghanistan, and ruthless dealings with satellite countries and republics have long contributed to the popularity of uniforms, badges and weapons from their military and paramilitary organizations. Under Gorbachev and his policies of *glasnost* (public awareness) and *perestroika* (restructuring) a wealth of information concerning the organization and tactics of the Soviet army became available. This information, so long a target of western intelligence services, was now being written about in the open press.

In the early 1980s the Soviet army incurred great losses in personnel and equipment due to its involvement in Afghanistan. As a result, captured equipment and uniforms became more available and eventually made their way to the collector via Pakistan. Such noted authorities as Stephen Zaloga, David Isby, and Gordon Rottman made inroads into the field of militaria collecting through their descriptions of the varied Soviet uniforms and equipment coming from Europe and Afghanistan. These experts provided the first modern guides to uniforms and equipment of the Soviet army and gradually filled the void for the collector and intelligence analyst alike.

At the time, books by the aforementioned authors gave collectors such as myself great insights into the Soviet army and its equipment; yet, they often failed to address the most basic questions about uniform issue dates, composition, and model numbers or designations. Due to the historical secrecy surrounding Soviet equipment development and fielding, such basic information was simply not available.

Right: Prior to the dissolution of the Soviet Union, authentic uniforms were difficult and expensive to come by. As a result, reproduction uniforms, such as this "Red Dawn" pattern were used to simulate Soviet forces in Opposing Forces (OPFOR) units.

As Gorbachev's *perestroika* brought economic hardship for the Soviet servicemen, *glasnost* brought a new openness about the Soviet military and its operations. Exacerbating economic difficulties was the Soviet government's reduction in military forces and subsequent withdrawal from the former Warsaw Pact (WARPAC)

Immediately after the reunification of East and West Germany, vendors hawking Soviet and East German military items sprang up throughout West Berlin offering previously hard to find items at reasonable prices.

countries. Few can forget the pictures in Western newspapers of Soviet soldiers rummaging through garbage dumps looking for usable refuse. With the prospect of no housing, meager wages, and subsistence living, it soon became commonplace for Soviet soldiers withdrawing from Germany, Hungary and Poland to sell their kit to local civilians in the hopes of earning enough hard currency to survive at home.

As the veil of secrecy was gradually lifted, Soviet professional journals began to describe little-known units and their heroic exploits in great detail, much as a grandfather would relate a good war story to his grandchildren. This new publicity elicited immense interest in the uniforms and accouterments of Soviet combat troops and special services.

However, uniforms and equipment from the former "evil empire" still remained largely unavailable to U.S. collectors until economic restructuring further began to erode the Soviet economy. Increased availability came about through attempts to improve the standard of living of the military through private (black market) sales in the former Soviet Union. Whole platoons and companies worth of equipment were illegally sold off by supply officers. Coupled with the steady stream coming from the East, Soviet militaria gradually made its way to the United States into the hands of collectors and speculators.

East Germany's collapse and the Bundesrepublik's subsequent reunification in 1990 provided a ready avenue for burgeoning entrepreneurs from all over Eastern Europe. In Berlin entrepreneurs could buy complete uniforms, field gear, and even-night vision devices at the *Polnische markt* in the morning and then shop for pistols and grenades in East Berlin from Soviet officers at *Karl Marx Platz* in the afternoon. This opened up a new opportunity for dealers of uniforms and equipment and spawned a new generation of collectors eager to assemble collections from the world's largest, most heavily-equipped army.

In the late 1980s interest in the Soviet Union increased as it became obvious that its survival was in doubt. While the USSR continued to crumble and hard-liners fought to maintain control, the special services charged with maintaining public order and eliminating crime were thrust into the limelight.

Worldwide, viewers were treated to films of special troops from the Ministry of Internal Affairs (MVD)[1] and the Main Intelligence Administration (GRU) combating dissidents in the breakaway republics. Then in 1991 and 1993, failed coups and attempted takeovers once again took center stage all over the world. As a result, foreigners scrambled to obtain souvenirs of the former world power in the form of watches, caps, flags and, yes, uniforms. Much as people sought to own a piece of the Berlin Wall when it crumbled, so too people flocked to flea markets and gun shows looking for hats, coats, pins and uniforms.

The desire to own a piece of Soviet history has increased continuously over the last ten years as travel to Russia has become easier and tourists are able to compete for military items to bring home as souvenirs. Economic hardships in Soviet Union and Russia, coupled with the military's willingness to sell issued uniforms, has led to a rapid increase in the supply of collectibles. Coupled with the relaxation of restrictions on private businesses and retail sales, collectors and dealers in the U.S. have reaped the benefits. Unfortunately, authoritative information describing these items has not been as forthcoming.

There currently exists a virtual flood of Soviet and Russian military and special service items throughout the world. Moreover, Russia's recent reorganization and expansion of its special services has yielded an even greater variety of patches, uniforms, badges and weapons, examples of which have made their way into U.S. collectors' hands. As a result, new units are identified more often than not through the purchase of patches and badges at Ismailovsky market in Moscow rather than through some top secret intelligence source. While there is no definitive source with which to identify all of this new material entering the collector market, this book will attempt to solve at least part of that problem, that is, the camouflage uniform niche.

Therefore to better understand camouflage uniform production of the last 60 years, let us begin with a brief discussion of the history of camouflage development. Then, we'll examine some important considerations in dealing with camouflage uniforms before attacking the specifics of each uniform.

ENDNOTES CHAPTER 1

[1] The MVD is responsible for the internal security of Russia. Units under its jurisdiction include *militsiia* (police units), counter terrorist units, traffic and automobile regulators, search and rescue, firefighters, and riot control troops.

2

HISTORY OF CAMOUFLAGE

"What is history but a fable agreed upon?"
– Napoleon Bonaparte

Although the German and Italian armies were among the first to issue camouflage shelter halves to their troops as early as 1935, the Soviet Union was the first nation to employ a variety of camouflage field uniforms in combat during the Second World War. Russian military planners developed the term *maskirovka* to encompass all forms of deception and concealment that an army might employ against its opponent. While virtually all modern armies have adopted camouflage uniforms as their primary field uniforms, the Soviet Union can be credited with not only being among the first to field a variety of combat overgarments, but fielding a larger variety than any of its contemporaries. To gain a better understanding of the importance Soviet and Russian camouflage has achieved, we'll look first at its historical development and subsequent evolution to become an important tool of modern warfare.

African tribesmen were undoubtedly the first to employ various forms of camouflage thousands of years ago to conceal themselves from their intended prey. Using natural dyes and vegetation, the earliest hunters adorned themselves with artistic designs to create fierce or bold patterns designed to increase their success during the hunt. Native Americans are known to have used grasses and tree branches to blend in with their surroundings and conceal their presence from opposing tribes or the many hoofed animals they hunted. However, it was not until the advent of modern warfare in the early twentieth century that artificial camouflage became an important tactical consideration on the battlefield.

The French are credited with the creation of the word "camouflage" from the verb camoufle' meaning: "to play a practical joke." It may also, as *Webster's New World Dictionary* indicates, come from the French "camoufleur" – to disguise. This term came to be used to describe attempts by armies to conceal their soldiers and weapons from the prying eyes of an opposing force. Early attempts at camouflage included painting tanks and seagoing vessels with various patterns and colors to either conceal or disguise them from enemy eyes. Camouflage soon was extended to the use of textiles and artificial substances to conceal soldiers under a variety of battlefield conditions. From early man's first use of natural means of camouflage to scientific development and implementation, man's need to conceal himself from enemies and prey has always meant success measured in terms of survival or death.

Artists and Camouflage

Camouflage is a direct descendant of both naturalist studies and revolutionary art movements which began in the late 1800s. Charles Darwin's work with natural camouflage and Abbot Thayer's studies of counter-shading in animals strongly influenced theories of coloration in wildlife and later contributed to studies of artificially camouflaging man-made objects.

During Darwin's travels he noticed that animals that possessed certain types of coloration survived better than those that did not. His most famous example demonstrated how dark moths in England were concealed from insectivorous birds on dark trees. Darwin also demonstrated the abilities of animals to mimic other species (moths with large eyespots), disrupt their outlines with colorful patterns (butterflies), or warn predators of their toxicity (poison arrow frogs). Darwin's observations led him to develop several theories on natural selection and survival strategies of animals. Although Darwin's theories earned him both praise and scorn, his belief in natural survival strategies laid a foundation for the study of natural camouflage.

Abbot Thayer took Darwin's theories further by proposing his theory of mammalian counter-shading; that is, when viewed from the side, animals with lighter undersides are difficult for predators to detect because of the resulting breakup of their outline in overhead lighting. Antelopes on the African veldt possess this type of counter-shading as do a wide variety of mammals throughout the world. Thayer also postulated that bright, conspicuous patterns may have the "disruptive" effect of concealing the animal against a convoluted background of shapes and shades. Thayer used zebras and certain parrots as examples of disruptive patterning. Like Darwin, Thayer was initially met with contempt for his theories. But that eventually changed.

In the late 1800s and early 1900s, anthropologists applied both Darwin's and Thayer's theories to humans as they studied the correlation between self-decoration by aboriginal tribes and concealment camouflage. Although little work was actually done on this topic, it nevertheless served to elicit greater interest in the scientific community. Considered too controversial, Thayer's ideas were largely ignored by the contemporary community until long after his death. However, at about the same time that Thayer postulated the concept of imitative camouflage, avant garde artists began to experiment with new forms of painting which challenged previously accepted ways of viewing the world.

At the beginning of the twentieth century a new type of art started to take shape. Pablo Picasso, experimenting with his Cubist renderings of realistic items, portrayed every day objects in abstract ways. Through the use of convergent and divergent lines, shading, counter-shading and a mix of colors, Picasso portrayed common objects in new and exciting ways. His unorthodox use of color and form presented with unusual perspectives served to confuse the viewer's previously accepted perceptions of reality.

Whereas modern art had previously dealt with the depiction of nature through realistic portrayals, Cubist art attempted to disguise and disfigure recognizable objects, making them almost unrecognizable to the observer. Lines, shapes and colors coalesced into a conglomeration of patterns which made discernment of the main object difficult; this type of abstract art eventually led to the development of theories involving disruptive camouflage.

At about the same time, Russian futurist artist Natalia Goncharova was experimenting with a new style of art, presenting common objects in uncommon ways. Dissatisfied with the realist art of the late nineteenth century, Goncharova created her own Slavophile type of cubist and futurist paintings, albeit with a heavy French influence.

Goncharova took her abstract cubism and paved the way for other Russian abstract artists yearning to break out of the commonly accepted Soviet creations. Another Russian artist who contributed to the future of abstract art and its practical application was V. Stepanova. Taking futurist abstract designs one step further, Stepanova created clothing that not only employed the cubist concept, but applied it to the concept of identifications of positions and professions of workers using specific colors and shapes.[1]

Thayer's premise that counter-shading offered mammals the chance to remain unobserved when viewed from the side eventually led to the development of camouflage for naval vessels and armored vehicles.

Disruptive patterning, such as the stripes on this zebra, serve to break up the outline of the object being camouflaged.

Stepanova's clothing used colorful fabrics and forming them into utilitarian designs for the socialist factory worker. Colored cloth insignia and splotches of color were added to denote what portion of the factory and what rank each worker held. If implemented, the clothing's purpose would have been to readily identify what assignments each factory workers held to any observer.

Stepanova eventually became well known for her textile designs for factory workers and athletes. Although never widely accepted and therefore not manufactured in any quantity, her clothing can be considered early versions of camouflage uniforms. Although intended for identification rather than concealment, Stepanova's creations marked a distinctive divergence from previously accepted bland factory uniforms. This undoubtedly contributed to Soviet understanding of disruptive patterning and may have influenced camouflage textile development.

Despite early research conducted by Soviet artists, the practical use of camouflage is generally attributed to the French, who undertook development of this new science. The initial studies of camouflage were due in large part to the influence of several French artists. According to Roy Behrens[2], such noted artists as Monet, Degas and Jean-Louis Forain worked with the French government to develop military camouflage.

As the political situation in Europe began to change so too changed the face of the world's armies. Up until the assassination of Archduke Ferdinand in Sarajevo in 1914, there was little practical application for the science of camouflage. However, as has been true throughout history, technical development usually finds a practical application during war. With the advent of the First World War came new weapons, new tactics and a new science called camouflage. This science would have far-reaching consequences and has remained an important part of military science even today.

This painting of Russian soldiers moving through the deep snows of the Caucuses during the Russo-Turkish War, show the earthen tones used in uniforms of the late 19th Century. From a painting by A. D. Kivshenko, 1886.

The First World War

The entry of Europe into a major conflict caused military leaders to re-examine well-established tactical and strategic doctrine and to look for ways to improve their war-fighting capabilities. Camouflage took on greater significance during this conflict, primarily as applied to disguising warships and combat vehicles.

Early camoufleurs painted trucks, tanks and ships with geometric shapes and bright colors to break up their outline thus making them less visible to the enemy. Known as dazzle paint, these brightly colored diagonal and angular shapes on the hulls of ships became the most widely used and most successful camouflage tactic during the First World War.[3] Based largely on Cubist concepts, dazzle paint found wide acceptance by 1918 with both American and French naval forces. The bizarre designs reduced the visibility of the combatants and helped to conceal them from the enemy until they could be effectively employed against enemy forces.

With the entry of the Americans into the war in 1917, camouflage development accelerated. While artificial means of camouflage was just being introduced, natural camouflage techniques became more refined. The French widely employed grass, leaves, and hollow trees to conceal soldiers and allow them to conduct reconnaissance unseen against enemy troops.

American snipers used natural materials to hide their presence on the field of battle and even wove strands of grass into their head-gear and uniforms, thus creating the first sniper ghilli suits.[4] Whereas cover protected the soldier, concealment permitted him to remain undetected while still performing his mission.

By the middle of 1918, camouflage production was proceeding full steam. A special factory was set up in Dijon, France to produce artificial trees and foxhole covers for use by the allied armies. While larger, mobile objects employed disruptive camouflage, soldiers used artificial objects to imitate existing conditions in order to conceal themselves. Examples of such objects included hollowed out trees, paper mache' horse carcasses, and rocks.

Combat engineers in the French, American and British armies took on the responsibility of employing camouflage techniques in their units. Within each engineer branch were specialized units that excelled in the art of camouflage; at the strategic level, special camouflage corps were created to perform camouflage duties in the theater of operations. The close association between engineers and camouflage remains largely unchanged today, in fact, many armies have maintained the special camouflage units in the form of battlefield deception units.

During the First World War, Abbot Thayer had become more involved with the notion of disruptive patterning and made recommendations to both American and British leaders concerning camouflage. Extending his concepts of counter-shading and disruptive patterning to practical use during war, Thayer described the possibilities of protective coloration and urged its use. Thayer contended that most animal coloration was designed to mimic the surrounding environment and that animal coloration is largely dependent upon the vantage point from which it is viewed, thus affecting shading and patterning. By dressing or coloring soldiers and equipment according to the vantage point from which they were viewed, soldiers could, in effect, hide in plain sight.

Thayer's ideas were largely ignored and few of them were ever put to use. While he maintained that his ideas were widely read by German military leaders, few allied leaders took Thayer seriously. His concepts were very advanced for the time and only found their niche decades later as armies modernized their forces for a potential European confrontation. It was only when the need to alter the combat soldier's external appearance was recognized that uniform appearances began to change.

Prior to World War One, most of the world's armies wore brightly colored tunics and breeches; their high visibility resulting in large numbers of casualties. Common to most armies of the time, these dress uniforms served more to identify units, branches and affiliations rather than protect soldiers engaged in battle. However, by the middle of the nineteenth century, as more and more nations became engaged in colonial wars of expansion, imperial armies were forced to adopt uniforms designed to reduce the visibility of their soldiers during combat.

In 1880, the British army exchanged its standard bright white tunics for a more subdued earthen color, thus making them less visible to enemy soldiers. By boiling their tunics in pots of tea, the British soldiers were able to more closely match the surroundings of the Afghan countryside.[5]

In this instance, the color was generally referred to as khaki or drab. The most commonly accepted reason for the change is that white tunics made the British soldiers more susceptible to snipers and enemy soldiers resulting in higher casualties; the change to the subdued color was therefore a defensive move. Another reason may have involved British experiences in India.

On long deployments in the Indian provinces, the bright white uniforms became dusty, resulting in an unkempt, dirty appearance. To offset this, the colonial uniform was changed to a more subdued color thus giving rise to the "drab" appearance of the uniforms. Whatever the reason, in the late 1800s the British army changed its field uniforms to the more suitable drab color as its standard field uniform for use throughout the empire.

Relying largely on British experiences in Afghanistan and India, most imperial armies had adopted similarly subdued uniforms by the late 19th century, the exception being Russia. For most of the 1800s, Imperial Russian soldiers still relied largely on brightly colored uniforms with elaborate headdresses and plumes. Coupled with the bright tunics and full-size medals, Russian officers and troops became highly visible targets against the drab mountains of the Central Asian highlands and steppes of southern Russia.

During the Russo-Turkish War (1877-1878), the great Russian artist Vereshchagin, depicted Russian infantry still wearing the white uniforms akin to British uniforms of the period. An additional drawback of the Russian uniforms was the habit of Russian officers wearing highly polished metallic helmets that reflected sunlight, making them more visible to their opponents.

Eventually, Russia's limited incursion into Afghanistan in 1885 led to its adoption of more subdued colors, incorporating a variety of greys and browns, yet still employing bright colors for insignia. However, it was not until Imperial Russia's experiences with the Japanese in the early 20th century that the army adopted a uniform which was a departure from the elaborately decorated versions of the 19th century.

Standard dress for officers in the Imperial Russian Army from the 1860s through about 1907. The white kitels, metallic buttons, and bullion shoulderboards were typical for the period. From a painting by L. V. Popov, 1904.

Weapons development during the 19th century also significantly influenced the development of subdued uniforms. According to Russian historians at the General Staff Academy, the move to subdued uniforms came about as a result of improved ranges and accuracy of rifles and cannon. While early engagements characteristically occurred at ranges of less than 300 meters, the development of rifled barrels and improved munitions (especially during the American Civil War in the 1860s), increased the distance at which engagements occurred. As a result, in the post-1880 period, soldiers were more susceptible to long-range weapons and, therefore, could be killed by unseen opponents.

As a result of the increased accuracy of hand-held weapons and field artillery, the need to remain undetected from enemy observation became an overwhelming concern. The high numbers of casualties from direct and indirect fire weapons caused a changeover from brightly colored uniforms to less conspicuous tunics and headgear. Typical names ascribed to these subdued uniforms included the U.S. olive drab, the French *changeant*, and German *feldgrau*.

Russian soldiers, fighting for Nicholas II in the Russo-Japanese War of 1905, first encountered Japanese soldiers wearing a dusty, yellowish uniform which they referred to as khaki (хаки). Although the word khaki is probably from the Persian word for dust, Japanese soldiers used this term to describe the uniform color which they employed throughout Asia. Russians eventually adopted both the word and the uniform color, using khaki to describe any uniform of a dull green or yellowish color.

Eventually the term *zashchitnyi tsvet* (protective color) replaced the foreign term and was used to describe any Russian uniform of a subdued or khaki color. Later this term was extended to cover the word *kamufliazh* to denote uniforms employing camouflage colors or patterns.[6]

While the world's armies had largely converted their field uniforms to make them more suitable for battlefield use, it was not until the First World War that camouflage was expanded to complete units and weapon systems. The first use of camouflage clothing did not occur until 1918 when H. Ledyard Towle introduced artificially colored clothing which mimicked surrounding foliage and terrain. Towle's "camouflage robes" were issued to members of New York's Women's Reserve Camouflage Corps.[7]

Towle and his artists painted the robes to resemble rocks, bark and grass in a natural setting. Thus Towle was responsible for introducing the first camouflage clothing for deceptive purposes. Generally, individual camouflage still employed natural substances to conceal the soldier during battlefield engagements. Grasses, twigs and mud were used more than artificially colored cloth to hide troops in the field. Most of the advances in camouflage occurred with artificial netting and the painting of weapons systems to conceal them from aerial observation.

Meanwhile, most of Europe's armies continued to apply camouflage technology to battlefield systems. Most commonly, camoufleurs applied various color patterns to aircraft and vehicles in order to conceal them from enemy observation.

Due to the fact that early aircraft were slow moving, and thus vulnerable to ground fire, their lower surfaces were painted to break up their outline against the brightly lit sky. As a result, blues and greys were the most common form of camouflage coloration applied to the undersides of biplanes in the First World War.

Conversely, when viewed from above, aircraft had to match the surrounding foliage in order to escape detection. German camouflage designers employed patterns such as the four-color lozenge camouflage, incorporating olive, brown and khaki, in a geometric pattern of small ovals, on a green field to break up the outline of the aircraft. The combination of camouflage patterns was necessary to protect the aircraft from varying points of observation.

Slow moving naval vessels encountered a similar problem. While many ships were painted in varying shades of greys and blues, dazzle paint schemes were employed as an additional measure of camouflage. Eventually, varying forms of patterning, mimicry, and deceptive camouflage patterns were applied to ships both in the First and Second World Wars.

The lessons learned during the First World War were not lost on the combatants of subsequent wars, rather, the skills developed by camoufleurs were further developed in the inter-war period and refined as the world moved closer to the next great conflict.

The Inter-war Period

After the end of the First World War, camouflage was largely forgotten and therefore, little information exists about its technical development from 1920 through 1937. This was due in large part to the post World War feeling on the part of most world leaders that large scale wars were a thing of the past. Although technological advances in armored and air forces were made, little money or time was spent in the development of personal equipment or the modernization of ground forces; the exceptions being Germany and the Soviet Union. In the rest of the world, although military tactics and history were studied in military academies, little effort was made to improve individual equipment or study the art of camouflage.

Left: Standard full field dress for Imperial Russian infantryman of the 1870s. Dark wool clothing and field gear were the norm for the conscript pressed into service during the 19th century. Right: Near the end of the existence of the Imperial Russian army, uniforms were at their final stage of development for the doomed army. The color of the shineli (overcoats) is referred to as "zashchitnyi tsvet", a term retained through the Soviet and new Russian periods. These privates, at the beginning of their service, show the differences in uniforms for the Russian army in 1916.

Meanwhile, in Soviet military academies the art of war was being intently studied and steadily improved resulting in new military strategies and advanced weapon development. With the advent of these new military doctrines came the development of individual camouflage clothing.

In the 1930s two major European armies began experimenting with new tactical operations and worked at improving their military preparedness: the Soviet Union and Germany. It has been fairly well established that the Soviet government cooperated in military matters with both the pre-Hitler Reichswehr and Hitler's Wehrmacht, and developed strong military relations.[8] Although Soviet-German relations were at first cold during Hitler's rise to power, they eventually improved to the point that a close military alliance was forged between the two nations.

Due to the prohibition against expanding its military capabilities or conducting military maneuvers, Germany was forced to develop its army and conduct training in secret. It was during this period that close relations between Hitler and Stalin grew and an exchange of technical and tactical information occurred. The Wehrmacht, and certainly Soviet Russia, benefited from this alliance and each was able to modernize its security and ground forces in the event of a future conflict. The concept of a conquered Europe, shared between Hitler and Stalin, may have evolved during this period, eventually leading to the invasion of Poland.

Stalin's desire for close relations with Hitler undoubtedly led to his decision to permit German officers to train in Russia and share military expertise. This exchange of information and joint training may explain many of the similarities between equipment, uniforms and weapons of Stalinist Russia and Hitler's Third Reich.[9] It was during this period that the Soviet Union and Germany developed breakthrough and blitzkrieg tactics and deep strike operations using airborne troops. Development of new tactics demanded improvements in the equipment of each country's combat forces, and the creation of suitable protective clothing for the field soldier.

As Thayer explained twenty years prior to the introduction of Soviet camouflage uniforms, the most suitable protective coloration was that which was in harmony with the environment in which an animal existed. Since most animals occupy a limited area, their camouflage need not be complex or highly variable; rather, most organisms require a protective cover which is suited only to their local environment. Animals faced with a highly variable environment usually have sufficient time to alter their appearance. Two examples are the summer and winter coats of arctic mammals, and desert ground lizards that have the ability to lighten and darken their ground color.[10] The camouflage needs of the combat soldier are much more complex.

Unlike animals which occupy a relatively limited area, modern combat soldiers move from one environment to another as the theater of operations evolves and the battle progresses. This means that soldiers must be able to conceal themselves in urban, desert, grassland, forest and snowy landscapes. Fortunately, these environments seldom coexist simultaneously and there is usually sufficient opportunity to alter one's external appearance. However, to accomplish this, soldiers must either modify their existing uniforms as they change environments or carry an additional camouflage uniform which can be donned or removed as the need arises.

Up until the advent of reversible and complex camouflage uniforms, soldiers occupying stationary positions wore field uniforms that matched their immediate vicinity; this was during the era of trench warfare. With the initiation of hostilities between Germany and Poland, and the subsequent lightning war in Europe, the need for variable camouflage arose.

As part of the tactical improvements made during the 1930s, European nations began to develop uniforms suitable for their rapidly expanding armed forces. The first camouflage overgarment was issued in 1935; the German *zeltbahn* – a shelter half that could also be worn as a rain poncho, served as a convenient way for soldiers to vary their appearance according to local vegetative patterns.

The pattern of the *zeltbahn* was relatively simple: a splinter pattern over large brown and green geometric shapes, on a tan or light brown background. In this same year the Waffen-*SS* was also issued a camouflage jacket designed to be worn over field tunics.[11] The pattern was disruptive in nature: several earth tones combined into a spotted and streaked pattern. The cut of the jacket was significant, however, in that it possessed a hood, thus providing limited concealment from overhead observation (this unique jacket construction and pattern provided the Soviets with an example they would copy subsequent to the first Eastern Front engagements in 1941).[12]

Also in 1935, the People's Commissariat for Defense (NKO) of the USSR issued a series of edicts which established rank insignia and authorized uniforms for the Workers and Peasants Red Army (RKKA). The NKO authorized increased research and development of new uniforms, which were gradually introduced over the next five years during a time when the Red Army underwent significant changes in its structure and doctrine.

As Stalin was able to clarify his position with Hitler, it became obvious that the Red Army required significant organizational and structural changes. Quantities of tanks, aircraft, and basic soldiering equipment grew rapidly from 1935 through 1940. Stalin was already preparing for the time when he and Hitler would dominate the European landscape. Soviet and German military leaders also developed new techniques involving the use of airborne troops; introduced into the enemy's support area, *desantniki* would wreak havoc with supply lines and destroy command and control centers. Highly mobile NKVD[13] and motorized army units were created which had the responsibility to destroy similarly structured units introduced into the Soviet rear echelon area.

In 1939, the Soviet RKKA Draft Field Service Regulations addressed the subject of camouflage, requiring commanders at all levels to take the initiative in camouflaging units and equipment. The regulations specifically stated that camouflage should be "... natural, constant and diverse."[14] The Soviets placed responsibility for camouflage operations under the control of the chief of engineers for larger operations; however, it was the responsibility of each soldier to exercise camouflage discipline. It was during this period that the term "*maskirovka*" came into use.

Maskirovka

The Soviet concept of *maskirovka* (camouflage, concealment, and deception) from the French, *masquer*, has more significance than just camouflage. Whereas most armies use the more common term camouflage to describe operations which conceal or disguise troops and equipment from enemy observation, the Soviet use of the term *maskirovka* is much broader in its application.

Maskirovka covers all operations: *strategicheskaia* (strategic), *operativnaia* (operational), and *takticheskaia* (tactical).[15] It not only relates to physical concealment and cover, but also informational, visual and electronic deception and diversion. *Maskirovochnye* operations also include deception operations, mimicry, and concealment actions such as camouflaging individuals, units and even whole areas through terrain alteration.

According to the Soviet Military encyclopedic dictionary, *maskirovka* involves a "...series of measures to mislead the enemy related to the presence and location of troops, military objectives, their formations, military preparedness and actions, and also the plans of the command; a type of operational (military) security."[16]

The term *maskirovka* also includes the capability of unexpected unit movements, maintaining military effectiveness and increasing survivability. Since its inception, the Soviet army has attempted to mask its intent and capabilities from the enemy through the use of intelligence collection, deception, electronic disinformation, radio-electronic jamming, and cover and concealment. Moreover, through the use of government misinformation, the intent and capabilities of its armed forces could be protected from enemy intelligence collection. Within the context of our discussion, *maskirovka* is also used to describe the techniques of concealing individuals and units through camouflage clothing.

While natural camouflage was the preferred method of concealment, the Soviets recognized the need for artificial means to deceive the enemy; this included camouflage clothing of various patterns and designs.[17] According to Soviet doctrine, the purpose of camouflage clothing is to: "... conceal personnel from visual observation, photography, and other optical reconnaissance."[18]

Uniforms developed in the late 1930s that meet the Soviet definition of camouflage are divided into two types: the camouflage coverall (*maskirovochnyi kombinezon*) and camouflage suit (*maskirovochnyi kostium*). Furthermore, camouflage patterns can be divided into three types: imitative, patterns which mimic natural foliage or objects (trees, leaves, bark, rocks); disruptive, bright or subdued geometric designs which break up the outline of the wearer (splotches, squares, triangles, intersecting lines); and a combination of the two.

This concept of camouflage and *maskirovka*, largely developed prior to the Second World War, provided the basis for the development of camouflage uniforms and led to its continued use and development to the present.

ENDNOTES CHAPTER 2

[1] Christina Lodder, *Russian Constructivism*, (New Haven, CT: Yale University Press, 1983), pp. 149-151, plate p. 142.

[2] *Art and Camouflage.* (Cedar Falls, IA: North American Review, UNI), p 9-10. Mr. Behrens gives a very detailed and thorough account of camouflage development which I would strongly encourage anyone interested in the subject to read.

[3] Behrens, pp. 39-45.

[4] Ibid, p. 28.

[5] Guy Hartcup, *Camouflage, a History of Concealment and Deception in War.* (New York: Charles Scribner's Sons, 1980), p. 12.

[6] V. M. Glinka, *Russkii voennyi kostium, 18 - nachala 20 veka* (Russian military uniforms from the 18th to the beginning of the 20th century). (Leningrad: Khudozhnik RSFSR, 1988). p. 225.

[7] Ibid, p. 29.

[8] John Dziak, *Chekisty, A History of the KGB*, (New York: Ivy Books, 1988), pp. 105- 106.

[9] The opposition to this unholy alliance by Stalin's officer corps may partially explain Stalin's purge of military officers during the late 1930s. After all, if Stalin felt that his alliance with Hitler guaranteed his place as a leader in Europe, there would have been little need to maintain an extensive military leadership who opposed close ties with the Reichswehr and could pose a threat to Stalin's leadership.

[10] This is as much a function of light absorption and reflectance as well as camouflage, a factor which has been considered for combat soldiers of the 21st century.

[11] Mollo, McGregor, Smith and Chappell, *World Army Uniforms Since 1939.* (Poole, England, Blandford Press, 1981). p. 28, plate 74.

[12] Andrew Mollo. *The Armed Forces of World War II*, (New York: Crown Publishers, 1981), pp. 189-190.

[13] People's Commissariat for Internal Affairs. The NKVD motorized units probably provided the concept for Hitler's formation of *Waffen SS* units during World War II.

[14] Major General V. A. Matsulenko, *Operational Camouflage of the Troops*, (Moscow: 1975).

[15] S. F. Akhromeev, (representative of the Chief Editing Commission), *Voennyi entsiklopedicheskii slovar'* [Military encyclopedic dictionary], (Moscow: Military Press, 1986), p. 428.

[16] Ibid.

[17] Throughout the text I will use the terms "pattern," to describe the color and designs of the camouflage, and "construction," to denote how the uniform is sewn and made.

[18] A. A. Beketov et al. *Camouflage of Actions by Ground Force Subunits*, (Moscow: 1976), p. 29.

3

PREWAR THROUGH POSTWAR DEVELOPMENT

"...You know for me this whole camouflage thing for me doesn't work very well. Because you go into the jungle, I can't see you. You know, you go into the jungle, make a statement. If you're going to fight, clash!"
– Robin Williams, *Good Morning Vietnam*

Although most Soviet war memorials designate June 1941 as the beginning of the Second World War, few would disagree that the Soviet Union's invasion of Finland (1939) and Poland (1939) and the annexation of the Baltic States (1940) marked the beginning of the Soviet Union's entry into the war in Europe. Germany's military buildup, its subsequent annexation of Czechoslovakia, and close relations with the Soviet Union, caused several nations to move to a war-time footing and modernize their armed forces. As part of this modernization and upgrading of forces, the major powers began to modernize their individual tactical equipment and as a result, research the development of camouflage uniforms and issue them to their combat forces.

Prior to the Second World War, Soviet military research was focused primarily on the duplication of successful weapons and tactics used by other countries. Typically, most Soviet military advances have been the direct result of other countries' efforts; the advances made in the 1940s were no different. Numerous training agreements and memorandums of understanding between Nazi Germany and the Soviet Union yielded a close working relationship between the two burgeoning superpowers. Subsequent involvement with the Hitlerites on its western boundaries caused a more rapid development of Soviet military power and tactics. The development of wartime camouflage uniforms was almost certainly directly related to this interaction.[1]

Prewar Development

During the first years of the war in Europe, the Soviet Union began to field new uniforms which were similar, if not in pattern, at least in tailoring, to German camouflage uniforms. In fact, due to a scarcity of uniforms among ground troops, it was quite common for soldiers of both armies to don the captured camouflage uniforms of the opposition. It is quite natural to expect, therefore, for some imitation to occur.

Although the exact date is uncertain, the Soviet Union began to issue a new winter camouflage overgarment – the *zimnoi maskirovochnyi kostium* (ZMK) to certain units as early as 1938. Commanders of the Red Army saw the need for both utility and concealment during the Russo-Finnish war and put over whites into service during the campaign. These were simple two-piece cotton suits with hoods and loose-fitting trousers and may have been copied from either German or Finnish designs of the period.

The ZMK proved very effective during the Russo-Finnish campaign, and by the middle of the Second World War, most of the armies fighting in Europe had adopted similar uniforms. The suit was issued in a grey, khaki or brown fabric bag in one of three sizes: 1, 2 or 3 and weighed between 600 and 700 grams.[2] Attached mittens concealed the wearer's hands and helped to protect them from the cold. This marked the beginning of Soviet camouflage development.

However, the first development of Soviet camouflage came in the late 1930s with the issuance of a one-piece coverall and a two-piece suit marked with large brown blobs on a green background. Tolochkov identifies the one-piece suit as a *maskirovochnyi kombinezon* or MK.[3] In his book, *Maskirovka soldata, oruzhiia, i boevoi tekhniki* [Camouflage of soldiers, weapons and combat equipment], Lieutenant colonel F. I. Myshak also refers to the one-piece as the MK.[4]

The two-piece version is referred to as the *maskirovochnyi kamuflirovannyi kostium,* or deceptive camouflage suit – MKK.[5] Both the one-piece and two-piece versions were issued to combat troops.

The 1938 MK and MKK "amoeba" uniform were the first Soviet camouflage overgarments specifically designed for concealment during combat operations.[6] The pattern, consisting of dark brown blobs (resembling amoebae) on a green background, was issued as a smock and a coverall to airborne, engineer, reconnaissance troops, and snipers. Special troops of the NKVD, referred to erroneously as "minelayers," also received the uniform as their primary camouflage issue.

Made of a lightweight, 100% cotton material, MK uniforms were issued with an attached hood and sewn-in face veil. The two-piece version came issued with a face mask and a small carrying sack. According to the aforementioned references, the uniform could easily be donned in a minute or less. In the event the suit became wet, it could be air dried in a matter of minutes. The 1938 MKK proved fairly effective and was issued well into the 191940s and 1950s.

The one-piece uniform was also issued in a single sided camouflage and a reversible version. The dual sided issue is reported to be green with brown blobs (*piatna*) on the "spring" side, and gray with yellow patterning on the reverse; it was designed for use in Central Asia and for fall usage in areas with deciduous foliage. Other one-sided versions were in the planning stages but may never have been issued: for areas with green undergrowth – yellow (actually, a sand color) with green blobs; for desert steppe regions – a gray uniform with yellow blobs; and for mountainous regions – grey with yellow blobs.

During its lifetime, the 1938 MKK continued to undergo modifications and redesign. According to some sources, the suit remains in use today by reservists and trainees; indeed, it is often seen in military publications being used as a training uniform by cadets. Reportedly there are stockpiles of the uniform held in warehouses, intended to be issued to reserves in the event of war. Furthermore, MOSFILM, a leading film production company in Russia, purportedly has several examples for use in historic films. Typically the MK and MKK are used as the premier example of camouflage uniforms in all subsequent reference books on *Maskirovka.*[7]

The 1938 MKK suit was the first attempt by the Soviets to use an artificially colored uniform for camouflaging combat troops. This set a precedent which led to the development of numerous other camouflage uniform patterns and designs, many of which are still in use today.

In the period just prior to the entry of the United States into World War II, European nations rearmed and reequipped for the impending conflict. Technical research and development yielded numerous advances in the area of weapons and personal protection. Yet, during this period few countries were prepared to expend the necessary resources to develop field equipment and armaments, never mind camouflage uniforms, and issue them to their troops in time for the upcoming world conflict. The majority relied on preexisting stocks left over from the First World War. As a result, only the Soviet Union and Germany were able to field a variety of uniforms at the start of the conflict.

Throughout 1939, and 1940, Germany issued several different camouflage patterns such as the *tiger jacket,* which was issued to *SS* units. Italy was also among the first to field camouflage coveralls in the late 1930s. This pattern, consisting of large colored blocks on a solid background, is still in service with some units. The only ally to issue camouflage uniforms was Britain in 1939 when it issued camouflage parachute coveralls to its SOE and OSS units and in 1941 issued its Denison smock to airborne units.[8]

The Second World War

By the time hostilities were in full swing during the summer of 1940, only the axis powers had managed to deploy fully equipped and combat ready divisions throughout Eastern and Western Europe. The allies were at a serious disadvantage totally unprepared for a full-scale conflict. The USSR continued to manufacture the amoeba pattern and introduced at least two more camouflage patterns, based on the same one and two piece cuts as before.

In late 1940, or early 1941, the Soviet army began to issue a camouflage uniform consisting of a shirt and pants with an oversized hood sewn to the jacket. While the construction of the smock may have been based on early German uniforms, the pattern was distinctly Soviet. Rather than being disruptive in nature, the "leaf-pattern" MKK was imitative with outlines of leaves, grasses and twigs on a green background. As with the earlier amoeba pattern, the leaf-pattern uniform was issued in one piece coveralls and two-piece suit versions and was eventually issued to Romanian troops in the post-war period.[9]

The one-piece variant of the leaf-pattern uniform was known as the *maskirovochnyi kamuflirovannyi kombinezon* – or deceptive camouflage coveralls – also MKK.[10] This suit was also issued in a reversible version with a sandy colored background for desert and mountain operations, thus establishing a precedent that would last through to the 1980s. This uniform was short-lived and issued on a limited basis only to special troops of the engineers, airborne forces, reconnaissance forces and some snipers.

While there are versions of the leaf pattern one and two-piece MKK that were made from the same cut as the 1938 amoeba designs, most of the new 1940/41 issues have improved smocks with redesigned hoods and frontispiece. Some of the redesigned shirts from the two-piece suits have

Reconaissance troops wearing the ZMK winter overwhites. First employed in the Russo-Finnish war of 1939, the ZMK has remained largely unchanged in sixty years.

open necks and lack the hood while others have a narrower cut. The trousers of the two-piece garments remained largely unchanged. The one-piece versions may vary from issue to issue. As with the 1938 MKK suit, the leaf pattern suit is still issued to reservists in the Russian Armed Forces and some Romanian reserve units.

Notwithstanding the 1938 and 1941 MKK patterns were issued on a limited scale to specialized troops of the Soviet army, primarily snipers, engineers, and airborne forces, some references to camouflage uniforms being issued to minelaying troops and airborne forces may, in actuality, have referred to the first special purpose forces of the NKVD – *spetsnaz*. Part of the Soviet Union's deception plan included hiding the existence of these specialized troops. Nevertheless, specialized troops having priority in receiving camouflage uniforms remained constant throughout the war and even into the present.

It was not until mid-1942, that the United States was able to convert its factories to bring about full military production. Britain was holding its own with U.S. help, and German forces were already struggling to maintain supremacy in Eastern Europe and Northern Africa. Meanwhile, the Soviet Union was attempting to fight a delaying tactic against the onslaught of German advances while relocating its military industrial resources. During this period, the United States continued to provide materiel support in the form of food, weapons, vehicles, and tactical equipment.

Meanwhile, in the far East, Japanese forces adopted their first camouflage uniforms (in 1943) and the U.S. issued its first simple camouflage patterns to the U.S. Marine Corps (in 1942). Although the U.S. Army had tried numerous camouflage versions, it didn't issue any regular issue camouflage until 1944 prior to the Normandy invasion. Other combatant nations continued to develop patterns that would eventually prove effective under various types of terrain and battle conditions later in the war.

With its focus changed to an offensive strategy in 1943, the Soviet Union under Stalin fought the Germans to a standstill in Leningrad, Stalingrad, and to victory in the great tank battle of Kursk. As the tide slowly turned in favor of the Red Army in the East, increased pressure was placed on the Afrika Corps by Allied forces bent on taking Italy. Thus the Soviet army was able to initiate offensive operations against the retreating German army.

No longer static for long periods of time, the modern Soviet combat soldier of the mid-1940s required a uniform which would conceal and yet could be altered depending on the locale and the season, the most likely answer was the development of two-sided camouflage uniforms.

While the German army had employed stand-alone reversible camouflage uniforms early on in the war, most countries had heretofore employed non-reversible overgarments worn over standard field uniforms. Soldiers donned camouflage overgarments as they moved from one environment to another, augmenting them with local vegetation, or removed them as they moved into urban areas. While relatively simple, this strategy often resulted in problems of camouflage uniforms being mismatched with the surrounding environment.

The unsuitability of a single type of camouflage under varied conditions was best described by Anthony Hopkins in the movie, *A Bridge Too Far*. In the movie, Hopkins, playing British airborne commander Lieutenant Colonel Frost during operation Market-Garden, noted that his forest camouflage wouldn't fool anyone in the city.

Lieutenant Colonel Frost's predicament was the result of a single type of camouflage uniform unsuited for changing combat locales. Despite this shortcoming, most countries issued only single-sided camouflage uniforms and then only to those elite forces most likely to be in contact with the enemy such as snipers, reconnaissance troops, and airborne forces. The Soviets, however, discovered the value of issuing reversible garments to its forces which could be used in multiple settings.

In order to improve the utility and appearance of these uniforms, both service and field uniforms were further developed and refined. As the Soviet army improved its service uniforms for standard forces, it also improved its camouflage field uniforms. Yet, the development of the MKK uniforms remained largely unchanged. Except for pattern trials and variations, the construction of the coveralls and two-piece suits remained relatively constant through 1945.

In addition to the artificially colored uniforms of the prewar and wartime periods, the Soviet Union also developed a uniform with artificial grass sewn to the suit, known as *mochal'nyi letnii maskirovochnyi kostium,* MLMK, or "summer camouflage suit garnished with bast."[11, 12] Because this uniform does not involve the dying of cloth or use of

The MKK two-piece Amoeba pattern was the first true camouflage overgarment placed into service with Soviet forces in World War II. Here a razvedchik (scout) confers with partisans.

artificially designed camouflage patterns, it will not be described extensively in this book.

Late in the 1944 or early in 1945, the Soviet Ministry of Defense issued the next camouflage pattern to its combat troops: a three-color (dark green, light green and yellow) disruptive-pattern suit. While the cut of the leaf-pattern suit was retained, the *tritsvetnyi maskirovochnyi kamuflirovannyi kostium* (TTsMKK) was the first camouflage uniform with a stair-step pattern to be introduced into the Soviet army. This geometric design served as the basis for future stair-step patterns which remain in use today.

The stair-stepped pattern, used on several uniforms from the 1940s through the 1980s is often incorrectly referred to as a "computer pattern." Even Carey Schofield mistakenly claims this pattern (found on the KLMK) was "... designed by computer."[13] This will be addressed further in the section on KLMK uniforms.

According to Tolochkov:

> "The material from which are prepared the coveralls may have either a one-sided or a two-sided coloration: a yellow color with green spots – for localities with green vegetation, or grey-green or grey-yellow color, corresponding to mountain-forest or desert-steppe localities."[14]

As in previous uniforms, this suit was issued in a one-piece and two-piece version, and then only to special troops such as snipers, reconnaissance, engineer and border forces. The two-piece suit retained the face-veil to reduce facial glare, especially for snipers and artillery observers. The coverall (*tritsvetniy maskirovochnyi kamuflirovannyi kombinezon*) was issued with a matching face mask throughout the 1940s and 1950s.[15] This uniform most recently made an appearance in Albania during the riots in the spring of 1997. numerous rebel factions fighting against government forces in Tirana and elsewhere have adopted one and two piece versions of the multi-colored uniform.

The Second World War afforded Soviet designers the opportunity to put into practice several theories of *maskirovka* and the effect of light and shadows on reflective surfaces. While the uniforms developed and fielded were in no way unique representations of the camofleur's art, they nevertheless incorporated the unique theories of Thayer and the original designs of Stepanova to create the forerunners to modern day camouflage uniforms. Much of what was designed in the late 1930s and during the early 1940s provided the basis for further development in the postwar period and the heyday of Soviet camouflage.

During uniform transition periods, it has become standard practice to issue new uniforms to officers and trainers and use existing stocks for trainees and enlisted personnel. This photo shows an enlisted soldier wearing the TTsMK while the officer standing behind him wears the newer paratrooper KLMK coveralls issued in the early 1960s.

The Postwar Period

The late 1940s marked the beginning of Soviet domination of Eastern Europe and the beginning of the Cold War. As independence movements in Hungary and the Baltics began to emerge, the Soviet government reached across its borders crushing all resistance; using as its tool the enormous and well-equipped Soviet army. Soon the mighty power of the Soviet Union extended well beyond its prewar boundaries to encompass several nations. As its armed forces grew, the Soviet Union expanded production of arms and equipment, to include uniforms.

While warehouses remained stocked with thousands of unused World War II camouflage uniforms, the Ministry of Defense felt the need to continue the development of new uniforms and camouflage for use throughout the Eastern Bloc. While many of the warehoused uniforms were issued to reservists and the rapidly expanding internal security forces, most were sent to client states for use in their armies. The result is a mixture of Soviet uniforms in use throughout Eastern Europe.

As with earlier issues, most camouflage uniforms were issued only those units likely to engage the enemy or to be located in forward combat areas. Those troops designated to receive camouflage were combat engineers (sappers and bridging units), reconnaissance detachments and companies, airborne units, including special-purpose units (*spetsnaz*) and diversionary sabotage units (RDG), naval infantry and naval *spetsnaz* units, and of course, snipers.[16]

Because camouflage uniforms were limited to only so-called elite units, camouflage continued to elicit greater interest from militaria collectors and the defense and intelligence communities. This increased interest resulted in a greater desire to acquire examples of new camouflage uniforms on everyone's part.

Equating camouflage with elite status also became common in other countries; typically, camouflage uniforms and equipment were issued only to scouts, airborne forces, police units and other specially trained military and paramilitary forces. It was not until the mid-1960s that Western nations began to issue camouflage clothing on a wide scale to all of its combat forces. Even the former Soviet Union did not begin to field camouflage uniforms to its ground forces on a broad scale until well into the 1980s. Today there are some countries that restrict camouflage issue to its special forces and strictly control its export. As a rule, camouflage equipment demands a higher price among collectors due to both its rarity and association with special units.

The next two-tone camouflage uniform to be issued was a simpler version of the leaf-pattern MKK. Large green leaves appear to grow out of a tan background. However, the base color of the cotton uniform is actually green, and tan stencils were used to paint leaves on the background in order to provide the appearance of green leaves and stems. On a sample I examined, there were several dye errors which led me to this conclusion, otherwise, it would have been easy to assume the base color of the fabric was actually tan. The process used to color the uniform fabric was a simple roller process as evinced by folding errors in the fabric.

Printed on the inside of the uniform is the word прокат (*prokat*) – meaning it was developed through a rolled process.[17] It is difficult to say whether or not this particular uniform was issued to any specific units since the markings on it indicate it may be an experimental piece. If we follow previous examples, one would suppose this uniform was issued in both one- and two-piece varieties. Nevertheless, the Type II leaf pattern MKK was in fact the beginning of the two-tone MKK series. I have yet to find photographic evidence which associates the Type II leaf pattern uniform with any specific unit and its origins remain a mystery.

During the 1940s the Soviet army experimented with two-color and three-color uniform patterns employing primarily earthtones: green, beige, brown and orange/yellows, in both imitative leaf patterns and disruptive stair-step patterns. As part of their camouflage research the simpler two-tone coloration was eventually combined with a stair-stepped uniform creating a benchmark style of camouflage which has lasted through to the present.

Perhaps in an effort to improve upon previous camouflage designs, the Soviet government issued one- and two-piece uniforms with combinations of previous patterns. These uniforms were issued in several different styles albeit in limited quantities, and they remained in use through the mid-1960s. The first such combination uniform issued was a cross between the amoeba-pattern MKK and the three color disruptive pattern TTsMKK.

In the late 1940s, two-piece and one-piece suits were issued with chocolate brown amoebas over the three-color stair-step designs. Despite claims by Mollo,[18] this uniform does not appear to have been the initial World War II issue; rather, it was simply an effort to exhaust existing stocks of the previous patterns or create experimental designs for use in the field. There are several variations of this uniform with its bizarre color combination, to include the standard one- and two-piece uniforms as well as an open-neck smock with large buttons. The open neck smock design was retained for later use but the combination pattern lasted only a short while.

During the postwar period the Soviets strived to improve the design of the uniform while simplifying the patterns. The TTsMKK was the most prevalent camouflage uniform during the 1950s and formed the basis for subsequent camouflage issues. Soviet designers modified the TTsMKK through the introduction of protective neck pieces, narrower hoods and more tailored pants. These design improvements continued over the next decade.

The next uniform to be fielded was in the early 1950s. Based on the cut of Type II leaf-pattern MKK, the new Paratrooper *kamuflirovannyi letnyi maskirovochnyi kombinezon* (KLMK) coveralls incorporated the improved cut of the tricolor MKK (TTsMKK) with a protective flap across the neck, narrower hood and other improvements detailed in the illustration section.

Perhaps the greatest change to the uniform was the pattern: irregularly shaped white splotches in a splatter pattern on a dark green background. This uniform was the logical follow-on to the amoeba MKK and the Type II leaf pattern. It became the most commonly issued uniform to airborne and reconnaissance units in the 1950s through the 1960s. One source indicated this uniform was in use with airborne units as late as the mid-1970s.

After the introduction of the KLMK paratrooper coveralls, little improvement was made to camouflage uniforms. In fact, no advances were made until 1969 when a new KLMK uniform was introduced for general use by specially trained combat units. The first to be issued was the *kombinezon* (coveralls). The color combination of the previous uniform was retained but the pattern was refined into a stair-step pattern identical to that of the World War II-issue TTsMKK. Resembling the pixels on a close-up graphic on a computer screen, the pattern of the KLMK eventually came to be known by its misnomer: computer pattern. It is unlikely this pattern was developed with computer technology; first, the pattern was designed long before computers came into general use in the Soviet Union, and secondly, the pattern had already been introduced as early as 1943 with stair-step pattern issues.

This uniform is generally referred to as солнечный зайчики (solnechnyi zaichiki), meaning sunshine rays, by some personnel who wear this uniform, describing the pattern sunbeams coming through a forest canopy would make on the ground. Few describe the pattern as a "computer pattern," especially since the majority of Russian soldiers had probably never seen a computer.

Subsequent to the development of the 1969 issue KLMK, new uniforms began to appear with surprising speed. Two new uniforms, the KZS and PMK were issued shortly after the KLMK coveralls. Both were short-lived issues and, in the case of the PMK, saw limited distribution.

After the introduction of the KLMK one-piece, a disposable version was created for special forces, mountain troops and rapid deployment forces: the *kostium zashchitnii cet'* or KZS for short. Developed in the mid-1970s, the KZS has been issued to numerous active and reserve units throughout the army and special services. As the name indicates, the uniform is a two-piece, camouflage suit made from loose-weave netting. The stair-step pattern is identical to that of the earlier KLMK but was much more variable in coloration. Because of factory variations, the range of color combinations seems almost infinite (see description in illustration section).

However, other than pattern similarities, the KZS lacks most of the other qualities attributed to the KLMK. It was obviously designed to be worn as an overgarment and due to its lack of color fastness, would appear to be a short-term, field issue uniform or disposable uniform for deployed combat forces. According to one officer, the uniform has special properties that permit it to be worn under adverse chemical and nuclear environments thus providing extra protection for the wearer. It is frequently seen being used as a training uniform with the former KGB's Quick Reaction Force of civil defense, the mission of which was to evacuate important documents from the Kremlin in the event of war.

Stocks of this uniform remain in warehouses throughout Russia and the Baltic States. Recently factory-sewn sacks been sent to the United States for sale to collectors. Uniforms shipped from the factory in these sacks varied considerably in pattern color. While the majority came from Latvia, a significant number of uniforms have been sent from Estonia, Lithuania and St. Petersburg, Russia. Some dealers (and collectors) mistakenly believed the uniforms were of Baltic origin. However, the manufacturer's label shows that the uniforms were produced prior to the breakup of the Soviet Union and are, in fact, Soviet-produced.

This uniform is now largely obsolete and is used as a training uniform or issued to reserve units. The manufacturing period for this uniform was between 1975 and 1991. It was issued to numerous units during the Afghanistan war and to mobile units in the Central Eurasian region of the former Soviet Union.

Based on the same construction as the KLMK one-piece, a desert version, called *pustinoi maskirovochnyi kombinezon* (desert camouflage coveralls – PMK), was soon issued for use in the sub-Saharan and African regions. The pattern incorporated the designs of the older Type I and Type II leaf patterns with minor color variations. Large leaves with rough edging were laid out on a sandy brown background, while dark green smaller leaves were overprinted randomly across the uniform. The PMK coveralls marked only the second time that a specially designed uniform was issued to conceal the Soviet soldier in a specific environment, the first being the snow coveralls.

The PMK's actual fielding remains somewhat uncertain. While it is believed the uniform was used by the same special purpose forces as received earlier camouflage issues, it is not known whether or not these units served in an advisory role in foreign countries. A former member of the Limited Contingent of Soviet Forces in Afghanistan (OKSVvA) admits to being issued the PMK during his service in Afghanistan. Another special service member claims this is a tropical issue KLMK for reconnaissance troops.

Unfortunately the PMK has not shown up in any recent publications and earlier, Soviet publications downplayed the role of its advisors in African and Middle Eastern countries, especially when those advisors also took part in combat operations against U.S. allies.

Issue of the 1969 KLMK and PMK were remarkable in that two-piece versions were not issued at the same time as in earlier issues. As it turns out, two-piece versions of the 1969 KLMK uniforms were indeed being developed, but would not be released until six years later. PMK two piece uniforms have yet to be seen although the MVD KLMK uniforms are the most likely candidates for follow-on versions.

Guard's Lieutenant Colonel Valerii A. Vostrotin was awarded the title Hero of the Soviet for bravey in Afghanistan in 1988. Although not stated, LTC Vostrotin was probably assigned to an airborne or spetsnaz unit while in Afghanistan judging by the KLMK and airborne tel'niashka.

When in 1975 the new two-piece KLMK was issued, most thought it was a new border guard uniform. Forgetting that all previous camouflage uniforms were issued in both *kombinezon* and *kostium* versions (the PMK did not actually come to light until several years after its issue), many in the intelligence community believed they were seeing a new camouflage issue. In reality, the two-piece KLMK version was so heavily reworked from previous designs and given a new designation, that, technically speaking, they really were seeing a new step in Soviet uniform evolution!

The *kamuflirovannyi letnii maskirovochnyi komplekt* (summer camouflage deceptive set – yes, KLMK again!) represented several advances in the area of camouflage development. First, the uniform was much more tailored; rather than being developed for wear over existing field uniforms, the new KLMK could be worn either as a stand alone uniform or over summer or winter uniforms. Secondly, the uniform was issued with a new detachable hood and a matching beret (in addition to the matching face mask). Pockets were added to the exterior of the uniform and scrim tabs provided for inserting natural camouflage. The result was a very modern camouflage uniform which would remain in service for the next two decades.

Development of the new two-piece KLMK may have resulted from the experience of Soviet special-purpose forces during conflicts in the Middle East and service in non-aligned countries in Africa. As Soviet advisors were exposed to foreign-supplied forces, they most likely adopted aspects of the uniforms which they thought usable; as far as camouflage patterns, the same can be said for the PMK uniform.

Another innovation that came about as a result of the creation of the new KLMK, was the introduction of camouflage accessories. In the past, only essential items were issued with the uniform: pants, smock, mask and attached hood, but with the issue of the KLMK 2-piece uniform matching camouflage items began to make their appearance as well. Baseball-style caps (*polevye furazhki*), boonie caps (*panama*), and other appurtenances soon made their way into the military kit. What's more, the new KLMK two-piece eventually gave rise to two entirely new branches of camouflage uniforms, KLMK varieties issued to the Ministry of Internal Affairs (MVD) and the KGB's *spetsodezhda*.

In late 1989 or early 1990 the two-piece KLMK underwent several revisions. The hood attachment buttons were removed and epaulettes were added for rank insignia. Open-faced plastic buttons replaced small metal buttons which now buttoned through the pocket flaps. Scrim tabs were removed as well. The result was a less complex, more utilitarian version of the previous model. While several intermediate variations and altered uniforms can be found, the reworked version is still in use with army special forces, reconnaissance forces and paramilitary units throughout the FSU.

Soviet combat engineers in Afghanistan wearing disposable KZS overgarments. Judging by the richness of color and relative cleanliness of these uniforms, this is most likely a well-prepared posed photograph.

The KLMK two-piece uniform was a departure from previous issues in that it provided a more tailored appearance and could be worn either as a stand alone or overgarment. Shown here configured for an airborne enlisted soldier of the Soviet army in the 1980s.

Uniform development from the 1930s through the late 1970s showed significant advances in camouflage uniform development. Loose-fitting, baggy coveralls and lightweight two-piece overgarments were eventually replaced by more sophisticated camouflage uniforms with numerous additions to protect and conceal the soldier.

As the Second World War progressed, experiences in the rapidly moving war caused armies to change their concept of concealment and camouflage on the modern battlefield. Modifications in construction and pattern, based on captured German uniforms and combat experiences, resulted in the rapid development of Soviet camouflage during the 1950s and 1960s.

At the height of the Cold War, as the Soviet Union spread across Eastern Europe, new uniforms were introduced for use in the Soviet colonies and abroad. More useful, less complex designs incorporating bicolor camouflage schemes became the rule as camouflage clothing was standardized. Since no major full-scale conflicts forced the USSR to change its designs, the one and two piece KLMK became the standard for the 1960s and 1970s.

Then, the Afghan War forced the Soviet Union to reexamine its uniform inventory and determine the best uniform for use in the near-abroad. With numerous examples to evaluate from the French-Indochina and then American-Vietnam war, several new camouflage designs were developed and tested in Russia's own Vietnam. This marked the beginning of the contemporary phase of Soviet camouflage uniform design.

ENDNOTES CHAPTER 3

[1] Although the camouflage patterns of World War II German and Soviet uniforms are not identical, the Soviet MKT-L fabric camouflage sets used for concealing vehicles and tents is very similar to patterns and colors used during WWII by the Waffen SS, (A. A. Beketov, figures 4 and 5).

[2] United States Air Force, Camouflage, *A Soviet View*, (Washington D.C.: Government Printing Office, 1989), p 198. Translation of A. A. Beketov et al. *Camouflage of Actions by Ground Force Subunits*, (Moscow: 1976).

[3] Ibid, p. 33. Tolochkov fails to use the term "*kamuflirovannyi*" which is generally understood.

[4] Moscow: Voennoe izdatel'stvo Ministry of Defense, 1954, p. 15.

[5] M. I. Tolochkov, *Maskirovka na voine* [Deception in war], Moscow: DOSAAF, 1958, p. 38.

[6] For more information on this uniform, see the illustration section.

[7] Although Tolochkov revised his book in 1975, he made no substantive changes to the text. Furthermore, he failed to update his discussion of specific uniforms or include any additional patterns that had been fielded since 1938. And you wonder why there aren't that many books on Soviet camouflage.

[8] Aleksei Ardashev and Liudmila Shchekotova, "*Snariazhenie Britanskikh Spetschastei*," [Equipment of British Special Operations Units], *Tekhnika-Molodezhi* ,5/94, p. 48.

[9] Gordon L. Rottman, *Warsaw Pact Ground Forces*, (London: Osprey Publishing, 1987), plate I-3, p. 58. Although Rottman fails to equate this uniform with Soviet development or issue, examples I have seen bear both Soviet and Romanian manufacturing marks.

[10] The last "K" in MKK can mean either *kostium* (suit) or *kombinezon* (coveralls); hence, the abbreviation MKK is used to denote both one-piece and two-piece camouflage uniforms.

[11] Bast are strings made from rope or hemp.

[12] L. L. Neliubin, *Illiustrirovannyi voenno-tekhnicheskii slovar'*, [Illustrated military- technical dictionary], (Moscow: Order of Labor of the Red Banner Military Press of the Ministry of Defense of the USSR, 1968), p. 406.

[13] Carey Schofield, *Inside the Soviet Army*, p. 118.

[14] *Maskirovka na voine*, 1958, p. 46.

[15] Although Andrew Mollo et. al., (*Red Army Uniforms of World War II*, London: Windrow & Greene, 1993) claim the combination pattern was the most widely issued version, photographic evidence suggests the pattern without the amoeba overprint was both the most common and the initial issue. The appearance of the combination uniform with the brown blobs overprinted on the stair-step pattern also suggests the patterns were combined later.

[16] Ministerstvo Oborony SSSR, *Podgotovka snaiperov* [Training of Snipers], (Moscow: Voennoe izdatel'stvo, 1987), pp. 93-97.

[17] In this instance, *prokat* could also mean "for hire", that is, it was used for rental purposes by a movie company.

[18] Andrew Mollo et. al., (*Red Army Uniforms of World War II*, London: Windrow & Greene, 1993) , p. 46.

4

MODERN SOVIET CAMOUFLAGE UNIFORMS

"When you're wounded and left on Afghanistan's plains,
And the women come out to cut up what remains,
Jest roll to your rifle and blow out your brains
An' go to your Gawd like a soldier."
– Rudyard Kipling, *The Young British Soldier*

The advent of the war in Afghanistan in 1979 marked the beginning of a new type of warfare for the Soviets. Unconventional warfare of course demanded unconventional tactics and equipment; as a result, Soviet designers undertook the development of new uniforms to fit the needs of the Soviet soldiers in Afghanistan. Knowledge gleaned from experience during the war significantly influenced later Soviet camouflage designs and can be seen in the camouflage uniforms worn today. Perhaps the greatest change during this period was the move from a lightweight coverall to a heavier weight camouflage two-piece suit designed to be worn as a stand-alone garment. The cut from which these uniforms were developed was the model 1981 khaki six-pocket airborne uniform.

1981 Six-Pocket Khaki Airborne Uniform

In previous years, soldiers wore uniforms which were ill-suited for field use. Aside from differences in color, the woolen Soviet, semi dress uniforms were reminiscent of Nazi uniforms of World War II. Restrictive, lacking sufficient pocket space, and poorly designed for sustained combat operations in the field, the standard *forma odezhdy* placed the OKSVvA at a severe disadvantage. Then sometime in 1980 or 1981, a new uniform was introduced which incorporated most of the features of NATO army field uniforms. The finished product was a sturdy utilitarian field uniform perfectly suited for war in Afghanistan.

According to one former Soviet army intelligence officer, Soviet intelligence personnel acquired numerous examples of U.S. camouflage uniforms during the Vietnam war. Members of the Soviet military echelons were so impressed with the design of the uniform, especially the numbers and locations of the additional pockets, that they initiated development of similar uniforms. As a result of the study, which took place from the late 1960s to the mid-1970s, the Soviet army developed and fielded the 1981 khaki airborne uniform.

The khaki six-pocket uniform worn by Soviet airborne forces first appeared publicly during the *Zapad '81* exercises. Made of cotton and with a much more tailored look, the uniform bore a definite Western appearance yet retained a lighter khaki color than Western designs. Designed to serve as a field combat uniform, it bore chest, cargo, and sleeve patch-pockets (closed by Velcro) on the shirt-jacket.

A new winter version was also fielded that incorporated button-in liners in the pants and jacket. A blue fake-fur (sometimes called fish fur – since when do fish have fur?) collar was added with both an enlisted and officer-quality version. Previously developed camouflage over-garments could be worn over the winter uniform making it versatile in all environments.

The pants were also significantly more comfortable than previous designs and possessed numerous patch-pockets for storage of ammunition and equipment. A *spetsnaz* variant, with pants pockets located on the front of the thighs, was also fielded; it remains in use by *spetsnaz* units today.

Previously, a khaki colored boonie cap, developed in 1937, was worn with uniforms issued for tropical areas. With the introduction of the 1981 six-pocket uniform, the boonie cap was reissued and a new field cap added to the inventory. Resembling NATO field caps, the new khaki field cap was made of sturdy cotton and came equipped with earflaps that could be unbuttoned and lowered to protect the ears. New subdued rank and branch insignia also made its appearance during this period, which helped reduce the possibility of identification by the Afghanistani freedom fighters (*Mujahadeen*). Ground forces continue to wear this uniform as a garrison, training and even combat uniform throughout the former Soviet Union.

The significance of the 1981 six-pocket airborne uniform was not only that it represented a new phase in Soviet uniform development, it also provided the basis from which virtually all future camouflage field uniforms up to the present would be developed. The first such uniforms to be issued were the KGB border forces' *spetsodezhda* and the army's woodland camouflage field uniforms. Like the six-pocket airborne uniform, these two designs would last, albeit modified, for the next decade and beyond.

KGB Developments

The first uniform developed subsequent to the six-pocket khaki uniform was the KGB *spetsodezhda* border guard camouflage uniform. Making its appearance between 1982 and 1983, the KGB *spetsodezhda* was based on the six-pocket airborne uniform but with certain styling differences. Designed to withstand adverse weather conditions and serve as a stand-alone field uniform, the *spetsodezhda* marked the first time a camouflage uniform had been developed for a specific unit.

Made of a sturdy cotton fabric, the standard, or first pattern, KGB border guard camouflage uniform was designed to serve as both a field and garrison uniform. Large plastic buttons, marked with a hammer and sickle, secure the front of the uniform and cargo pockets. Patch-pockets, located on the chest, are held closed with similarly marked small plastic buttons which button through a pocket flap. Sleeve pockets close with small flaps of Velcro. Two special pants pockets are located at the hips to allow the wearer to carry extra AK magazines. Instead of a waist cinch, many of the uniforms came with elasticized cloth casings inside the jacket. Strikingly similar in construction to U.S. and NATO field uniforms of the period, the pattern of the *spetsodezhda* differed in that it retained the bicolor stair-step pattern which had been developed during the Second World War and remained in continuous service since the late 1960s. However, rather than green and white, the new color pattern combined a more yellowish geometric pattern on an olive background.

Initially the border guard green service peaked cap (*furazhka*) was worn with all border camouflage, but by the mid-1980s *spetsodezhda* camouflage caps began to shows up in border units. Soft peaked caps (*furazhki*), boonie (*panama*) caps, and berets, all with the KLMK stair-step pattern, have been issued to border units throughout the former USSR. Although soldiers continued to wear patterns from the 1950s, 1960s, and 1970s, most border units adopted the first pattern KGB camouflage uniform. Several transition patterns of the lightweight KLMK two-piece uniform with characteristics of border guard uniforms as well as patterns of the heavier weight KLMK were also tried during this period.

This unidentified reverse KLMK pattern is relatively uncommon and appears in only a lightweight shirt and trouser variant. While it superficially resembles the woodland bicolor uniform, the pattern is of the stair-stepped pattern typical of KLMK's. The history of this uniform's development and issuance remains unclear.

These border guard kursanti (cadets) were photographed in Leningrad in 1991 on Nevskyi Prospekt. Each wears the two-piece KGB/MVD spetsodezhda with matching cap. Border guard patches and shoulder-boards are visible on each kursant's uniform.

As was typical of Soviet equipment development, the military scientific research institute (VNII) made continuous technological improvements to the KGB uniform. In the mid- to late-1980s the KGB/MVD or second pattern *spetsodezhda* camouflage uniform was introduced. The cut of this uniform was much closer to the six-pocket khaki uniform than the first, indicating the possibility that the first KGB border pattern was developed either before or simultaneously with the khaki uniform.

While the color and design of the camouflage pattern remained unchanged, the second pattern KGB/MVD uniform underwent several tailoring modifications that distinguished it from the first pattern. Epaulets were now present on the shoulders so rank stripes or stars could be worn more easily. Large cargo pockets replaced the magazine pouches and small plastic buttons were added to close all but the sleeve pockets. The large plastic buttons used to close the jacket were replaced by small, unmarked plastic buttons protected by a flap; this may have been the result of the larger buttons catching on twines and branches in a field environment. The second pattern or KGB/MVD *spetsodezhda* uniform was truly an improvement over previous special service uniforms and represented a significant advance in Soviet camouflage development.

In addition to the camouflage items already associated with the uniform, a camouflage field cap (*polevaia furazhka*) was added to the list of available headgear; which was patterned after the cap developed for the khaki uniform. By the mid-1980s, virtually all of the KGB's field and garrison units adopted this uniform as their primary field (and even garrison) uniform. As late as 1993, I observed KGB Kremlin guards within the confines of the Kremlin wearing the second pattern *spetsodezhda* with subdued rank and insignia.

Other units subordinate to the KGB also adopted the second pattern *spetsodezhda* to include *spetsgruppa* "A" (also referred to as *Al'fa* – a very un-Russian word which journalists introduced), *spetsgruppas Vympel'* and *Kaskad* and other anti-terrorist and counter-terrorist KGB subunits. Other non-KGB units that adopted the second pattern KGB/MVD *spetsodezhda* included Moscow's counter-terrorist special-purpose *militsiia* Detachment (OMSN); separate units of the MVD's Dzerzhinsky division,[1] and the counter-terrorist special-purpose company (RSN) of the MVD.

The *spetsodezhda* represents a remarkable step forward in the development of Soviet camouflage uniforms and stands as a significant representative of modern camouflage development. This was the first stand-alone camouflage uniform designed to withstand adverse weather under all field conditions. It has been so successful that it remains in use even today with units of the foreign intelligence service (SVR) successors to the KGB.

As the special services were developing the *spetsodezhda* for operational use, the Soviet army was also pursuing the development of its own, more specialized camouflage clothing and equipment.

Type I Woodland Pattern

In 1982 a new three-color camouflage uniform, unlike any previous Soviet camouflage designs, was introduced for use by airborne and army *spetsnaz* forces; thus was born the Type I woodland camouflage pattern. Classified for several years, the new combat uniform did not appear in public until the 40th anniversary of the Great Patriotic War military parade in Moscow in 1985. Until then the new uniform remained relatively unknown to U.S. intelligence and defense agencies. Ostensibly this was due to the fact that it had been directly copied from U.S. camouflage uniforms and the Soviets Ministry of Defense was not eager to publicly display its new uniforms.

According to a former member of the GRU, on the orders of the Soviet leader Brezhnev, U.S. Army camouflage uniforms, worn primarily by U.S. Army rangers and special forces, were sent back to the Soviet Union during the Vietnam conflict. Marine camouflage, Army battle dress uniforms, and special forces tiger stripe "cammies" were seriously studied and eventually, reverse-engineered. The acquisition of the American uniforms was kept a closely guarded secret as was their exploitation.

The tailoring of the new "desant" uniform, as in the 1981 khaki field uniform, was a departure from previous KLMK styles and instead paralleled the KGB *spetsodezhda* issues. As with the KGB versions, these new uniforms had additional cargo and slash-style pockets, belt loops, epaulets for rank, and bore a much more tailored appearance than the early KLMK styles. When compared to previous U.S. Army issues of the 1960s and 1970s, the similarities are obvious.

Members of the 106th Guards Airborne Division were among the first to receive this uniform and other units soon followed. Although the one-piece and two-piece KLMK's were still widely used, new winter and summer versions of the woodland pattern gradually made their way into the system. Soon the woodland uniform was issued to several elite units in two distinct color variants and with branch-specific configurations.

Initially the tricolor woodland pattern uniform color variations were limited to two versions: brown (mountain-desert), and green (forest). Although many collectors believed these color differences were due merely to manufacturing variations, it soon became clear the variations were intentional. In early 1989 I determined that there were

The first published photo of the 1982 woodland pattern uniform worn by a Guard's airborne unit on parade in Moscow in 1985. Note that the personnel wear parade beret flashes and airborne patches on their right side, facing the reviewing stands. Unusual dress brown gloves are also worn.

additional variations within the uniform issues, not just colors, but styles as well. These differences appeared to be related to Soviet branches of service.

From photos taken in the Soviet Union I observed that Soviet army personnel tucked in their uniform shirts while naval infantry personnel wore the shirts untucked, wearing their belts around the shirt waist rather than through belt loops on the pants. At first I felt this was simply a custom each service had incorporated as part of its service tradition, much as U.S. Army, Naval and Marine units adopt certain uniform customs associated with their branches of service. With the uniforms running about $500 a set, it was difficult to obtain them in any quantity to look for differences. Fortunately, while I was stationed in Germany from 1989 through 1991, the Berlin Wall fell and I was able to acquire several examples to inspect further.

Upon examining several examples of the woodland uniform, I noticed that there were two specific variations: one, an army version; and another, a naval infantry variant. The army version possessed suspender openings, an internal holster with a lanyard, two chest pockets (button) and two sleeve pockets (Velcro). The lack of cargo pockets on the jacket and the presence of suspender openings helped clarify the matter of which units wore their shirts tucked in. On a visit to the USSR in 1991, I was able to further validate my assertions.

While in Leningrad (now St. Petersburg), I also discovered naval variants lacked the holster and suspender openings but had both cargo pockets and epaulets for rank. A drawstring cinch cord was located on the waist of the naval jacket which helped with tightening of the jacket. The presence of the additional cargo pockets also helped to clear up the question about proper wear of the naval variants. Of course, with the issue of the 1988 Soviet regulations concerning the proper wear of military uniforms, much of this became clearer through diagrams; since the book did not hit the collector markets until the early nineties many of the explanations remained unclear.

While the naval infantry uniform appeared to be closest in design to the khaki six-pocket airborne uniform, from which it was no doubt derived, other versions of the woodland camouflage uniform were eventually created using the original woodland Type I uniforms as models. Crewman's uniforms, tanker variants, and air force *kombinezons* (*kombis*) were fielded to the various support services over the course of the 1980s. Woodland camouflage field caps or branch-specific colored berets were issued as part of the uniform initially, but, by the early 1990s, these were replaced by camouflage berets. By late 1989 numerous ground and special operations units began to adopt the new woodland uniforms as their primary field apparel. In addition to branch of service variants, other Type I variations have also come to light in recent years.

One such variation is the so-called reconnaissance uniform. Based on the Type I naval uniform, the "reconnaissance" uniform possesses a new camouflage design not recorded prior to the fielding of the woodland patterns. The pattern, consisting of five pastel colors bleeding into one another, are arranged in a vertical pattern rather than a loop or whorled pattern. According to the original owner of the uniform, it was issued only to reconnaissance personnel of combat units. However, according to a Belorussian military officer, the uniform was issued to soldiers operating in the steppe regions of Central Asia beginning in the 1980s.

Recent evidence suggests this uniform has been issued only to reconnaissance and GRU *spetsnaz* units of the Soviet and Russian Armies. The development of this uniform largely parallels that of the KGB *spetsodezhda* and represents a specially-produced version of the six-pocket khaki uniform. While there is no open source material to suggest this uniform was anything other than a limited-issue item, its design and coloration are remarkably advanced.

The reconnaissance uniform has yet to be described in any official or unofficial military publications; to date it has been published in only a few publications, primarily in a civilian context.[2] One newspaper showed a *spetsnaz* soldier wearing the uniform without any visible insignia, while another showed the uniform worn by an unidentified soldier. Perhaps more information will be forthcoming concerning its use and fielding in some future Russian publication.

Fielding of the new woodland uniforms accelerated in the late 1980s and numerous ground units began to adopt it as their standard uniform. For example, in 1988 when Gorbachev announced the formation of special units to counter terrorism and organized crime, there were no special uniforms available for their use. Therefore, the MVD's special-purpose *militsiia* detachments (OMON) adopted the army's camouflage uniform for operational use until unit-specific uniforms became available.[3]

Members of the OMON in the Baltic states adopted this uniform as their standard field uniform – usually with the airborne blue-striped T-shirt (*tel'niashka*) to show their elite status. As a result, news media and local officials wrongly identified riot suppression units as regular airborne forces, a claim the army was quick to deny. Previously, the OMON, while in covert status (they were referred to as special motorized *militsiia* units), wore uniforms of other services for precisely this reason, just as the Soviet intelligence (GRU) *spetsnaz* wore the uniforms of combined-arms troops to hide their affiliation. When the OMON became overt riot suppression and anti-crime units in 1988, there was no longer a need to conceal their identities. By 1990, the OMON detachments were issued sleeve patches, new helmets, and eventually OMON-specific crests and badges.

One of the few published photographs of the woodland reconnaissance uniform, worn by a member of the armed forces in the Predenestrov region of the former Soviet Union. The subject is armed with an AK-74 and a sidearm.

Initially, because unit-specific items had yet to be produced for the OMON, several units adopted naval infantry berets with *militsiia* devices as their standard headgear. According to an officer in the Main Administration for Internal Affairs, since the first units were formed in St. Petersburg, black naval berets were the only berets available at the time. Those OMON members unwilling to remove the red flash, simply inserted their *militsiia* insignia through the flash.[4] Thus were born the "black berets," a symbol of repression known throughout the USSR in the late 1980s and early 1990s. While OMON troops in Saint Petersburg have largely replaced their black berets with smoky-grey berets, Moscow OMON units continue to wear both black berets and grey berets with either Soviet *militsiia* oval flashes or Russian tricolor flashes.

In addition to the OMON, other special units of the MVD's internal troop and crime-fighting units began to acquire camouflage uniforms as their main field uniforms, many of these were replaced with other, more specialized camouflage uniforms. However, at least one variation of the Type I woodland pattern was instituted as a standard uniform for the MVD's Eighth Guard's Administration (GUO MVD) as early as 1991. This uniform, a four-color urban woodland variation, was issued in St. Petersburg to guards serving as auxiliary protection for banks and private companies. Known as the MVD KKO camouflage uniform, it will be discussed in more detail in a separate section.

Development of the patterning on the woodland camouflage uniforms is reportedly achieved through a complex dye process which incorporates standard dyeing techniques with infrared suppressing chemicals. Rather than using a simple screening process the woodland pattern uniforms are produced through repeated coloration of each whorl over and over. According to a military source, this process reduces infrared signatures by at least 30% and prevents observation with night vision devices at distances greater than 100 meters.

The Soviet woodland camouflage uniform was a great step forward in the development of combat uniforms. Despite its probable development from U.S. designs of the 1960s, it nevertheless represented a move toward more advanced, combat systems rather than stand-alone uniforms. Of course, as with all Soviet technological developments, the Type I camouflage was soon improved and a new version fielded with numerous improvements.

Three enlisted soldiers of the Russian army in Moscow in 1994. Each wears the Type II woodland uniform. Each soldier wears a sam browne belt and an enlisted cap device on the field cap. Not the various footgear and generally unkempt appearance of the soldiers in the nation's capital.

Type II Woodland Pattern

In late 1989 or early 1990, the Soviet Military Scientific Research Institute began to work on improving and standardizing woodland camouflage uniforms. The result of this research was a combined army-navy variant that provided a suitable utilitarian camouflage uniform for the 1990s. This hybrid uniform featured an internal holster, epaulets for rank, and four pockets; this uniform gradually replaced the previous two variants as the standard camouflage field uniform for the ground and naval forces. Although the tailoring of the uniform had been standardized, there soon began to appear a wide range of color variations that couldn't be explained as manufacturing inconsistencies.

A few separate airborne units began to appear on Soviet television and in magazines sporting a new "pink" version of the woodland camouflage. The color was very obviously not related to factory variations as the pink color was consistent among units. Curious about this new version, I met with a colonel of the Soviet airborne forces at Leavenworth, Kansas who was attending the Command and General Staff College there in the fall of 1991. He explained that the pink version was to become the standard issue for Soviet airborne forces in the near future. He also indicated that the brown and green versions would remain in service with ground and naval forces, at least for the time being.

In addition to the pink version, by mid-1992, numerous versions began to appear with various paramilitary and security forces throughout the Soviet Union. Colors ranged from light green, forest green and mud brown tints, to brighter shades of green, reddish brown, blue, orange, and lavender. These variants made their way to several military and security units within the former Soviet Union and several were adopted by republic armed forces, most notably Ukraine and Belarus. Many of these variants remain in service today with former republic ground forces, replete with their Soviet and Russian factory markings.

In 1993 the MVD also updated and modernized its camouflage uniforms, following the lead of the ground and naval forces. The result was a series of four modern combat uniforms similar to the Type II woodland camouflage. The differences between these and the woodland issues are such that I have opted to place them in a separate category; MVD combat uniforms.

All of the color variations mentioned thus far were derived from the Type II version of the woodland camouflage field uniform. While several of the variations have since been adopted by various paramilitary and security organizations, most of these were doomed to be replaced by several new uniforms developed for the ground and security forces just prior to the collapse of the Soviet Union.

The period 1979 through 1991 was an important period in the development of Soviet camouflage uniforms. Moving away from the baggy, pajama style overalls of the past, more tailored, stand-alone designs made their way to the forefront of Soviet uniform development. Several new trends also arose during this period, specifically, the development of uniforms for each branch of service tailored to meet the demands of the field, and variations in pattern based on conditions under which the units would operate. Furthermore, several uniforms came into being which, although largely developed from existing Western designs, still showed ingenuity and demonstrated the capabilities of Soviet research designers. As in the past, this experience was not lost on the developers of Russian camouflage uniforms and would form the basis for the next series of camouflage uniforms, that is, the uniforms of the reborn Russian state.

ENDNOTES CHAPTER 4

[1] Since renamed the Separate special-purpose division (ODON).

[2] Nataliia Gorbunova, "*Nad chem smeemsia*," (At what are we laughing), *Sputnik* - Digest of the Soviet Press, p. 69.

[3] There are indications that the OMON existed prior to 1988 but their activities were kept secret. By announcing their formation, General Secretary Gorbachev may have attempted to prove to the public his desire to bring the growing crime rate in the Soviet Union under control. The OMON's use of army camouflage may simply have been a ruse to conceal their true organizational status.

[4] Several "OMON berets" created by unscrupulous dealers have the justice shield instead of the *militsiia* insignia on the flash, an unlikely occurrence considering that the OMON is strictly a police unit, and OMON members have police uniforms but not justice ministry uniforms. Also, all authentic OMON berets have the flash on the wearer's left side since these berets, unlike those in the airborne and naval forces, are not worn during parades.

5

RUSSIAN ARMY CAMOUFLAGE UNIFORMS

"First we act, then we explain."
– Alexander Lebed, Russia's former national security chief

By early 1991, the Soviet Union's military and special services had gone through several phases of uniform development. The end result was a series of well-tailored, utilitarian camouflage combat uniforms that met the changing needs of the military and special services according to their missions. While these uniforms varied widely in color, due mainly to the environment in which the forces were deployed, they became standardized in construction.

While most other nations had adopted specific uniform styles for their armed services and retained those designs for several years, the Soviet Union fielded a series of new uniforms after only just completing the standardization of its woodland camouflage uniforms. The impetus for this change was an attempt to improve the image of the armed forces of the Soviet Union and present a more professional appearance to the public. The collapse of the Soviet Union in 1991 certainly hastened this process. Rising nationalism and a drive toward a more stable identity were certainly part of the desire to develop and field a new line of dress and camouflage uniforms, security was another.

Incorporating aspects of uniforms of the major European armies, proven U.S. designs, and the old Imperial Russian heritage, the new uniform designs were largely a departure from the old, staid designs of the 1960s and 1970s. Dress uniforms are distinctly Western in appearance and although the cut of the field uniforms is reminiscent of older designs, the patterns are certainly unique. What we see today throughout Russia and some republics of the FSU is the result of this change, that is, the Russian Armed Forces or VSR camouflage uniform.

Russian Armed Forces Pattern

In early 1991, army designers were experimenting with new camouflage designs for the ground and air forces. Appearing in mid-1991, was the Russian Armed Forces (*Vooruzhennie sili Rossiia* or VSR) camouflage uniform. This development stemmed largely from an attempt on the part of the Ministry of Defense to standardize the uniforms of the fighting forces in order to create a general "smartening up" of their appearance, with each service having specific camouflage uniforms and insignia to inspire more *esprit de corps*. This was also an attempt to improve the military's standing with the public at large by providing a more professional image.

Another reason for the changeover to a new camouflage design may have been related to problems associated with confusion of military ground units with the security forces, especially in the Baltics and in the Georgian

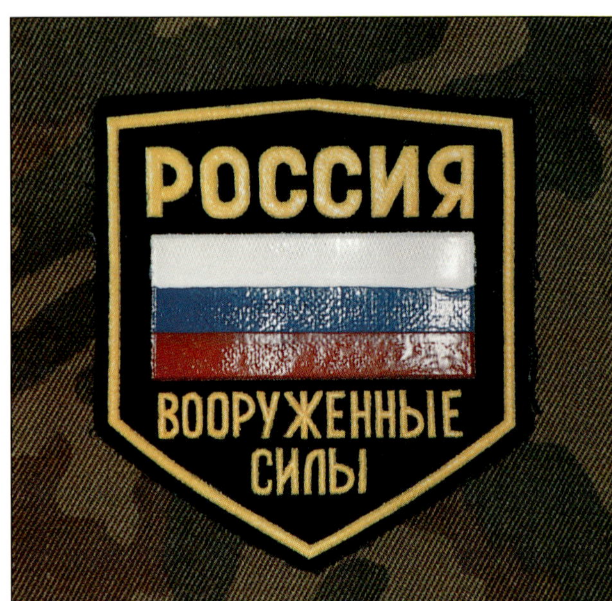

The patch of the Russian armed forces adopted for use on all field and service uniforms of the Russian ground forces. The background is the VSR or "Schofield" pattern.

Russian troops of the 27th motorized rifle division and American soldiers of the 3rd Infantry division train together as part of the Partnership for Peace program. The Russian soldiers are wearing the VSR pattern uniform and "peacemaker" patches on their left sleeves.

republic. Due to the sometimes bloody actions of army and security units during the suppression of insurrections in these unstable areas, the need for unit-specific uniforms also arose. The VSR uniform satisfied this need.

Initial development of the VSR pattern probably occurred simultaneously with that of the Type II woodland pattern, with the first uniforms going to airborne units. Earlier patterns of woodland camouflage were eventually abandoned for a new look, one radically different from other camouflage styles. Even the pink woodland camouflage uniform, first fielded to airborne forces, were gradually replaced with the new VSR designs. However, in keeping with the Soviet tradition of upgrading existing equipment, the new camouflage pattern was fitted to an old uniform design, the 1981 khaki airborne uniform.

First appearing in two open source publications in late 1991, the VSR pattern gradually caught the notice of collectors. The first source was in Carey Schofield's *Inside the Soviet Army*, published in 1991. On the inside back cover, Ms. Schofield is shown wearing a new three-color, six-pocket uniform with vertical green and brown splotches on a tan background. This first full-color uniform photo caused me to refer to the pattern as a "Schofield Pattern," a term quickly adopted by the collecting community. Based on the publication date of the book and taking into account the length of time to design and field new Soviet equipment, I estimated the inception date of the uniform to have been as early as 1990.

Jane's Intelligence Review was the next publication to carry a photo of both the garrison and the field uniforms that were about to be introduced into the then transitioning Soviet army.[1] The camouflage uniform shown in Jane's had the same pattern as that in Carey Schofield's book. Although there was no detailed supporting text, the inference was that these uniforms were to be fielded in the near future. Of course, this was before the attempted coup by Gorbachev's military and security chiefs, an event which undoubtedly affected the fielding of the new uniforms.

After the collapse of the Soviet Union and the subsequent creation of the Russian Armed Forces, the uniform began to appear more and more often in use by ground force units of the Russian army. Since these units were the first to receive the uniform, I began to equate the new pattern with ground and combined arms units. A new patch, bearing the Russian flag and the inscription: "Armed Forces of Russia", also began to appear on the sleeve pockets of the new uniforms. In order to standardize references and to clarify the differences between the woodland and

VSR patterns, I began to use the terms "Schofield" and "VSR" interchangeably, designations which have generally been accepted within the militaria collecting community. Some mistakenly refer to the uniform as a pattern 1993 uniform, believing it was not released until that year. The designation "VSR" is probably the most accurate.

In August 1991, the attempted military takeover in Moscow led to the eventual downfall of Gorbachev and the collapse of the Soviet Union. Due to the utter collapse of the Soviet government and subsequent rise to power of Boris Yeltsin, several of the former republics declared their independence. By December of 1991 Yeltsin, now leader of the newly created Russian Federation, began to reorganize the Soviet military and special services forces.

Although Yeltsin sought to create a joint military organization which combined several armies of the FSU, the Unified Armed Forces of the Commonwealth of Independent States (OVS SNG) turned out to be strictly an ill-fated dream. With the creation of new republic armies in Ukraine, Belorussia and the Baltic States, Moscow found itself faced with the prospect of its forces wearing the same uniforms as those of potential foes. With these thoughts in mind, Yeltsin's Minister of Defense no doubt accelerated the fielding of the new VSR patterns.

Beginning in 1992, VSR pattern uniforms began to appear more often in the open press. Members of the 14th Army in action in Nagorno-Karabakh and in Ossetia appeared on Russian television wearing the new pattern with the new sleeve patch. Although most soldiers still wore the 1982 woodland pattern, a few combatants were shown wearing the new design. Finally, in the United States, the television program, *World of Valor*, which first aired in October 1992 on the Discovery Channel, showed winter and summer versions being worn by airborne units. It was becoming more apparent that the VSR pattern was replacing the standard and pink airborne variants of the woodland pattern.

In 1992, during a military parade honoring the creation of its ground forces, the Azeri government showed its paratrooper assault units (*Vozdushniye shturmovie desantniki*) wearing the new camouflage. This indicated wider fielding among certain republic armed services, specifically those that had become de facto members of the SNG.

While visiting Russia in June 1993, I saw several members of right-wing political groups such as *Pamyat* congregating near the Kremlin wearing the new uniform, both in civilian and military versions. I also noticed soldiers of the Russian army in Moscow and St. Petersburg wearing the new uniform with "Armed Forces of Russia" patches on their right shoulders. Yet it was not until July

A member of the Russian Federal Border Service (FPS) in Moscow in 1993. Here the border guard wears a combination of Russian armed forces camouflage and a Soviet KGB dress cap with officer's cap device. Soviet items can still be seen worn by a large portion of the military and special service forces.

1993 that the Russian Ministry of Defense announced that the Armed Forces of Russia would officially adopt the new camouflage uniform as its standard field uniform.

In the announcement, published in the July 27 issue of *Krasnaia Zvezda*,[2] the chief of the Central Equipment Administration of the Ministry of Defense of the Russian Federation (TsVU MO RF), General-Lieutenant Mikhail Khrenov, said the new camouflage was fielded to provide a uniform which was "... markedly different from service uniforms of soldiers of nearby countries."[3] General-Lieutenant Khrenov also stated the new pattern was to be issued in a forest variant (dark green) and a mountain-desert variant (brown or tan).

VSR patterning bears little resemblance to either U.S. or previous Soviet patterns. Although highly variable, the tricolor pattern consists of rough-edged, elongated, brownish and greenish splotches on a tan or khaki background, and bears more resemblance to a hunting uniform sold commercially in the West. Base colors of the uniform range from a light tan background to a dark forest-green with dark green and reddish-brown splotching. Construction of the new uniform is based on the 1981 khaki six-pocket uniform rather than the light-weight KLMK and is made of the same 100% cotton material. Despite official claims that only two distinct variations were developed, factory inconsistencies have resulted in several off-color versions being released with a range of shades and colors.

Although General-Lieutenant Khrenov stated that factories could supply only 10% of the orders as of 1993, this number began to stabilize upward as the economic situation in Russia began to stabilize. As of this writing, the new VSR pattern has been fielded to the most of the Russian ground forces and some motorized units of the Ministry of Internal Affairs. Airborne forces continue to wear pink and other woodland variants, a bicolor woodland variant, and the VSR pattern.

Peacemaking units in Bosnia-Herzegovina have largely adopted this unit as its standard field uniform. Moreover, some of the Russian special services, OMON units from around the Moscow and Saint Petersburg districts, have fielded the new uniform as their standard operational camouflage.[4] Therefore, it would appear that, although the woodland uniforms may not entirely disappear over the next few years, they will definitely be reduced in number as the VSR pattern becomes more common.

ENDNOTES CHAPTER 5

[1] August 1991, volume 3, number 8, p. 384.

[2] *Krasnaia zvezda*, "About the New Military Uniform without verbal camouflage". Ivan Ivaniuk in an interview with General Lieutenant Mikhail Khrenov, Chief of the Central Clothing Administration for the Ministry of Defense of the Russian Federation, July 27, 1993, #168, p. 2.

[3] Ibid.

[4] Personal observations, 6/93, and 10/94.

6

MVD COMBAT CAMOUFLAGE UNIFORMS

"If racing in an APC (armored personnel carrier) through this region and peering out the windows at it means controlling it, then we control it."
– Capt. Sergei K., 29, said of the army's grip on the (Chechen) capital.
Los Angeles Times, February 15, 1995

"After all the atrocities I've heard of here, I would agree with Stalin," he said. "The entire Chechen nation shouldn't just be deported, it should be exterminated."
– Col. Sergei P., commander of an ODON regiment.

During the politically unstable period of 1990 through 1991, under Gorbachev's leadership, the military and special services faced uncertain futures. While the army and strategic forces were experiencing the results of the drawdown brought about by Gorbachev's peace initiatives, the security forces experienced unprecedented growth. This was the natural result of the rise of crime in the Soviet Union and expansion of democracy movements in the Baltic States and the south. The collapse of East Germany signaled the eventual downfall of the Soviet system and provided an impetus for KGB Chief Kriuchkov and MVD Chief Pugo to expand their powers and strengthen their security forces. Part of this strengthening included the development of new weapons and equipment to outfit combat troops of the KGB and MVD.

MVD KLMK Uniforms

A major change occurred in 1991, with the development and introduction of a series of lightweight KLMK uniforms for the MVD. While this new series was an refinement over earlier two-piece KLMK uniforms, it appears to have been a dead-end program. The new MVD KLMK's were an improvement in that the Russian government attempted to develop several camouflage patterns directly tied to vegetative and terrain conditions under which its units would be fighting, thus further departing from previous camouflage development strategies. Although the uniforms deviated in pattern and color from previous KLMK uniforms, there was no real difference in uniform construction.

Initially, the new uniforms were a curiosity due to both their novelty and the fact that they had not been shown in any open source material. In May 1992, when a dealer began offering the four new types of lightweight camouflage suits, it was natural that they should attract the attention of militaria collectors. However, due to a lack of information concerning their fielding, the uniforms remained unpopular with the collecting public. To counteract this unpopularity, militaria retailers came up with some interesting explanations for the uniforms' origins and use. Still, the design of the uniforms and the presence of MVD markings left little doubt as to their true purpose.

The uniforms were issued in three color variants, one of which has two versions. The first style, or European version, is a four-color uniform with black, rust and mustard on a greenish/beige background. The second, or tropical style, is a tricolor design with forest green and orange on a peach background. This style also comes in a mountain variation with lime green and bright orange on a yellowish background. The third style, or desert pattern, is a two-color camouflage with brown splotches on a peach or orange background.

The patterns themselves, although simple, are a departure from previous stair-step or multiple-color pattern designs fielded after World War II in that they present a more jagged appearance, with the designs running horizontally rather than vertically. Orange and yellow splotches appear broken as though painted through overlying twigs or sticks. Color differences notwithstanding, the MVD KLMK uniforms, although similar to the KLMK versions of the 1980s, show some striking differences in construction.

Specifically, as with the previous two-piece KLMK uniforms, the jackets possess four pockets on the front, held closed by plastic buttons, each of which is covered by a flap. Several scrim tabs (*nashivki*) on the jacket allow the soldier to insert twigs or branches to improve his concealment. Matching lightweight pants, as in earlier models, have two slash front pockets and one hip pocket, with no other cargo, magazine or utility pockets. As in the two-

Members of the Separate special purpose division at Balashikha. The special purpose forces soldiers are wearing, left to right: SMK - light urban, SMK - daytime green, SMK - nighttime green, KKO Type 2 urban variant, KKO Type 2 forest variant, MVD KLMK European variant, KKO Type 1, MVD KLMK tropical variant and KKO Type 2 forest variant (wearer's back is to camera). To the right the wearer has a short coat version of the SMK Nylon uniform with matching cap and woodland camouflage trousers.

piece KLMK uniforms, each MVD *spetsnaz* KLMK uniform comes with a matching beret and large sniper face mask. A hood, provided as part of the outfit, is fastened by two buttons at the rear of the collar of the jacket. The beret may be worn as a complement to the uniform or other headgear may be substituted.

At first look, differences in construction of the new uniforms seem puzzling. Unlike the KLMK two-piece uniforms, the belt loops on the pants are too small for the standard army field belt. Secondly, there are no magazine pouches or cargo pockets; however, there is one right hip pocket, of the type for carrying identification papers. The thinness of the material also brings into question whether or not these are stand-alone uniforms (most likely) or are designed to be worn over a more rugged field uniform.

The differences in manufacture are compounded when one attempts to ascertain the origins and uses of these uniforms. Although advertised by many dealers as Afghanistan combat uniforms, undoubtedly with the intent of getting higher prices for them, this is unlikely. The uniforms did not come into existence until 1991 or 1992 and there is little evidence that anyone other than the MVD has or will use these uniforms.

All of the uniforms I have examined bear the factory marks and the name of a plant in Saint Petersburg (not Leningrad, but St. Petersburg). They also bear the initials "МВД" (MVD in Cyrillic) on the pants and jacket in large block letters. This alone was a significant occurrence; seldom in recent history has any Soviet uniform been hallmarked with an agency's initials (let alone a security agency).

Other countries, such as the former East Germany (DDR), marked large numbers of their equipment with agency initials (MdI, MfS, NVA etc...), obviously not being as concerned about security. Soviets, however, were always sticklers for secrecy and seldom identified their uniforms with anything other than the factory name, symbol, and approval (OTK) marks from the plant. Apparently, the Russian government holds different views as more and more of its uniforms are marked for specific ministries; most collectors will say this has been amply demonstrated by the flood of new Russian unit patches issued in 1995 and 1996.

When I discussed this matter with a member of the Main Administration of the Internal Troops (GUVD), he mentioned that some uniforms are produced on contract for the ministry in limited numbers by such companies as Vera in Saint Petersburg. In the case of the MVD, uniforms may be issued to commanders of local detachments based on guidelines provided by the GUVD or the Chief Administration of the Command of Internal Troops (GUKVD). While policies governing the issue of army uniforms are more strict than for the security services, patches and unit insignia are often acquired for these units based on the same guidelines, such as with *spetsnaz* and airborne units.

The MVD *spetsnaz* KLMK camouflage uniforms reportedly were developed specifically for the MVD's special-purpose units, which operate under various conditions. A factory located in St. Petersburg handled the contract and produced limited numbers of the uniform sets for MVD units deploying to southern republics of the former Soviet Union. Only one or two units adopted these uniforms for general use in the central and southern republics of the FSU. As a result, few of the sets actually made it to the field units, the rest being exported for sale to collectors.

Information gathered from open-source material and conversations with members of the MVD, indicates the main customers for these uniforms are the *osnaz* troops of the MVD's Brigade of Special Designation of Internal Troops (BON-VV). First, the July 23, 1992 *Krasnaia zvezda* showed an officer wearing the European style pattern with a 1982 woodland pattern field cap. Next the November-December 1992 issue of *Na boevom postu*[1] showed the desert variant worn by a soldier of the MVD in a southern republic. It soon became clear that these uniforms were indeed fielded to MVD units operating in combat regions. Although they are still worn in some regions, they have largely been replaced by new nylon combat variants (see below) and upgraded versions of earlier woodland patterns. Nevertheless, due to their suitability for varied combat conditions, the MVD *spetsnaz* KLMK uniforms were an important step in the development of Russian camouflage.

Recently members of the MVD leadership admitted they were introducing new uniforms and equipment to help with the battle against organized crime and to stem the rising violence in several republics of the FSU. It is a fact that in 1991 the Minister of Internal Affairs, under Gorbachev's direction, created several new organizations to fight terrorism, economic crime, hijacking, and a host of other criminal activities which were plaguing the emerging democracy. Therefore, it seemed logical that new uniforms would be among those items procured for use by these new organizations in their effort to put an end to the rising tide of crime and violence.

A gunner in Chechnia wears the PFO Tiger stripe version of the KKO Type 2 uniform with matching field cap. The large number of Internal Ministry forces deployed to Chechnia required significant logistical support and was complicated by the varied units and their individual unit requirements - including operational uniforms and equipment.

MVD Special Operations Uniforms

As previously mentioned, the MVD has since its inception used variants of the army's uniforms and more recently, uniforms specific to the MVD. In the last few years the MVD has adopted a green and urban four-color version of the army woodland uniform, and lightweight KLMK uniforms for its special operations detachments deployed to southern republics. Also within the last few years, the MVD has introduced additional camouflage uniforms that bear little resemblance to any designs in use by other ministries; one of these is the nylon SMK combat uniform.

Although marketed by a Russian dealer as a SWAT uniform, the *spetsial'nyi maskirovochnyi komplekt* (or SMK) actually has a much broader use. Generally this uniform has been associated with members of the Administration for Combating Embezzlement of Socialist Property and Speculation (BKhSS) which has since devolved to the 6th Administration responsible for organized crime. Certain OMON units and members of the Dzerzhinsky (now Separate Motorized Rifle Division – ODON) division's *spetsnaz* unit *Vitiaz'* also employ this uniform. In order to simplify matters, I have chosen to refer to this uniform as the MVD's Special Operations Uniform (SMK).

The SMK which has an unusual construction and pattern, is produced on contract by the *Laboratoriia spetsial'nykh materialov i tekhnologii* (Laboratory of special equipment and technology) in St. Petersburg. This company produces a wide variety of equipment for law enforcement units in Russia including vests, holsters, helmets and tactical assault equipment.

Construction of the SMK consists of a nylon outer shell with a dark cotton lining. The suit is issued in both lightweight summer versions as well as heavier winter versions. Winter suits are very heavy and are marked in the interior with the word *"SNEG"* or "snow". Although the uniform is highly variable in its construction (see illustration section), it is quite suitable for special operations. There are green (forest), dark grey (urban), and light grey (low-light urban) variations available for operational use. In addition to the standard coat, bib overalls, and caps, the SMK also has matching assault vests, riot helmets and bullet resistant vests available in both forest and urban variations.

What is so unusual about the SMK is its heavy reliance on foreign-designed materials. Plastic couplers, obviously not made in Russia, or at least not designed there, play an important part in the SMK construction (as well as in MVD combat boots and vests). Most likely, portions of the uniform were either contracted out or designed, whole or in part, by foreign factories, probably in Germany. The sudden appearance of uniform items, marked with Roman letters, is a strong indicator that the items are not wholly domestic. Since other items, such as riot helmets used by certain *spetsgruppa* units, were produced in Germany, it does not seem unlikely that other items may have been produced there as well; or at least with a European country's assistance. With the privatization of factories that used to produce uniforms for the state, another variable has been introduced as well, specifically, civilian copies.

A privatized company in St. Petersburg recently began to offer civilian versions of SMK uniforms and accessories. Jackets, pants, backpacks, caps, book bags and even umbrellas are all commercially available in the grey, green and even brown versions. In 1993 a complete set of civilian summer camouflage was available in St. Petersburg for about 26,000 rubles ($26), whereas the price had increased to about 70,000R ($35 due to inflation) in 1994. Hunters, security guards, and private citizens are able to purchase these uniforms for personal use.

As with earlier woodland variants, it has now become common to find civilian variants of military issue SMK uniforms everywhere one goes in Russia. Unfortunately, these civilian issues are often sold to the American collecting public as military combat uniforms without a disclaimer. As a rule, civilian variations have English size markings or labels in them, or to hide the fact that they are civilian, lack any labels at all. Most military issues are plainly marked in Russian on the inside of the jacket or trousers with factory and/or approval (OTK) marks.

Since the 1993 Parliament standoff between Boris Yeltsin and supporters of Aleksandr Rutskoi and Ruslan Khasbulatoff, the SMK has been issued to a large number of units of the MVD. Yeltsin's well-publicized visit to military and security units prior to the standoff gave many people the chance to see several of the new SMK combat uniforms in use by *spetsnaz* units of the Dzerzhinsky division. Numerous units from the MVD including *Del'fin* and *Vitiaz'* used these uniforms as their primary combat outfits during the standoff and also the attack against Ostankino television station. Other units using the SMK include members of the Special Department of Quick Reaction of the Regional Administration for Combating Organized Crime (*Spetsotdel bystrogo reagirovaniia regional'nykh upravlenii po organizovannoi prestupnosti* – SOBR for short), and *Iaguar* (Jaguar) a *spetsgruppa* assigned to the MVD's ODON.

The future of the SMK is uncertain. During a visit to Russia in 1994, I purchased a combat assault vest from a member of *Vitiaz'* and was quite impressed with both its quality and its technical usefulness. It is apparent, at least to me, that the new Russian special operations uniforms and equipment are quite sturdy and well constructed for the rigors of combat. It remains unclear whether this marks the beginning of a new phase in uniform development or, like the MVD *spetsnaz* KLMK, it is merely a short-run production item for the MVD. Based on recent news reporting, MVD units appear content to remain with the SMK as its primary tactical uniform.

However, as with all uniform development in the former Soviet Union and Russia, only the future will provide the answers. Nevertheless, the SMK is definitely not the last in the line of newly developed MVD special operations uniforms. Modern innovations, recently incorporated into MVD uniforms, indicate the future looks very bright for collectors of Russian camouflage uniforms. The MVD's series of woodland camouflage-derived uniforms provide ample evidence of a continued effort to improve the selection of uniforms available to the MVD.

MVD KKO Four-Color Combat Uniform (Type 1)

First appearing within collecting circles in 1993, and then more widely in open source publications of that same year, the MVD *komplekt kamuflirovannogo obmundirovannogo* (KKO) four-color combat uniform is based on the Type I woodland patterns which arose prior to the collapse of the Soviet Union. Rather than placing this uniform within the section on army combat uniforms, there appeared to be sufficient differences to merit its placement in this section on MVD combat camouflage uniforms.

Originally the bright forest version was misidentified by retailers as a "Peacekeeper" uniform, named for units deploying to the former Yugoslavia. There is no evidence it has ever been worn by any army or special service units deployed to the region; rather, it appears to be the sole purview of the MVD. In fact, virtually all of the KKO uniforms examined to date bear the initials MVD in Cyrillic on the inside of the jackets and pants.

Initially, urban variants, consisting of two shades of gray, white/cream and black, were listed as separate issues and not equated with the four-color forest versions issued to MVD units. Since few were available for inspection, the urban issues were regarded as new army issues. However, after comparison of these uniforms and discussions with members of the MVD's Eighth Guard's Directorate, it became obvious that these were urban four color MVD issues and simply mirrored the development of the Type I woodland issues of the late 1980s.

As in the case of woodland Type I woodland camouflage, KKO uniforms were issued in two variants that possessed aspects of the Type I navy woodland camouflage uniforms or Type I army uniforms. Similarities to the navy uniforms include six patch-pockets – two breast (closed by velcro), two cargo, and two sleeve pockets; epaulets for rank stars; and no internal holster. However, the KKO lacks the drawstrings of the Type I woodland navy uniforms and has elastic sleeve bands in place of buttons.

Type I army woodland jacket similarities include the missing cargo pockets and versions without epaulets. To date, none have been examined that possess the suspender openings or internal holsters. KKO Type I trousers may be issued with or without patch-pockets; when present, they are similar to GRU *spetsnaz* issue uniforms in that the pockets are present on the front of the legs at or above knee level. The waist construction is identical to army woodland issues whereas Type II KKO issues have a much higher waist. When the cargo pockets are absent, standard slash pockets and a single right hip pocket are present on the trousers.

The urban version of the Type I KKO is simply a subdued four-color version of the Type I army woodland uniform minus the holster in white, light gray, dark gray, and black. It remains unclear as to whether the KKO was designed specifically for the MVD or if it was intended to serve as an urban combat uniform for other services. Since army units have yet to be identified wearing this uniform, it can reasonably be assumed that it was intended solely for MVD use.

There is both a bright and a subdued forest woodland version of the uniform. The bright version possesses red-brown, cream and black on a dark green background, whereas the subdued version incorporates chocolate-brown, black and tan on a dark green background.

Aside from the obvious color and tailoring differences (see also the illustration section on MVD combat uniforms), what also separated this uniform from standard woodland issues was the fact that it was issued with several new matching accessories, unlike previous woodland uniforms.

Previously, units adopting woodland camouflage were forced to wear whatever headgear was available. Typically, units donned headgear associated with their branch service, either field caps or full color, branch-specific berets (blue, green, nettle or black). This pretty much defeated the purpose of wearing camouflage when the most vulnerable part of the soldier was displayed in full view of the opponent. In contrast, the MVD four-color combat uniform was actually issued with a beret matching the pattern of the uniform and could be modified with the addition of a flash and a cap badge for specific units. Additionally, a matching camouflage assault vest was also issued with the uniform, which set a precedent for future MVD issues. The practice of issuing matching berets and assault vests continues to the present and has been adopted by ground, naval, airborne and special service units.

In June 1993, I observed six individuals wearing the bright forest version of the KKO uniform in St. Petersburg, all of whom bore new MVD *spetsnaz* patches on their sleeves. Several articles in Ogonyek, *Krasnaia zvezda*, and *Na boevom postu* during 1993, also showed internal affairs troops wearing this uniform during combat and law enforcement operations, thus verifying its usage.

Most of the units associated with this four-color woodland variant are those units of the MVD involved in crime suppression. Specifically, special-purpose units of the Moscow region of Internal Troops (MOVV) of the Russian MVD,[2] *Spetsotriadi* of the Federal MVD,[3] and some units of the Moscow criminal investigative department (MUR) have adopted this uniform as their primary operational uniform (prior to the issue of the new MVD variants). This uniform is also worn by MVD detachments in the Caucasus[4] and other southern republics.[5] In 1993 this uniform was modified and reissued as a MVD combat variant; several enhancements are discussed below.

MVD KKO Type II (Woodland and Tiger Stripe Uniforms)

As mentioned previously, members of the MVD's ODON unit *Vitiaz'* (knights) have been using the SMK as their primary uniform since 1992. In 1994, however, a new uniform appeared which, at present, is associated only with this MVD *spetsnaz* unit. To differentiate between the woodland versions and army woodland camouflage issues of the 1980s and early 1990s, I have chosen to refer to these issues as MVD combat uniforms or MVD KKO Type II.

While it may be assumed the construction of the KKO Type II is based on the 1980s woodland camouflage uniforms, this uniform is in fact of a much higher quality and far superior in design to those early issues. It therefore remains a distinct class of uniforms.

Like the KKO Type I, the woodland version superficially appears to incorporate the same camouflage pattern as the 1980s army patterns; however, as with the KKO Type I, it incorporates a four-color rather than a tri-color woodland pattern.

If the army and the recent MVD camouflage woodland uniforms are compared, it becomes quite obvious the new MVD version differs significantly from all previous army woodland and VSR issues. Aside from the stated color differences, the MVD combat uniform has a much improved construction and incorporates several modifications making it a more comfortable and functional uniform.

The KKO Type II is a well-constructed, heavy-weight uniform and is issued as a four piece set: shirt, pants, assault vest and field cap in lieu of a beret. Specially designed for combat operations, the new MVD uniform has modifications making it more suitable for a combat environment.

The addition of numerous pockets for carrying additional magazines, flares or shotgun rounds allow for increased firepower by the wearer. Removable knee pads have been added which are an innovation previously incorporated only in *militsiia* uniforms of the post-Gorbachev period.[6] Each uniform possesses reinforced elbows and seats and adjustable cinches to permit comfortable sizing by the wearer. But perhaps the most innovative design of these uniforms is the addition of inner pants-leg liners that permit the pants legs to be easily bloused over the boots without having to tuck in the heavy outer portion, a design other countries would do well to adopt.

In keeping with the *spetsnaz* tradition of front-facing pants pockets, the KKO II variants have the cargo pockets on the front of the pants leg at the thigh level. Pockets for a survival knife (or bayonet) and batons (or pepper gas canisters) have been added to the right and left side respectively. The pants waist has been lengthened and larger belt loops added to facilitate standard military belts.

The combat assault vest is configured wholly for combat. In the front of the vest are three pouches for AK magazines, two grenade pouches, an external holster for a makarov 9mm, a gas cannister pouch, and two non-specific utility pouches. The rear of the vest has three large pouches for carrying additional ammunition, food or the usual things combat soldiers carry with them in the field.

The special knife pocket on the KKO Type 2 uniforms is suitable for various types of edged weapons, including this spetsnozh, used by special operations forces.

The vest is secured by a series of subdued metal snaps in front and a nylon belt in front. There is a nylon belt to adjust the fit of the vest on each side.

The MVD KKO Type II combat uniform is issued in a four-color woodland camouflage pattern and a design incorporating uneven horizontal stripes, almost like tiger striping. Both the woodland and the tiger stripe pattern are issued in a four-color forest and urban coloration.

One of the two camouflage issues, the *Vitiaz' Piatnisto-fioletovoe obmundirovanie*, or spotted violet uniform (PFO for short) resembles French or Portuguese patterns issued in the 1960s through to the present. Due to its striped appearance I have ascribed to this uniform the obvious nickname of "Tiger" pattern. Russian service personnel have also used this moniker to describe the pattern.

The PFO Tiger pattern appeared first in collecting

circles as an unidentified uniform thought to belong to either the MVD or possibly Russian advisors in Africa. Its strong resemblance to Portuguese patterns made its origins suspect. Fortunately, samples brought to the United States were well-marked with Russian factory stamps and MVD initials, thus improving the chances of these new uniforms being authentic. The dubious origins of the uniforms didn't make them any more popular with collectors, especially with their $250 a piece price tags.

In the summer of 1994, pictures in the journal *Stolitsa* showed members of *Vitiaz'* wearing both the PFO Tiger pattern and the MVD Combat woodland pattern lending credence to the theory they were specific to units of the MVD. Still, many collectors were reluctant to spend the money on the new finds.

Subsequent to these articles I traveled to Russia and saw the forest-green version of the PFO Tiger pattern for sale which included a combat vest. I also saw members of a MVD *spetsnaz* unit wearing assault vests made of the same material with the urban coloration; thus reinforcing my beliefs that the uniforms were authentic Russian issues. I was able to visually inspect several of the uniforms that were for sale in Moscow and verify their authenticity.

Having looked at several of the uniforms and studied their construction in detail, I am generally impressed with the composition and design of the new MVD combat uniforms and would not be surprised to see certain characteristics adopted for use by the army or special operations units of the ground and naval forces. These uniforms have been fielded extensively to units throughout the FSU and most recently appeared in Chechnia worn by members of an MVD special weapons unit and *Vitiaz* team members deployed to the region.

Vitiaz' and its subordinate platoon of "black masks", commanded by senior lieutenant Yurii Drobushevich, are the primary users of the Tiger patterns.[7] More recently, however, several other units have adopted the woodland versions of this uniform. For example, the fourth platoon of OMON, or subunit of the North-Caucasian Administration for Internal Affairs for Transport as it is also called, recently adopted the woodland version of the MVD KKO Type II combat uniform.[8] Under the command of Sergeant Major Viktor Kravtsov, this special transport police unit counters organized crime, bomb threats, and highjackings of aircraft, buses and trains.[9]

Other units have also adopted the new MVD KKO Type II uniforms as their primary operational uniform. Some of the additional units who are using this uniform include the GUVD's quick reaction force (*Gruppa nemedlennogo reagirovaniia* – GNR), and members of the GUVD's SOBR units. The urban version is most prevalent among OMON and *militsiia* special-purpose units in Moscow, especially *podrazdeleniia* (subunits) of the Moscow OMSN and Internal Troops. Several civilian guard units such as GROM and MVD guard units of the Eighth Main Administration also use the subdued woodland pattern for their duty uniform.

This security guard working in Moscow is wearing the MVD KKO Type 2 forest pattern uniform. The maroon beret and special operations boots indicate he may work as an employee of the MVD's 8th Guards Administration (Directorate).

MVD Reed Pattern Camouflage

Just when you thought you knew everything... In early to mid-1996, the MVD of Russia issued a new lightweight uniform for use by its combat troops in Chechnia. Rather than being an improvement of an existing design, the reed pattern camouflage represents another step in Russia's uniform evolution.

First making its appearance in the open press in 1996, the uniform appeared as part of the field duty uniform with Interior Ministry troops of ODON and *militsiia* subunits. A Ministry of Internal Affairs video (*krapovie berety* – Mottled Berets) showed some members of OMON wearing a field jacket with a strange combination of jagged green and brown lightning bolts on a tan or yellow background. From the video it was difficult to discern much about the uniform and what its possible uses might be.

Soon, however, it began to make its way into collector's hands and into the general press.

Later in 1996, Alan Wise, in his book *MiG Pilot Survival*, published a photo of a new pattern camouflage boonie cap with green face netting. Although associated with flight personnel as a survival item, the cap was a complete departure from earlier aircrew issues and camouflage designs. The pattern, however, was definitely the same as the earlier described "lightning bolt" patterns of the MVD.

The December 1996, issue of *Orientir* showed General Lieutenant Viacheslav Tikhomirov wearing the new camouflage pattern shirt with a Chechen combat badge displayed prominently above his right breast pocket. Tikhomirov served as the federal commander in charge of the Russian forces in Chechnia. As such, Tikhomirov controlled both the conventional armed forces as well as the special services contingent on the ground. Since Tikhomirov was an army lieutenant general, this served to add further to the confusion surrounding the origin of the new uniform.

Then in early 1997, Mike Powlen and Alan Wise provided examples of the uniform and a boonie cap, respectively, for further study. Upon examination, the source, and the customer for this uniform was immediately apparent: on each button of the uniform and the cap was inscribed МВД РОССИЯ – Ministry of Internal Affairs of Russia.

Dennis Salakhov, a former member of the Vitebsk Division in Russia, confirmed the use of this uniform when a photo of the pattern was sent to him for identification. According to Salakhov (and others), the uniform, known as "kamysh" (reed), or "*kamyshovy risunok*" (reed pattern), is strictly a Ministry of Internal Affairs tropical issue uniform for use in hot climates. The main units to receive this uniform are the motorized combat elements of the ODON, members of OMON, and the quick reaction units in and around Moscow (SOBR).

The boonie cap, initially described as a survival accessory, may actually have dual usage as both a sniper's accessory and a means of protection against biting insects in swampy or arid lands. As a sniper's mask, the cap is used by the MVD's special sniper units assigned to OMON. It significantly reduces glare from the wearer's face while also reducing the signature when in a concealed position.

Additional issues in this pattern include a combat assault vest (see uniform text), and a short, zippered front jacket, made from nylon similar to the U.S. MA-1 aviator's jacket, but slightly longer. The uniform is also issued with a lightweight field cap, resembling for the most part, a combination of the VSR flight field cap and the standard woodland field cap. The cap also possesses two MVD-marked buttons that hold the ear flaps up. There is also a frontispiece for attaching cap insignia.

The uniform is issued in both a forest and an urban version. Other nicknames for this uniform include lightning bolt pattern, shadow pattern, and tropical MVD uniform. As there has been no official mention of the uniform's designation, reed pattern (*kamyshovy risunok*) will suffice until overruled by the Ministry of Internal Affairs.

General-lieutenant (Russian two-star) Vyacheslav Tikhomirov, former commander of the Russian armed forces in Chechnia, wears a MVD Reed pattern uniform while in Chechnia. The fact that an army commander would wear a pattern designed for a special service ministry indicates the liberal attitude toward uniform regulations as well as the usefulness of the newly introduced tropical uniform.

ENDNOTES CHAPTER 6

[1] *Na boevom postu, Zhurnal vnutrennikh voisk,* issue 11-12, 1992. Inside front cover.

[2] Major Aleksei Petrov, " *'Zaslon-93' ChP ne zastanet vrasplokh*" (Barrier 93 - the emergency situation will not catch them unawares), *Krasnaia zvezda*, June 4, 1993, p. 1.

[3] Karpov, B. "*Kavkaztsi*", (Caucasians), *Na boevom postu, Zhurnal vnutrennikh voisk,* 5-6, 1993, pp. 10 -15.

[4] Ibid, p. 13.

[5] Ibid, p. 17.

[6] In fact, these uniforms are basically camouflage versions of the smoky grey OMON combat uniforms currently in service.

[7] Igor' Smelkov, Major of militsiia, "*Rozhdennye Oktiabrem, spravliaiut iubilei v iiune*" (Born of October, they are celebrating the jubilee in June). *Shchit i mech*, June 16, 1994, number 23, pp. 1, 10-11. The photo on page 10 shows Drobushevich wearing an SMK jacket over the Tiger pattern uniform. Page 11 clearly shows members of the *Vitiaz'* "black masks" wearing SPECIAL FORCES tabs over the *spetsnaz* sleeve patch on the right side.

[8] *Shchit i mech* (Sword and Shield), "S riskom dlia zhizni," (With a risk to life), January 13, 1994, p. 6.

[9] Part of a larger company-sized unit of OMON, commanded by *militsiia* Captain Mikhail Ivanov, their mission includes general crime suppression and fighting organized crime (mafia) gangs in the North-Caucasus region.

7

CONCLUSION

"Camouflage and magic have a lot in common: they confound and deceive. A coin, an army disappears; the whole world is a stage where the goal is TO HIDE IN PLAIN SIGHT."
– Unattributed

The concept of Russian camouflage, deeply rooted in the studies of naturalists such as Thayer and Darwin, has grown to an immense industry providing uniforms to military, security, and special operations units. Since its earliest pre-war years of the 1930s, the Soviet camouflage uniform evolved from a lightweight, baggy, bicolor overall to a complex tactical assault system incorporating durable uniforms, assault equipment, riot helmets and protective vests.

Up until the Gorbachev period of the 1980s, much of this information was hidden from the public and few details, if any, were available about the uniforms employed by the Soviet army. Today, professional journals are literally crammed with photos and descriptions of Russian military and security units and their uniforms. This has provided a bonanza to the collector of Soviet and Russian militaria.

The impetus for the development and modernization of Soviet camouflage uniforms was always conflict. Historically, Russian involvement in the far east and near-abroad resulted in drastic changes in both foreign policy and military tactics. Conflicts in Afghanistan and the Baltics resulted in a gradual move away from the more brightly colored tunics and headgear associated with Tsarist imperial forces.

Russia's catastrophic involvement in the Russo-Japanese War undoubtedly convinced the Imperial Russian forces to adopt the more subdued khaki coloration for its field uniforms. Upon the collapse of the Russian army, and then Russia itself, the emerging Soviet Union radically altered its dress and field uniforms. With its first full-fledged deployment during the Second World War, with its devastating weapons and changing combat conditions, the Soviet army began to introduce a series of camouflage uniforms to meet the needs of modern warfare under varied conditions.

Next, the Cold War, with its numerous low intensity conflicts and advisory roles, required the Soviet military to incorporate new designs for use in its various client states as well as new uniforms for its advisors in far away lands.

American involvement in Vietnam provided modern examples of western uniform development and provided a further impetus for military research facilities to improve the outdated field uniforms of the 1950s and 1960s. The Soviet leadership, using American camouflage uniforms as models, forced the development of more modern uniforms while the conflict in Afghanistan caused designers to further re-examine outdated Soviet designs.

Finally, the end of the Soviet Union and the creation of the Russian state offered the special services the chance to improve the development of their tactical uniforms during deployments to the many hot spots around the FSU. Today, the military and special services are fielding equipment and uniforms at a surprising rate of speed. As opposed to the long-term, generalized issues of the 1940s and 1950s, today's combat troops can expect new uniforms and equipment to be fielded as the need arises in the course of combat operations. The result of all this experience is the development of a series of modern and technically advanced combat uniforms.

With such a profusion of camouflage uniforms, the militaria hobby has grown immensely over the last few years. Larger numbers of collectors are scrambling to acquire examples of Soviet and Russian uniforms and are paying higher prices than ever for them. As Russia matures and the republics of the former Soviet Union are able to further codify their positions within the Commonwealth, an even greater diversity of uniforms and equipment will be forthcoming, offering the collector of the future the chance to own a piece of history.

8

SPECIAL PURPOSE UNITS OF THE SPECIAL SERVICES

"When going into a combat assignment spetsnazovets take off their beret, place it over their heart, and don their helmets."
– Militsiia Colonel Bagatovym of the MVD

Discussing camouflage uniforms without discussing the units that employ those uniforms as part of their operational equipment is incomprehensible. Since the two subjects are so closely intertwined, the remainder of this book will provide and overview of the special units of the Ministry of Internal Affairs (MVD) and former Committee of State Security (KGB).

Spetsnaz troops

The two questions most people ask are: what are *spetsnaz* troops and how do they differ from other, specially trained forces of Russia and the former Soviet Union? The question of Soviet and Russian special operations forces is a complex one. One of the greatest challenges is even translating all of the variations of the terms special operations. Depending on what author you read or to whose ideas you subscribe, the terms *spetsnaz* and *osnaz* (as well as a host of others) may be translated as special operations, special purpose, special designation, or even specially named.

Unfortunately, after the collapse of the Soviet Union in late 1991, and subsequent *glasnost* (public openness), military and special services units literally jumped on the bandwagon to announce to the world that they had been operational special units for years. Unit commanders and reporters went into great detail to describe the formation and history of these units and how they came to be formed from units of the NKVD prior to the Great patriotic war. Numerous others simply sprang up during the cold war period.

With the notoriety that these numerous early units of the various services achieved, came the formation of several new modern special units, each with its own special designator. As a result of the more open press, those units previously unknown or classified were embodied with histories and exploits far out of proportion to reality.

As with some Americans who claimed service in Vietnam, Russians claiming to have served in *spetsnaz* or *osnaz* units started cropping up everywhere. As a result, stories about these units, their activities, their capabilities and training, and even their insignia, have been clouded with suspicion and misinformation.

In reality, any unit used for any special task can be considered a special operations or unit of "special purpose." The only thing special about the unit is its makeup and its mission; that is, it has a task for which it is specifically organized or trained. The designation *spetsnaz* has grown so far out of proportion to its actual importance that any unit of any service specially organized for a specific mission has been called a *spetsnaz* unit.

Within the context of special purpose units there is also the translation issue. Several phrases are used to denote special purpose units, depending on whether they are military or from the "special services" as the Russians call them: SVR, FSB, FAPSI, FPS, MVD and GUO and so forth.

Special purpose units are divided into two categories: *spetsnaz* and osnaz. Several of the better known Russian variants denoting special purpose units are listed below. All of their monikers derive from two terms:

[Unit size] *spetsial'nogo naznacheniia – spetsnaz* (special purpose unit, such as a company, brigade, etc...).

[Unit size] *osobogo naznacheniia – osnaz* (special purpose unit, company, etc...).

Within military units, *spetsnaz* units are divided into brigades, these are subdivided into *otriadi* (detachments) which are comprised of companies. Each company is further subdivided into *spetsgruppi* (a *spetsgruppa* is a smaller unit which often varies in size but would be equivalent to a U.S. platoon). Within the *spetsgruppa* are smaller *spetsotedelyi* or teams. This organization generally holds true for SVR (former KGB), and FSB special operations units. Typically, *spetsnaz* and *osnaz* have equal meaning and both are used to denote special purpose units according to their special service headquarters.

As you will see, the types of units afforded the term special purpose are quite varied. Some of the units designated as special purpose include those placed in anti-terrorist and counter-terrorist roles, intelligence units, special assassination and deep insertion units (also called diversionary and sabotage units), numerous special police (MVD) task forces, and several other units engaged in signals collection (*Kaskad*) and counter-intelligence operations.

MVD equipment display at Balashikha near Moscow, Russia. Nearest the camera are KKO Type 2 assault vests. Also on display are a standard SSh-60 steel helmet, a titanium riot helmet, and the MVD's version of the German GSG-9 assault helmet in the background.

Spetsnaz troops of the MVD

The Ministry of Internal Affairs equals or surpasses the combat capabilities of most armies of Western Europe. Equipped with ground forces, air support, and special operations units, the mission of the MVD is to safeguard the interior of the Russian Federation from all enemies internally and externally. Its recent missions, to counter terrorism, organized crime, and narcotics trafficking, takes up the bulk of its responsibilities. MVD forces also took part in the Chechen conflict, deploying several special purpose and support units.

The qualities which an Internal Ministry *spetsnaz* soldier embodies includes physical strength, intelligence, stoicism, and the ability to make independent decisions. He must also be able to master to perfection the martial arts. One MVD *spetsnaz* colonel valued self control as much as knowledge and emphasized the value of the eastern martial arts discipline; the Russian martial art of *Rukopashnyi Boi* therefore became an important tool for combat. Despite their physical prowess, the *spetsnazovtsi* of the MVD are forbidden to use their weapons against women, children or invalids, and weapons were only to be used for self-defense or to safeguard an objective.

Spetsnaz troops of the MVD typically transfer from Soviet army units or KGB field units and undergo six months of additional training, primarily in hand-to-hand combat and crowd control. They must pass a suitability test for maturity and earn the right to wear the nettle beret, a sign of elite status in the MVD. Upon graduation, the new *spetsnazovets* solemnly swears not to tarnish the honor of *spetsnaz*.

Typically, *spetsnaz* soldiers have been attributed with a great many qualities which may or may not be accurate; the *spetsnazovets* assumed strength and abilities in the minds of his opponent, which far outweighed reality. Military operations during the Gorbachev era showed many of these assertions were inaccurate; moreover, the MVD, as with many peacemakers, often found itself caught between warring factions with little to do but sit idly by. One facet which has not been overrated, however, is the *esprit de corps* and unit traditions which the MVD holds dear. Colonel Bagatovym described one such tradition held by *spetsnazovtsi*:

> "When going into a combat assignment *spetsnazovets* take off their beret, place it over their heart, and don their helmets."[1]

Some of the more well-known MVD special purpose units are described below. Their structure and composition have changed considerably since their inception and with the subsequent demise of the Soviet Union and combat operations throughout the FSU, continues to change even today.

Dzerzhinskii Separate Special-Purpose Motorized Division

Officially created in June 1924, the Order of Lenin, Red Banner Division in the name of F.E. Dzerzhinskii was one of the most elite, yet secretive combat units of the Ministry of Internal Affairs under Gorbachev. Under the command of General Bosov, it acquired a fearsome reputation known throughout the Soviet Union's republics.

On June 17, under Stalin's direction, Felix Dzerzhinskii created an internal troops division by joining sections of special designation (ChON) of the OGPU and Detachments of special designation (*osnaz*) of the Cheka. Lenin had formed the original units to fight armed opposition to the young Socialist Republic and to guard railroads, waterways and industrial installations.[2] The new division consisted of three rifle regiments and support units.[3] Dzerzhinskii equipped the new internal troops division with the combat capability to suppress armed uprisings at a moment's notice.

After Dzerzhinskii's death in 1926, the unit was renamed the *Otdelnaia motostrelkovaia diviziia osobogo naznacheniia im. Dzerzhinskogo* (Separate Motorized Division of Special Purpose named in honor of Dzerzhinskii). The NKVD mechanized the division in 1934 and provided it with heavier armaments; the firepower of the division increased by ten times.[4] As part of its restructuring, the chief of armaments provided armored cars and artillery as support for the newly refurbished combat division.

From the original division were created at least two other similarly equipped and organized units and support elements. As the Soviet Union expanded and the need for internal control increased, the MVD expanded its influence over the country through the deployment of several numbered separate brigades and divisions. Currently, each MVD district has its own motorized MVD division and at least one separate brigade.

Shown is the uniform configuration for a member of the Dzerzhinsky Division ca: 1988. Worn as part of the riot gear ensemble is the two-piece spetsodezhda with matching helmet cover on a titanium helmet, and a MB610 defensive (flak) vest.

Located in the town of Balashikha, near Moscow, the Dzerzhinskii Division under Gorbachev had many functions, not the least of which, according to Victor Suvorov,[5] was to counter a revolution against the Central Committee by the army.[6]

This role was one for which it had already been prepared; upon the death of Stalin in March 1953, security chief Lavrentia Beria combined the MVD and the Ministry of State Security (MGB) into one powerful organization. In his attempt to consolidate power, Beria deployed troops of the Dzerzhinskii Division[7] and Taman Motorized Division throughout Moscow.[8] The military responded to Beria's move by sending in the Kantemir and other divisions. According to Dziak, there may have been isolated fire-fights between the *Dzerzhintsi* and army units in Moscow. Another source related the story that the Dzerzhinskii Division was prevented from entering Moscow by the Kantemir Division and told to stand down under threat of "elimination of the entire division."

Eventually the Dzerzhinskii Division stood down and the combined special service dismembered. The MGB was dropped from ministerial level and renamed the Committee for State Security (KGB) while the MVD emerged as a separate ministry under the control of the Communist party. The MVD thus became responsible for internal law enforcement functions.

The subordination of the MVD to the precursor of the KGB in 1953 lends credence to Suvorov's most startling claim that the Dzerzhinskii Division was controlled not by the MVD Internal Troops Administration, but by the KGB. Victor Yasmann,[9] an expert on the special services of the USSR, also claims the KGB controlled the Dzerzhinskii Division unit through its Department "V".[10] Although members of the Dzerzhinskii Division with whom I spoke denied KGB control, some former members of the KGB and GRU agree that personnel within Dzerzhinsky were often recruited into the ranks of the KGB and that such control existed.

Currently there are indications that career progression within the ODON may also be influenced by the intelligence community, that is, persons in the Russian Security Council and the foreign and domestic intelligence services (SVR and FSB respectively).

Configuration for trainee of OMSDON (Dzerzhinsky Division, now ODON) in 1990. Large numbers of the Amoeba pattern uniform reportedly remain in warehouses for use by reserve and training units (Na Boevom Postu, 3/90, color insert p. 32-33).

Nevertheless, the Dzerzhinskii Division was not only well-trained and well-equipped, but considered more politically reliable than regular army units. Some of the Dzerzhinskii soldiers were housed within the same Kremlin walls and provided the same rewards as the troops of the 9th Guards Administration of the KGB. Since the *Dzerzhintsi* were used for conducting crowd control and suppressing ethnic uprisings, they were considered undoubtedly more reliable and trustworthy than their army or KGB counterparts.[11]

Yet, there appears to have been a close relationship between one Moscow-based army unit and the Dzerzhinskii Division. The Guard's motorized rifle Taman Division named after Kalinin (Second Motorized Rifle Division) apparently has a training and cooperative relationship with the Dzerzhinskii unit.[12] Most recently, mutual cooperation was very apparent between the Taman and Dzerzhinskii Divisions during the Parliament standoff in October 1993.[13]

Suvorov also mentions the role internal troops performed during training exercises with special-purpose forces of the Soviet army (GRU *spetsnaz*) in suppressing internal dissent and destroying forces of national liberation. Motorized NKVD units performed this type of operation behind the front lines during World War II, seeking out Nazi sympathizers and airborne troops inserted into the Red Army's support areas. The Dzerzhinskii Division undoubtedly maintains several close relationships with other units that may not yet be fully understood outside of Russia.

Under Gorbachev, the division was comprised of three motorized rifle regiments and support units. Although the unit was equipped with artillery and mortars, it lacked the organic tank support found in most Soviet rifle divisions.[14] In a recent article, Dr. Mark Galeotti states the 1st Separate Special Purpose Division (ODON – the follow-on to Dzerzhinsky), now has an organic tank battalion.[15] Whether this battalion is truly organic to the division or is attached from the Taman division remains unclear. General Kulikov maintains the division has no organic tank or fixed-wing support.

The Dzerzhinsky division's primary transport vehicle is the model 70 series of armored personnel carrier (BTR-70). Reported to have been equipped with airborne combat personnel carriers (BMD's) in the Baltics, these most likely were transferred to them by the 106th guards Airborne division who took part in the suppression of ethnic unrest. Recently, however, the division has acquired BMDs as part of its organic inventory.

At its height, some authorities estimated the size of the ODON to be as high as 18,000 soldiers and officers.[16] Based on discussions with Victor Yasmann and MVD personnel, I estimate the strength to have been closer to 12,000.[17] However, there are several *spetsnaz* subunits and separate brigades which comprise the division and are deployed separately that combine to give the ODON more personnel than a standard motorized division. Additionally, at least two operational regiments are used independently from the Division.[18]

As of 1994, the commander of the separate special purpose division (ОДОН in Russian) A. Denisov, was responsible for the training and deployment of what has become the MVD's largest and premier operational group. The division, which is still located at the combined training center (OUTs) at Balashikha, has acquired several special purpose subunits used for counter-terrorism, hostage rescue, and riot suppression. During wartime, ODON's separate units can be employed as combat units fighting alongside the Russian army's *spetsnaz* and motorized infantry units. This was evinced during the numerous combat engagements in the separatist republic of Chechnia.

The uniform of the ODON, although not necessarily distinctive, made personnel easily identifiable as soldiers of the Internal Troops Administration. Upon the introduction of the 1982 woodland camouflage uniform, *Dzerzhintsi* wore it as their standard field camouflage but donned the round internal troops patch on their left sleeves. They also wore a maroon-colored beret which gave them their nickname of *krapovye berety* or "nettle berets," after the flower of the thistle plant.

Subunits of the Dzerzhinsky have alternatively worn *spetsodezhda*, army woodland camouflage, VSR camouflage, and SMK patterns. The most common uniform worn today by ODON is the VSR camouflage pattern with the MVD district patch worn on the right sleeve pocket. With the introduction of the specialized KKO uniforms, numerous subunits of the division now wear one or more variants depending on their operational mission.

Other, more specialized, units have also existed within the Internal Troops Administration in the 1980s. Many of these were subordinate to the Operational Troops Administration under GUKVV.[19] These specialized units were created as needed, usually out of the motorized divisions of the internal troops, and equipped accordingly. Although their missions varied, their primary duties included riot control, countering terrorism, and hostage rescue operations. Today they are much more likely to be involved in separatist wars and ethnic conflicts. Several of these units survive today and will be discussed in more detail.

This photo represents a soldier assigned to the Separate special purpose division (ODON) assigned to Balashikha. The uniform is the standard VSR forest issue with matching cover for the titanium helmet. The uniform also incorporates the maroon and white tel'niashka used only by members of this division.

MVD Special-Purpose Divisions and Brigades

The units of special designation, collectively known as MVD special-purpose forces or simply, *spetsnaz*, grew in number during the Gorbachev administration. Rising ethnic tensions in the Baltics, and the Georgian, Armenian and Azerbaijanian Republics, and general dissent within other autonomous *oblast's* and republics, created the need for specialized units that could deploy rapidly and intervene where trouble occurred. Today, each MVD district has its own MVD special operations division.

From the original Dzershinsky division were created other similarly equipped and organized units and support elements. A second division, the 43rd, was mentioned as being located in Latvia in January 1991.[20] Another division may have been numbered the 44th (after a regiment which was highly decorated by the *Komsomol* for its part in the civil war in the 1920s).

Another division was identified in a report by Senior Lieutenant Igor' Bolotov who claimed to be a member of the 1561st motorized MVD division. This division was described as a *spetsnaz* division which had previously been deployed to the Caucasus.

One unit identified as being in Ossetia since 1988 was the special-purpose Brigade of the Internal Forces of the MVD (BON VV MVD). Commanded by a lieutenant colonel (*podpolkovnik militsii*) of the MVD, this unit has deployed to several "hot spots" in the USSR including Baku, Tbilisi, Fergana, Dushanbe and others.[21]

Listed as a brigade, it is not clear what the actual size of the unit was nor how many personnel served in the unit. The commander indicated that a maneuver group (MMG) also existed within the unit, as did some type of infrastructure for support. He described the makeup of his unit as consisting of Russians, Ukrainians, and Byelorussians, with an average age of 18 to 19 for soldiers, and from 26 to 28 for officers and *praporshchiki* (warrant officers).

Another unit, commanded by colonel of the MVD (*polkovnik militsii*), G. Bagatovym, was engaged in peacemaking duties in one of the southern republics. Colonel Bagatovym stated his various roles as: "...removing barricades, implementing security of colonies, providing food, fuel and medical supplies."[22] He also said he had the responsibility to tame bandits, disarm fighters and generally to defend the interests of the "simple people."[23]

Rusich Special-Purpose Detachment

The Rusich (РУСИЧ) special purpose detachment of the internal troops of the MVD, is part of the *Sofrinskaia* division stationed in Rostov on the Don. During the October, 1993, standoff between supporters and detractors of President Boris Yeltsin's government, allegations were made that this unit supported the opposition of Rutskoi and Khasbulatov. As a result, attempts were made to stand the unit down or place it under the command and control of the President. Its present strength and operational status is unknown.

These units were controlled by the operational arm of the Internal Troops Administration and later by the Administration of Operational and Special Motorized Units of the MVD (UOCMCh MVD).[24] During the turbulent period of the late 1980s and early 1990s, most recently during the Chechen conflict, several of these separate brigades and subunits were deployed to various regions in the former USSR to serve as peacemakers during rising tensions and to quell ethnic violence. Other subunits of the former Dzerzhinsky division have attained notoriety due to their service and well deserved reputation for efficiency and ruthlessness. These are described in more detail below.

Special-Purpose Companies

Two company-sized units, the special-purpose company (RSN) and the special-purpose *militsiia* Detachment (OMSN), which emerged prior to 1980, achieved greater importance during the Gorbachev years. These companies, like the *spetsnaz* Brigades, were created for special missions and were trained and equipped to accomplish those missions in a professional manner.

Each company had similar origins and was designed to counter terrorism at the 1980 Moscow Olympics should it arise. Although subordinated to different administrations, each eventually served similar functions in the Gorbachev administration.

Special-Purpose company (RSN) – *Vitiaz'*

The first unit, the RSN, was created in December 1978 from the famed Dzerzhinskii Division. A company was freed from patrol and told to strengthen itself and improve its readiness. This company became the first counter terrorist unit of the Soviet Union.

Originally the unit was created as a counter terrorist unit prior to the Moscow Olympics of 1980; the events of

Members of the Special purpose company (RSN) - Vitiaz'. Subordinate to the Separate special purpose division, members of the RSN wear a variety of uniforms depending on their operational needs. Shown in the photo are combinations of KKO Type uniforms, PFO Tiger stripe uniforms, and SMK urban uniforms.

the Munich massacre driving its creation. Sergei I. Lysyuk, reportedly one of the first *spetsnazovets,* commanded one of the platoons of the company.[25] He contributed to this company with special training including a style of hand-to-hand combat which he himself developed. The unit also adopted weapons training and hostage rescue techniques as practiced by European elite counter terrorist units.

The company was not provided the opportunity to put its skills to the test until 1982 when it was deployed to rescue children from a hijacked school bus. Although not as polished as its Western counterparts, the RSN proved its worth several times in the course of its history.

Lysyuk took command of the unit in 1986 and concentrated on making it an extremely professional and capable organization. Eventually the RSN adopted a nettle-colored (maroon) beret as a sign of elite status; this beret, developed by the father of one of the recruits, was soon adopted by the entire Dzerzhinskii Division. Members then became known affectionately as the "nettled berets," referring to the color of the beret.

Lacking the equipment and uniforms necessary to conduct the unit's missions efficiently, its commander contacted the criminal science laboratory (VNII) and requested specialized helmets for dangerous situations. A metal helmet was developed for the company's use which included a special visor for assault situations. A glass shield protected the wearer's face yet still permitted clear viewing of the opponent. After a suitable testing period, the new riot helmets were approved for all units under the GUKVV.

The structure of the unit included six officers and 84 enlisted personnel. It was comprised mainly of conscript soldiers who served for a period of two years. Under Gorbachev the company grew to battalion size, but was later reduced to a detachment, still under the command of Lysyuk within the Dzerzhinsky Division. During this period its mission requirements broadened and included suppression of organized crime and riots of both an anti- communist and pro- communist nature.[26] One such mission, widely reported in the Russian press, involved RSN's participation in the assault in Sukhumi, Georgia along with the KGB's *Al'fa* spetsgruppa; this operation resulted in several deaths of civilians.

Prior to 1991, the unit may also have been subordinated to the KGB. A patch issued in Moscow shows the KGB sword and shield with the inscription "KGB * SSSR" above and the unit designation "RSN" below. Operating as a strategic asset, and part of the Dzerzhinsky division, it is likely the RSN was used as a Kremlin anti-terrorist asset. Vitiaz' (RSN) may now be subordinate to the Federal Protection Service (*Federal'naia sluzhba okhrany* – FSO) which operates in conjunction with Directorate T of the FSB, the anti-terrorist center, which has control over Al'fa and Vympel anti-terrorist units.

Liusuk was next reported as commander of the unit in January of 1992 as a lieutenant colonel.[27] Recently he was referred to in an article as being a lieutenant colonel in command of MVD Special Purpose Unit number 6, responsible for storming Ostankino television station in October 1993.[28] During an engagement in Kizlyar, private Yevdokimov, Dmitry Mikhailovich, 6th unit, was listed as a casualty. Based on these reports, it is believed the numerical designation of the RSN is the same.

Graham Turbiville in his article, "Soviet Union: The Enemies Within,"[29] reported that the unit had adopted Che Guevara as its hero. Although unusual, this subject comes up again in 1994 when a member of the Dzerzhinsky Division's special-purpose unit *Vitiaz* mentions Che Guevara as their honorific.[30] The RSN has apparently undergone several changes in its relatively short history and has since evolved into the *spetsgruppa Vitiaz* (ВИТЯЗЬ).

Still commanded by Sergei Liusuk, *Vitaz'* while assigned to ODON at Balashikha, Vitiaz' falls under the operational control of the Federal Protection Service (FSO), a large security organization responsible for the protection of the Kremlin leadership. *Vitaz'* has also developed a cooperative training relationship with the Austrian commando group Kobra, a special counter-terrorist squad responsible for resolving conflicts in which hostages are involved. One officer of *Vitiaz'* spent a year training with Kobra in order to learn the western techniques of hostage negotiation, conflict resolution, and crisis management.[31]

One of the subunits or *podgruppa* assigned to Vitiaz' is Commanded by Yuri Drobyshevich. This six-man platoon operates independently as an anti-terrorist and special purpose unit within the Vitiaz' unit. These "black masks" have worked in conjunction with the *Al'fa* anti-terrorist unit in hostage rescue and anti-terrorist operations.[32]

The black-masks have adopted the tiger stripe version of the KKO as its operational uniform along with the standard issue vests and assault gear. Recent photographs show the team using a mixture of KKO and SMK uniform components. The name stems from the unit's common practice of wearing balaclavas issued with the uniforms, to protect their identity and reduce the likelihood of reprisals from criminals and terrorists.

Special-Purpose *Militsiia* Detachment (OMSN)

The other unit which was created as a deterrent to terrorist activity for the 1980 Moscow Olympics was the OMSN. Like its brother the RSN, this unit was also created from a company in the Dzerzhinskii Division. However, instead of serving as an internal troops unit, the OMSN became a tool of the Moscow *militsiia*.[33]

Established in 1979, this unit's mission was centered around hostage rescue and especially dangerous situations when "... other measures [didn't] work.[34] The unit trained for situations involving highjackings and armed groupings of criminals, using as its role model the West German GSG-9 and Austrian Kobra counter terrorist units. When it was created, only 30 personnel were accepted out of hundreds of applicants, all of whom were master sportsmen. Training was demanding and stringent incorporating weapons skills, self-defense, and physical fitness.

Whereas most units of this nature had officers performing the same basic functions as the enlisted personnel, the majority of the OMSN's members were non-commissioned officers. Soldiers assigned to the OMSN made about 15 rubles a month more than other *militsiia* – for quite a bit more risk.

The OMSN was subordinated to the Moscow Criminal Investigative Department (MUR) and received instructions through the Main MVD Administration in Moscow.

Under the Gorbachev administration, the OMSN reached a level of approximately 1500 men. Its primary duties involved countering terrorist threats, prison uprisings, and organized crime in the USSR. The detachment deployed as a whole but broke down into an "*antiterroristicheskaia spetsgruppa*" for operational use.[35] This included smaller, numbered "*podgruppa*" or subgroups.

Although it did not participate in any counter terrorist operations during the Moscow Olympics, the OMSN nevertheless participated in other dangerous situations in its history. Of course, due to the proliferation of specialized units, it was sometimes difficult to tell which unit actually participated in a given crisis.

Other MVD Units

There are of course, other, less well-known operational units assigned to the MVD. Special police battalions, known as *spetsial'nyi motorizirovannyi batal'on militsii*, SMBM for short, are highly mobile police units that assist the local *militsiia* during crises. According to Dr. Mark Galeotti, there are four such units around Moscow and each has approximately 1,000 personnel assigned; their primary duty is to maintain law and order in the countryside and assist city units with regular law enforcement duties. While the majority wear the smoky grey *militsiia* uniforms, they can also be seen wearing woodland, VSR and SMK uniforms depending on their mission and unit of assignment.

Members of the Special purpose militsiia detachment (OMSN) a counterterrorist unit subordinate to the Separate special purpose division. This photo, taken in 1991, shows OMSN members wearing a combination of spetsodezhda and six-pocket khaki airborne uniforms. The "krapovie" berets are standard for MVD special operations troops.

Members of the Special Department of Quick Reaction of the Regional Administration for Combating Organized Crime (*Spetsotdel bystrogo reagirovaniia regional'nykh upravlenii po organizovannoi prestupnosti* – SOBR for short), are detachments of approximately fifty personnel subordinate directly to the Moscow mayor. There are ten such units, one in each of the city's raion's (police region). As previously mentioned, members of SOBR wear both the SMK and woodland uniforms as their operational uniforms.

Another special purpose *militsiia* unit – the detachment of operational reaction – (POR) was a special subunit of the Main Administration for the execution of punishment (GUIN/GUPIN) under the Soviet GULAG system. Falling under the control of the MVD's Main Administration for Internal Affairs of the Moscow District, it came under the direct responsibility of General-Major Y. Kalinin, commander of the GUIN for the Moscow District as of 1995.

The mission of this "SWAT" unit, is mainly preventative. It serves as one of many so-called "anti-crime" units in the Moscow area. As such it also acts as a quick-reaction unit, responding to prison riots and hostage situations.

As with other Russian units, its operations are based largely on the experiences and capabilities of Western special operations units. Upon its creation, POR trained with Austria's Kobra group, thus acquiring many of the skills and techniques already in practice by this well-known group. As of 1995 the strength of the POR detachment was 60 personnel and was subdivided into platoon-sized elements. It was commanded by Captain (Internal Service) Vladimir Shtanenko while the commander of "A" platoon was lieutenant (Internal Service) K. Pankov. POR's field uniform consists of the standard MVD internal troops woodland camouflage with either a beret or field cap as the standard-issue headgear. The titanium riot helmet and flak vest helmet are worn during operational missions.

Another, more specialized unit recently came to light in an article on the MVD's reaction to the increased terrorist threat posed by nationalist groups in the former Soviet Union. ODON's seizure group (similar to the FBI's Hostage Rescue Team – HRT), is commanded by Ivan Tsisar'. This platoon-sized unit is responsible for quick reaction responses to hostage and crisis situations. The *gruppa zakhvata* is likely to wear standard issue camouflage and green raid helmets worn by other anti-terrorist groups. It is unknown whether or not any unit-specific patches or equipment have been issued to the unit. Because of its low profile nature, little else is known about the unit or its makeup.[36]

Special Purpose *Militsiia* Detachments

The last unit in the category of specialized combat troops of the MVD is also the most notorious – the OMON or black beret troops. OMON, standing for special-purpose *militsiia* Detachment,[37] achieved notoriety when several of its detachments conducted brutal attacks against customs personnel and communications facilities in Riga, Latvia and Vilnius, Lithuania. This brutality established the OMON as the primary riot control force in the Soviet Union.

Generally the establishment of the OMON is set as 1988 and Vadim Bakatin is credited with its creation. However, there are several units that rose from the OGPU that can be considered ancestors of the modern OMON; furthermore, according to officers in the MVD, OMON detachments have always existed albeit in a covert state. Nevertheless, officially the OMON is said to have arisen as a federal asset under the control of the Council of Ministers in St. Petersburg in 1988.

Under the direct command of *militsiia* Colonel Eduard Riazanov, deputy head of the USSR MVD Main Administration of Protection of Public Order (GUOOP), OMON units were tasked by the Council of Ministers and the General Secretary in Moscow with riot suppression and crime fighting tasks. Orders were issued to OMON units only with the approval of the General Secretary of the CPSU and then approved by the council. Republic-level MVD leadership had no control over OMON operations in individual republics.

Each unit, consisting of five squads totaling 150 men,[38] was responsible for cooperation with the KGB and local procuracy in crime prevention and criminal apprehension.[39] According to MVD Minister Boris Pugo, they were also to have been used during natural disasters and to detain armed criminals.[40] According to the commander of the Vilnius detachment, Major B. Makutinovich, the missions of the OMON were positive crime fighting measures and he blamed Moscow for "... embroiling them in inter-ethnic struggles."[41]

Nevertheless, the OMON detachments were used extensively throughout the Soviet Union both in the RSFSR and in the satellite republics. Subsequent to the OMON's violent suppression of independence movements in the Baltics, the 34 OMON detachments located in the capitals, *oblast's* and *krai* centers were subordinated to local militsiia under the republic MVDs.[42] As of 1991 there were an estimated 9,000 OMON troops deployed throughout the USSR outside of Moscow.[43]

During Gorbachev's rule, the average age of an OMON militiaman was 25 and of Russian, Baltic or Polish descent. Each *Omonovets* was well trained and ruthless, caring for little other than his mission. One author, whose views were probably echoed by Lithuanians and Latvians, described the OMON simply as "thugs."[44]

Despite the events of January 1991 in Vilnius and July 1991 in Riga, the number of OMON detachments was increased. The OMON under Gorbachev became a powerful tool for implementing state policy against civilians in the independent-minded republics but only as tools of violence, not of reform.

Today OMON units are still under the control of the federal government in Moscow although city and regional MVDs deploy OMON units as the need arises. The Moscow OMON, largest of the OMON units, is under the direct control of the GUVD in Moscow.

Initially, the OMON detachments wore the standard woodland camouflage issued since 1982. Since 1992, the special police units have alternatively worn the SMK, VSR and Tiger pattern camouflage uniforms. Today each OMON unit selects uniforms according to the desires of the unit commander. As of 1994, units in Moscow wore the MVD Combat uniform in the urban coloration while those in St. Petersburg wore the VSR pattern.

Of course OMON is not the only unit that has responsibility for security in Russian cities. The MVD's Eighth Guard's Administration has assumed responsibility for guarding important government buildings and designated sites within Russia.

Internal Guards (Eighth) Administration of the MVD (VOKhr MVD)

The Eighth or Guard's (Okhrana) Administration of the MVD was established sometime prior to Gorbachev's rule and included the guard units employed to protect government buildings and Communist Party property. The actual strength of this unit under Gorbachev is difficult to determine; as of July 1990, Vadim Bakatin reports that the number of troops engaged in guard duties was 80,000.[45] By April 1991, this number was reported as 200,000.[46] Subsequent to the attempted coup much of the Eighth Administration's duties shifted to private companies.

In 1992 the designation of the Eighth was changed to Main Administration for Security (*Glavnoe upravlenie okhrani* – GUO) and it began to increase both its private security and installation security duties. The GUO's members are responsible for VIP security, installation and building security within the Russian Federation. Its symbol is the owl with outstretched wings and most of its members wear the VSR pattern camouflage.

Here a member of the Eigth Guard's Administration secures the entrance to a bank in Saint Petersburg in June 1993. His uniform consists of an early KKO Type 2 urban woodland uniform with matching field cap. No patches or insignia are visible on this uniform although other guards wore "team special" tabs on the sleeve shoulders.

ENDNOTES CHAPTER 8

[1] Ibid, p. 5.

[2] A. Gorlov, *V karaule bessonnom*, (Moscow: Molodaiia gvardia, 1984) pp. 21-29.

[3] I. G. Belikov, I. K. Boiko and M. S. Logunov, *Imeni Dzerzhinskogo*, (Moscow: 1976), pp. 3- 37.

[4] Gorlov, p. 41.

[5] Having recently come out of the shadows, Vladimir Bogdanovich Rezun, aka "Viktor Suvorov," is responsible for much of the factual and misleading information we have about the recruitment, training and operation of military *spetsnaz* personnel. While I won't subject the reader to an endless debate over the merits and flaws of Suvorov's writings, suffice it to say that much of the author's books contain a fair amount of fiction, open-source material, and suppositions that have recently been proven false.

[6] Suvorov, Viktor. *My Life in the Soviet Army, The "Liberators."* (New York: Berkley Books, 1988), p. 168.

[7] Fuller, p. 26.

[8] Dziak, p. 149.

[9] Victor Yasmann, "Where Has the KGB Gone?," *RFE/RL Research Report*, (Vol. 2, No. 2, January 8, 1993), p. 17.

[10] This may also be the 5th Department of the KGB responsible for monitoring internal dissent.

[11] Knight, p. 226; Suvorov, p. 168.

[12] I. G. Belikov, pp. 181-182.

[13] Christopher Bellamy, "Troops and Parliament in Showdown; Yeltsin orders disarming of guards in Parliament as Russia and eight other CIS States form an economic union," *The Independent*, September 25, 1993, p. 10; John Lepingwell, "Russian Army on the Offensive," *RFE/RL Daily Report*, October 4, 1993; Witold Zygulski, "Yeltsin fights back: Commando Democracy, *The Warsaw Voice*, October 10, 1993.

[14] Press Briefing by Russian Federation Interior Minister Victor Yerin, Official Kremlin International News Broadcast, October 7, 1993.

[15] Moscow's armed forces: a city's balance of power. Jane's Intelligence Review, February 1997, pp. 51- 53.

[16] Suvorov, p. 168.

[17] Department of the Army, *FM 100-2-3, The Soviet Army*, (Washington, D.C.: U.S. Government Printing Office, 1991), pp. 4-38.

[18] William C. Fuller, *The Internal Troops of the MVD SSSR*, (College Station, TX: 1983), p. 47.

[19] Main Administration for Command of Internal Troops.

[20] I. Andreyev, Interview with Victor Pugo, Minister of Internal Affairs, *Izvestiia*, January 23, 1991, as reported by *FBIS-SOV-91-015* (January 23, 1991), p. 27.

[21] Sergei Fedorova, "*spetsnaz*: There will not be a new Karabakh in Northern Ossetia," *Krasnaia zvezda*, June 23, 1992

[22] L .M., "*spetsnaz* Save Us From Misfortune," *Voennye znaniia*, 1/92, pp. 4-5.

[23] Ibid, pp. 4-6.

[24] Boris Karpov, "You Can't Get Along Without Internal Troops in the Country," *Krasnaia zvezda*, December 30, 1992, p. 2.

[25] Major V. Gerashchenko, Three Days With *spetsnaz*, *Na boevom postu*, 1/92, pp. 1-7. (in Russian).

[26] In October 1993 the unit was referred to as "Special Purpose Unit Number 6," under the command of Lieutenant-Colonel Lysyuk. This unit distinguished itself by guarding Ostankino Television against armed supporters of the parliament in Moscow. (Kremlin press briefing of October 7, 1993).

[27] Major V. Gerashchenko, "*Pervie: troe sutok so spetsnazom*" (The Originals: three days with *spetsnaz*), *Na boevom postu*, 1/92.

[28] Press briefing by RF Interior Minister Viktor Yerin, Official Kremlin Int'l News Broadcast, October 7, 1993.

[29] Graham Turbiville, "The Enemies Within," *Army*, April 1991, pp. 30-41.

[30] Valdimir Voronov, "*Strana 'spetsnazia,'* " (The country "*spetsnaz*"), *Stolitsa*, number 8, issue 170, 1994, pp. 9-12.

[31] *Shchit i mech*, June 16, 1994, p1, 10-11, Number 23.

[32] *Shchit i mech*, June 16, 1994, p1, 10-11, Number 23.

[33] Oleg Aksenov and Valerii Kulik, "Riskovie liudi" (Risky people), *Sovetskaiia Militsiia*, January, 1991, pp. 1-6.

[34] Aksenov, p. 1.

[35] Unattributed, *Na boevom postu*, 1/93, pp. 2-5 (in Russian).

[36] Ibid.

[37] There is frequently confusion concerning the use of the words "Special Designation" or "Special Purpose." In these instances the role of the units is of prime importance and therefore, based on the standard dictionary definition, I feel the word "purpose" is more appropriate.

[38] James Carney, *Time*, (August 26, 1991), p. 30.

[39] Sergey Ostanin of *Tass*, in Interview with Commander of OMON in Vilnius on January 18, 1991 as reported in *FBIS-SOV-91-014* (January 22, 1991), p. 46.

[40] Kondratov, p. 60.

[41] Ostanin, p. 46.

[42] Kondratov, p. 60.

[43] While 34 units with 150 soldiers does not add up to 9,000, certain of the Baltic republics maintained larger force structures, probably on the order of 2,000 to 3,000 each, while Moscow possessed approximately 6,000 soldiers.

[44] Michael Meyer, *Newsweek*, (September 9, 1991), p. 29.

[45] V. Prokopenko, "V. Bakatin: There's No Ground For Optimism," *Komsomolskaia Pravda*, July 17, 1990, p. 1, as translated by Russian Digest Press, RUSSICA Information Incorporated.

[46] "Soviet Union: The Police State's Policemen," *The Economist*, April 6, 1991, p. 48.

9

SPECIAL UNITS OF THE KGB

"I don't think they play at all fairly," Alice began in a rather complaining tone, and "they don't seem to have any rules in particular; at least, if there are, nobody attends to them-and you've no idea how confusing it is..."
– Lewis Carroll, *Alice in Wonderland*

A discussion of special units involved in crime suppression and counter terrorist operations would not be complete without a brief discussion of some of the former KGB's special-purpose (*spetsnaz* and *osnaz*) units. Created for diversionary actions during wartime, countering terrorism and suppressing crime, most of these units have been largely disbanded or moved directly under presidential control. Nevertheless, some of these units are still actively engaged in operational activities and wear camouflage uniforms during their missions.

Spetsgruppa "A"

Established in 1974, under Yuri Andropov, *spetsgruppa "A"* was primarily a counter terrorist force under the control of the KGB's seventh administration. Seventh Administration Chief Aleksei Beschastnov patterned *spetsgruppa "A"* after Charles Beckwith's Delta Force and gave it the same clandestine mission of countering terrorism and effecting hostage rescues.

The first commander of *Gruppa "A"* was major Vitalii Bubenin who earned the award Hero of the Soviet Union for bravery. His deputy commander was major Robert Ivon. Their leadership led to the development of the best trained and well-equipped anti-terrorist unit in the former Soviet Union.

According to author Mikhail Boltunov, in his book *"AL'FA"-Sverkhsekretnyi otriad KGB*,[1] the *spetsgruppa*'s first mission involved the seizure of Darulaman palace in Kabul, Afghanistan and the "elimination" of the Afghan president and his family. Reportedly, the *spetsgruppa* lost two of its members in the raid in Afghanistan (one purportedly due to friendly fire).[2] *Spetsgruppa "A"* also had additional combat roles as well: the group participated in clandestine operations in Tblisi, Baku and in Vilnius, Lithuania during which it suffered the lost of one of its lieutenants.[3] Eventually *spetsgruppa "A"* took on the role of countering terrorism and crime fighting for which it was designed.

The detachment achieved notoriety when it reportedly refused to storm the Russian White house and seize Boris Yeltsin. Some members of the group claim the orders were never given while others maintain subordinate members of the task force (including members from the Dzerzhinsky Division and OMON) refused to carry out the orders. The group was rewarded by being transferred to presidential control later in 1991, and then became part of the presidential guard under the Main Security Administration (GUO) of the new Ministry of Security

By 1993, the head of presidential security, Aleksandr Korzhakov, had put together a massive security service which included *spetsgruppi Al'fa* and *Vympel*, a motorized rifle brigade, the former Kremlin Guards (KGB's Ninth Directorate), a portion of the KGB's Fifth Directorate, and other KGB technical services units. Creation of this mammoth unit was due partially to Korzhakov's lust for power and partially to Yeltsin's fear of a military coup.

On the 4th of October, 1993, Yeltsin was met by his head of security, Mikhail Barsukov, and Barsukov's first deputy and head of presidential security, Aleksander Korzhakov. Barsukov reportedly told Yeltsin that officers from units *spetsgruppa "A"* and *Vympel'* (see below) wished to meet with Yeltsin to discuss the situation in the Russian White House. Yeltsin agreed to meet only with the senior officers of the two elite units.

Yeltsin asked the 30 or so officers gathered there if they were prepared to carry out his orders, no one answered. Yeltsin asked a second time as the officers stared at the floor. It was during the ominous silence that Yeltsin made up his mind to send in troop units from the Army's (GRU) *spetsnaz* and airborne troops to storm the building.

As in the August, 1991 putsch, the security ministry's elite troops refused to carry out the orders of their leader. It was not until Barsukov acquiesced to Yeltsin's demands that a show of force be made that Barsukov was able to talk several of the *spetsgruppa "A"* members into "volunteering" to approach the building in BMP's. The volunteers agreed to approach the building but not enter. As four BMP's approached the building one stopped near a wounded individual in order to render assistance. A junior lieutenant, by the name of Gennadii Sergeev, exited the vehicle and immediately came under sniper fire. A bullet penetrated his flak vest striking him in the back. Soon both the initial victim and his intended rescuer died.

Seeing their lieutenant mortally wounded by sniper fire, virtually the entire unit from *spetsgruppa "A"* prepared to storm the White House. Barsukov spoke with Interior Minister Victor Erin and requested BTR support for the assault. With sufficient firepower at their disposal, *spetsgruppa "A"* assaulted the building with support from the MVD and Barsukov and Korzhakov in the lead.

In 1993, President Yeltsin order the creation of the Directorate for Special Operations (USO) within the Ministry of Security (forerunner to the FSK and then FSB). *Al'fa* was still assigned to the Main Security Directorate (GUO) with the task of presidential protection. Approximately one hundred members of the Vympel anti-terrorist unit were transferred to the USO.

Late in December 1993, the Ministry of Security became the Federal Counter-intelligence Service under Sergei Stepashin. After events in Budennovsk, the Russian President ordered the creation of an anti-terrorist center which came to be known as Directorate "T." This directorate fell under the control of the FSK, and included troops from both *spetsgruppi* "A" and *Vympel.*

In 1994, the FSK ceased to be a power ministry and was changed to a special service. Then, in April 1995, the FSK was renamed the Federal Security Service (FSB) and became responsible for all internal counter-intelligence matters. As of this writing, *spetsgruppa "A"*, and *Vympel* (see below) were still part of the FSB's Anti-terrorist Center within Directorate "T."

From its creation in 1974 through the 1980s, members of *spetsgruppa "A"* wore uniforms that were indistinguishable from standard airborne forces. This remained true through to the mid-1980s whereupon members of this elite unit were issued the KGB/MVD green and yellow *spetsodezhda*. From then on, the *spetsgruppa "A"* operational uniform consisted of the camouflaged *spetsodezhda*, a green riot helmet developed in Germany, and blue striped t-shirts. Other headgear worn included the camouflage *polevaia furazhka* and light blue airborne beret.

Here two members of the special Kremlin presidential regiment (PP) walk through Red Square in October, 1994. The soldier on the left carries a winter KGB spetsodezhda jacket and wears a VSR pattern uniform. The left sleeve patch is a royal blue and has the inscription: РОССИЯ (RUSSIA) above with ПРЕЗИДЕНТСКИЙ ПОЛК (PRESIDENTIAL REGIMENT) below.

Of late, *spetsgruppi* members assigned to Directorate "T" are issued army type II woodland camouflage with matching vests, ammunition pouches, and assault equipment. Patches, unit insignia, and rank, are rarely, if ever, worn by *spetsgruppa* A members.

Spetsgruppa Vympel and Kaskad

Spetsgruppa Vympel was created to serve as a diversionary/infiltration unit under the KGB's First Chief Administration (now largely making up the Foreign Intelligence Service of Russia – SVRR) and was designed to operate during wartime. Created on August 19, 1981, the intelligence and sabotage group was largely the creation of KGB Directorate S (illegals) Chief Yuriy Drozdov and was referred to as *Gruppa B* (not to be confused with the training center unit).

Vympel's first commander, Evald Kozlov, worked to prepare the unit to conduct intelligence collection and sabotage missions deep in enemy territory. Its wartime missions included assassinations and kidnapping of unit commanders and intelligence officers. Prior to its creation, members of the special purpose group *Zenit* (with spetsgruppa *Al'fa*) took part in the assault on the Darulaman Palace in Kabul in December 1979. *Zenit* veterans were later recruited into Vympel in order to fill its rank with experienced and qualified individuals.

Vympel personnel were well-versed in foreign languages, survival, weapons handling, and of course, airborne operations. The main delivery method of *Vympel* teams was through airborne insertion although they were fully capable of being landed via heliborne or waterborne (submarine) methods as well.

By 1987, *Vympel*, consisting of approximately 500 combat veterans, served as part of the domestic anti-terrorist package and was deployed to various hot spots around the Soviet Union. While it typically performed clandestine entry missions for the KGB, Vympel is best known for its use as Russia's first nuclear anti-terrorist unit.

Subsequent to its refusal to attack Boris Yeltsin or participate in the 1991 coup, *Vympel* was rewarded by being transferred to the Main Guard's Administration along with *spetsgruppa "A"* in August 1991.

Due to the unit's leaders refusing to assault the Russian White House, it was subordinated to the MVD.[4] Morale in the unit fell to an all-time low and the unit's capabilities deteriorated rapidly.

Subsequent to the move to the MVD, the majority of *Vympel's* members quit in protest. Several of the former *Vympel* members went into business working in the security arena or as personal bodyguards. The remainder of the unit was transferred to the control of the Anti-terrorist Center within the Special Operations Directorate along with *spetsgruppa "A"*. Recent reports indicate *Vympel* has now been fully reconstituted under the Federal Security Service as an anti-terrorist force, creating yet another special operations unit.

A new unit, comprising some of the former Vympel members was also reformed and renamed. It is now located at Balashikha under the new name "*Vega*." This force, ostensibly a counter-terrorist unit, is under the control of the Ministry of Internal Affairs.

Relatively unknown in the intelligence community, the SVRR special group Grom (Thunder) was created under the KGB's 1st Chief Administration and was responsible for overseas and behind-the-lines operations. A combat assault unit, Grom is responsible for so-called 'Wet Affairs', that is, assassinations. Also within its purview are intelligence collection, reconnaissance against strategic targets, and sabotage and diversion missions in foreign countries. While there is little evidence to support the idea that members of the SVRR in foreign embassies are in any way affiliated with Grom, it stands to reason that in time of war, ad-hoc subunits could be created, using Grom team-leaders, to direct operational activities in the target country.

Spetsgruppa Kaskad, created in 1981, came under the control of the Eighth Administration of the KGB and was administered under Vladimir Kriuchkov through 1988. Its mission was to collect enemy radio signals and transmissions deep behind enemy lines. Like other *spetsgruppi* of the former KGB, *Omega*, *Zenit*, *Grom*, and "B" group (probably a training unit), *Kaskad* was designed to perform counter-terrorist and security missions.[5] Kaskad was reportedly dissolved upon the creation of the Federal Agency for Government Communications and Information (FAPSI), the successor to the KGB's Eighth Administration. Whether or not a similar unit has been established under FAPSI's control remains to be seen.

These units employed a variety of equipment uniforms during their history, their accouterments depending primarily on the mission. Both *spetsgruppi Al'fa* and *Vympel* were indistinguishable from regular airborne troops in the 1980s. *Spetsgruppa "A"* members wore the khaki six-pocket uniforms with blue *tel'niashkas*, and blue berets (probably without any army insignia).

When last seen publicly, *Al'fa* members were wearing both the *spetsodezhda* and woodland uniforms with green riot helmets. Although several types of insignia and patches have appeared in collector circles, no special indicators associated with *Al'fa* or *Vympel* have been seen on unit members while operational.

KGB Border Forces

Vladimir Il'ch Lenin created the border guards of the KGB ostensibly to defend the borders of the Soviet Union from external threats and, later, to prevent its citizens from escaping to the West. Structured along the lines of army brigades and divisions, these forces had provided the KGB with a powerful army to guard the state and the massive frontiers of the Soviet Union and Russia. Equipped with tanks, helicopters, armored personnel carriers, and mobile assault groups, the KGB border forces were equivalent to or exceeded the capability of the armies of many nations. Its personnel were generally more politically reliable and capable of serving the Communist Party (CPSU) unquestioningly.

Subsequent to the coup in August 1991, Gorbachev removed the border forces from KGB control and placed them under military control. His fear of their capabilities being used against the government moved Yeltsin to restrict their employment to strictly border matters.

In 1994 President Yeltsin brought the border forces back under the control of the new Russian Ministry of Security (MB). By bringing these combat and security forces back under control of the security agency, Yeltsin increased the power of the MB and was able to significantly increase his personal influence and military capability.

The border forces under Yeltsin temporarily became a committee again (KPV) and then were redesignated the Federal Border Service (*Federal'naia pogranichnaia sluzhba*). These forces were commanded by Colonel General Vladimir Shliakhtin until July 1993 and then Shliakhtin was replaced by Colonel-General Andrei Nikolaev. The FPS remains a powerful instrument of control and influence in Russia and provides the president with a significant amount of firepower and influence.

Border units are divided into regiments, battalions, companies and outposts (*zastava*). There are also assault maneuver groups (DShMG) designed to react quickly to hot spots along the border. Each *zastava* is equipped with armored personnel carriers, mortar and artillery support, and aviation support units.

The uniform of the border troops has progressed from the simple one- and two-piece KLMK light-weight uniforms to the heavier KGB/MVD variants. Currently, most of the federal border troops wear the two-piece KLMK uniforms, especially in tropical regions. The woodland and VSR patterns are also in use with some units.

During the 1980s it was standard practice for KGB and GRU special operations forces to go into combat areas disguised as ordinary airborne forces. This photo represents one such special operation troop of the KGB: SSh-60 helmet, MB610 defensive (flak) vest, "6x5" AK-74 bayonet, jump helmet, and woodland camouflage.

Special Purpose Separate Training Company of the Twenty Seventh (27th) Separate Guard's Motorized Sevastopol Red Banner Brigade

In July 1990, the separate reconnaissance company, serving as part of the special-purpose Twenty Seventh Guard's Motorized Brigade of the KGB, USSR was redesignated a special-purpose training company. For distinguished officers and soldiers of the company, pulled from other branches, the commander of the brigade, Colonel A. N. Egorov allowed them to wear with their field uniform a black tanker beret and *tel'niashka* of the airborne forces.

On the beret is worn the star in a wreath (for privates and sergeants) or cockade in a wreath (for warrant officers and officers), and on the left side is sewn a red "flash" with the emblem of the airborne forces (VDV). After 1 1/2 months of service in the company, new recruits have the right to take an examination which tests their knowledge and combat skills. Having successfully passed the examination the new recruits earn the right to wear the black beret.

In May of 1991, the commander of the company, O. A. Mitrofanov offered to establish a sleeve patch of special-purpose Forces (*Spetsnasovskoi*) qualification which they would also receive after passing an examination. In order to receive the patch, servicemen must serve their initial service obligation of not less than one year. Taking part in the designing of the patch, aside from the commander of the company, were: Captain I. V. Mishin, Sr. Lt. Makarenko, and the platoon leader Sr. Lt. O. V. Nevzorov.

Assigned personnel adopted the patch for wear during their term of service within the company. In the center was placed the head of a white eagle[6] "borrowed" from the emblem of the 101st Air Assault Division of the U.S. Army (101st Airborne Division (AASLT)). The patches were embroidered by one of the businesses in the Kaliningrad area (Moscow region). The size of the patch is 75x85 mm.

At the end of June the commander of the brigade approved the initiative of the *spetsnazovtsi* (special-purpose troops) and by the beginning of the following month was developing the qualification examination. It was administered to 4 officers (all successful), and 20 sergeants and privates (9 successful).

What follows is a brief historical background of the company:

Historical Information

Aug 1940: 535th Rifle regiment of the 127th Rifle Division

28 May 1943: Regiment changed to 6th Guard's Rifle Regiment

10 May 1944: By order of the Supreme command for outstanding performance in battle for the liberation of Sevastopol, the regiment was awarded the honorary title (honorific) Sevastopol regiment.

17 Aug 1944: By decree of the presidium of the Supreme Soviet, USSR for valor in the liberation of Shiauliai, the regiment was awarded the Order of the Red Banner.

26 March 1957: The directive of the command of the MVO the regiment was renumbered the 404th Guard's Motorized Regiment.

In 1980 the regiment was deployed as the 27th Separate Guard's Motorized Brigade.

In July 1990 the brigade transferred to the organization of the KGB of the USSR under the designation special-purpose 27th Separate Guard's Motorized Brigade.

22 Aug 1991: The unit was returned to the armed forces in accordance with the directive of the General Staff and was reorganized. At the beginning of September 1991 this decision was canceled.[7]

GROM (AOZT) Security Company

Although not a subunit of the former KGB, most of this security agency's members are former members of the KGB's elite teams. With a strength of over 1,000 personnel, GROM (Thunder) provides security for trains, aircraft, personnel and important buildings on contract with the Russian government. It is a public stock company but of a so-called "closed type" which means it does not pay out dividends and is licensed and partially funded, on contract, by the Russian government. The initials AOZT stand for "public company of a closed type."

GROM members are knowledgeable in personal security and highly skilled in the use of firing weapons and blades. One member of GROM, a former member of a KGB *spetsgruppa*, informed me that the employees learned their skills in Afghanistan and in combat around the former Soviet Union. Each member is licensed and permitted to carry concealed weapons in the performance of his duties.

Uniforms of GROM include the VSR and army woodland patterns. *Okhrana* patches and TEAM SPECIAL/SPECIAL FORCES tabs as well as GROM patches, identify members of this organization. Cap devices, when worn, are the standard Soviet army type.

Other security agencies operating in Russia whose members wear military style camouflage on occasion include Wakenhut, Alex, Pinkerton and several private companies. Generally employees of these companies can be distinguished from those of government agencies by the presence of company patches, tabs and cap devices. Unfortunately, virtually all MVD subcontract security companies as well as private security agencies have taken to wearing SPECIAL FORCES, TEAM SPECIAL, and the various *okhrana* patches, making identification difficult.

ENDNOTES CHAPTER 9

[1] Moscow, KEDR, 1992.

[2] According to two former KGB members, one of the units involved in the seizure was named *spetsgruppa* Vympel, since resubordinated to the MVD and renamed Vega. See the section on Vympel later in the chapter.

[3] M.E. Boltunov, *"Al'fa" - sverkhsekretnyi otriad KGB.* [Al'fa, supersecret detachment of the KGB], (Moscow: KEDR, 1992), p. 16.

[4] Yeltsin, p. 11, and *FBIS-SOV-94-035*, February 22, 1994, p. 32.

[5] Yevgenia Arbats, *The KGB, The State Within a State*, (NY: Farrar Straus Group, 1994), p. 25.

[6] Bald Eagle.

[7] This narration and history is taken from A. Stepanov's article: "*Narukavnye znaki VS Rossii* (1)"(Sleeve patches of the Armed Forces of Russia - in Russian), *Tseikhgauz*, January 1993, issue number 2, p. 44.

10

SPECIAL UNITS OF THE MINISTRY OF DEFENSE

Hence, when able to attack, we must seem unable; when using our forces, we must seem inactive; when we are near, we must make the enemy believe we are far away; when far away, we must make him believe we are near.
– Sun Tsu, *The Art of War*

The *Spetsnaz* Soldier

Previous discussions of special forces focused on those forces of the special services, that is, the former KGB (now SVR), FSB, FAPSI and MVD. The main differences between *spetsnaz* forces of the special services (*spetssluzhbi*) and those of the military (ground and naval forces), are their missions, armament, and command and control. While both types of *spetsnaz* fulfill peacetime and wartime missions, special services *spetsnaz* perform execute their duties (anti- terrorist, crowd control, crime-suppression) primarily during peacetime. Military or GRU *spetsnaz* units are only fully operational during war or the period immediately prior to hostilities. Moreover, military *spetsnaz* units are typically better trained, better equipped, and are more tightly controlled than those in the special service units. To get a better idea of the differences and similarities between the two groups, we'll look briefly at the operational units employed by the Main Intelligence Directorate (GRU) of the Russian Ministry of Defense.

Much of what we know about military *spetsnaz* units comes from the former *spetsnaz* officer who identified himself as Viktor Suvorov. Subsequent writers and *spetsnaz* members have written more definitively on the subject of *spetsnaz* and have corrected many of our earlier presupposed beliefs. In the course of this discussion, I will provide comparisons of some of the earlier writings with those produced later.

Spetsnaz personnel with whom I have spoken consider much of what has been written to be far out of proportion to the actual capabilities and abilities of the units in which they served. Moreover, Carey Schofield, in her book, *Inside the Soviet Military*, was able to provide greater insight into *spetsnaz* operations through her first-hand observations of *spetsnaz* training and interviews with personnel who serve in active *spetsnaz* units. It has been her assertion that the West has greatly overestimated the abilities of the Russian *spetsnaz*. Nevertheless, Soviet and Russian *spetsnaz* has long held a fascination with Western writers and devotees to the military and espionage genre and therefore, details of *spetsnaz* operations and structure are provided here for the reader's interest.

Organization

During the Soviet period, the basic strategic level operational unit was the *brigada* or brigade. Virtually every military district (MD) was assigned one *spetsnaz* brigade of 900 to 2,000 *spetsnazovtsi*.

Most of these units have either devolved to the new republics in which the MD was located or they have been relocated to other cities. Both Kazakhstan and Belorussia are known to have taken Russian airborne units and converted them to *spetsnaz* brigades employing former Soviet military personnel who swore and oath of loyalty to the newly independent republics.

Perhaps the most well known of the *spetsnaz* units is the 16th Special purpose brigade, headquartered in the Teplyi Stan. During the October 1993 coup, the 16th was placed on alert and readied for an assault against the parliament; it did not actually participate in the assault of the Russian white house.

Recently there have been allegations that the members of the 16th *spetsbrigada* were moonlighting as Russian mafia hitmen. The 16th has a separate otriad which serves as a guard force for the headquarters of the GRU (military intelligence) in Moscow.

There is currently only one full-strength *spetsnaz* naval brigade, at Ocharkov on the Black Sea, although during a war the Russian MOD could deploy one brigade for each fleet; there are several bases that would accommodate these brigades if necessary. These are located at

Severomarsk; Primarsk at Baku; and on a Russian Island near Vladivostok. During wartime, the 42nd Naval *spetsnaz* brigade would be situated there.

Each *spetsbrigada* includes a brigade headquarters, a signal battalion, and support units. During the Soviet period, in contrast with typical active army units, most of the *spetsnaz* brigades were maintained at full strength, and would generally be further augmented during a mobilization. However, due to severe budget constraints and economic limitations, Russian *spetsnaz* units are currently maintained at much lower strength levels.

Spetsnaz brigades are divided into battalions (called *otriadi* in Russian). Highly variable in their structure, an *otriad* may have between 180 and 410 or more *spetsnazovtsi* assigned. Each *otriad* consists of a headquarters company (called a *rota* in Russian) with medical and support sections, and three airborne companies. Each company is comprised of between nine and ten *spetsgruppi* or teams. *Spetsgruppi* may be further subdivided into sections (*spetsotdeleni*) each with ten to twelve men. Depending on the mission, sizes of units and types of equipment will vary. At peacetime strength, the typical *spetsrota* has 40 personnel equaling about 111 personnel in the *otriad* (battalion). During wartime, this number may increase two or three times.

According to *Spetsnaz* magazine, a typical Russian *spetsnaz* reconnaissance unit (*razvedyvatel'naia gruppa – RG*) consists of five *spetsgruppi* with three to five persons each. The *spetsnaz* RG consists of a strike group, an elimination group, an explosives group, a hostage liberation group, and a diversionary group. The entire size of the unit amounts to 19 personnel, including the commander.

Within each brigade is an administrative *otriad*, responsible for training reservists to bring other battalions up to strength. Moreover, each brigade includes a separate battalion (*otdel'nye otriadi*), which provides direct support to an army (combined arms or tank) commander. Each battalion would field thirty to forty-five groups capable of operating as independent *spetsnaz* units in direct support of the army commander.

In wartime, military districts are converted to fronts and army groups. Within each military district is an intelligence directorate – the Second Directorate of the Military District Staff. The chief of the Second Directorate of the Military District becomes the chief of the front for intelligence during hostilities. This chief controls all intelligence collection within his military district or front. Reporting directly to this chief of intelligence, *spetsnaz* battalion commanders pass important intelligence information gleaned from battlefield collection or prisoner interrogation as soon as it becomes available.

Members of the GRU's special operations forces (spetsnaz) during training (note full-color Guard's badges and blank adapters). Each soldier wears the woodland army camouflage, airborne tel'niashka, and airborne beret without flash.

Each fleet is approximately equivalent to a military district and has its own Naval Staff Second Directorate responsible for intelligence collection and dissemination. Naval *spetsnaz* unit commanders are similarly responsible for providing intelligence information to the fleet intelligence officer or chief.

The Main Intelligence Directorate (GRU) of the Russian army has the overall responsibility for intelligence collection by the military. This includes GRU agents stationed in embassies and military intelligence and reconnaissance units during wartime. Within the GRU, the Fifth Directorate manages operational intelligence, and intelligence organizations within fronts, fleets, and military districts. Within the army, all of the chiefs of the military district intelligence fall under the command of the Fifth Directorate head. In the case of the navy, fleet intelligence officers (Naval Staff Second Directorate Chiefs) fall under the control of naval intelligence which in turn falls under the Fifth Directorate of the GRU.

Within the Second Directorates (front intelligence) are several departments responsible for various aspects of intelligence collection and dissemination. The First Department controls reconnaissance at the tactical level. The Second Department manages agent recruitment and the development of agent networks. This is not to be confused with the development of agents abroad; rather, at this level, MD's are responsible for agent recruitment from areas adjacent to or in their area of responsibility in wartime. The Third Department is responsible for *spetsnaz* operations within the target country; this includes sabotage, kidnapping, assassinations, destruction of power plants and weapons delivery systems, and diversionary acts in time of war. The Fourth or Information Department is responsible for intelligence collection management and analysis. The Fifth Department is responsible for signals intelligence (sigint) and radar emissions by the enemy. Schofield mentions two additional departments, the Sixth, which is responsible for special signals; and the Seventh, which involves ciphers.

Although the *brigada* is the primary operational *spetsnaz* unit, independent *spetsnaz* companies can also be assigned to operate within enemy territory. A *spetsrota*, consists of three reconnaissance platoons and one signals platoon with a strength of between 140 men and officers. Typically the independent *spetsrota* has a more limited operational area, 150 to 200 miles behind enemy lines.

Separate *spetsnaz* battalions (*otdel'nye otriadi spetsial'nogo naznacheniia*) may also be formed in the event of hostilities, formed from experienced commanders and new recruits. These may operate primarily as reconnaissance units or engage in the elimination of strategic weapons and communications facilities. Like the green berets during Desert Storm, teams from *spetsotriadi* would target enemy missile launchers and communications facilities far behind enemy lines.

Another, possible ad-hoc organization might comprise *spetsnaz*-trained GRU officers within the diplomatic community, assigned to embassies and consulates. According to one source, all GRU officers undergo *spetsnaz* training, including parachute training, wilderness survival and language training. GRU officers graduating from the voennaia diplomaticheskiaia akademiia (VDA) who are subsequently assigned to the Ministry of Foreign Affairs or Russian embassies and consulates abroad, also further receive diplomatic training.

A GRU officer stationed in a foreign country might be responsible for the activation and direction of sleeper agents, long-term illegals responsible for sabotage, assassination, and the direction of underground movements in the host-nation during a conflict. GRU officers assigned to diplomatic establishments or using non-official cover (NOC) as business representatives, may also form ad-hoc teams during wartime in order to execute strategic level missions against the host-nation military leadership and communications facilities.

Spetsnaz-like units

Reconnaissance battalions assigned to motorized rifle and tank divisions perform some of the same functions as *spetsnaz* units. Within this battalion is a sabotage company, fully capable of performing the same functions as a *spetsnaz* unit. However, unlike *spetsnaz* units, reconnaissance units are more heavily equipped and designed to operate for longer periods of time behind enemy lines. Furthermore, reconnaissance battalions are comprised of soldiers with average abilities and training and seldom comprise airborne-qualified personnel.

An exception to this was the reconnaissance battalion assigned to the 103rd Guards Airborne Division. Stationed in Vitebsk, the 103rd Guards VDV was subordinated to the KGB Border troops; as a result, its personnel wore green berets and green collar tabs with airborne insignia. Although not readily available in the late 1980s, members of the unit were also instructed to wear the green and white striped *tel'niashka* t-shirt. In this case, the reconnaissance unit was comprised not only of airborne qualified personnel, but better trained and more politically reliable personnel as well. As a special note, also entitled to wear the green beret were several *moto-manevrennye gruppi* (MMG) stationed in the south of the U.S.S.R., and some companies from the Moscow Border Guard School. The Assault-landing maneuver groups (DShMG's) of the Border Guards Directorate, while outfitted with the KLMK uniforms generally wore the blue and white airborne *tel'niashkas*, and KLMK field caps instead of the green berets since the latter was largely unavailable to them.

Training

During the Soviet period only about 20 percent of the soldiers recruited for airborne forces were chosen to participate in *spetsnaz* training. Since the collapse of the Soviet Union, recruits on a contract basis can actually enlist for *spetsnaz* training, assuming they meet the minimum qualifications.

Within *spetsnaz* training several subcategories or specialties exist to which the recruit will be assigned. Additionally, those showing a special aptitude for leadership or technical knowledge can be sent to a non-commissioned officers training or communications training school. Unlike the U.S. or western military tradition, Russian NCO's simply have more training than the typical conscript and perhaps a few months more experience. The career NCO, a backbone of western military services, is largely nonexistent in Russia.

As with all recruits, *spetsnaz* soldiers undergo a basic orientation course designed to acquaint the soldier with basic army procedures. Marching, standing at attention, and basic military drilling and reporting procedures are emphasized. It is here that the recruit gets his first taste of discipline and the army life. While the failure rate of new recruits is high, due to the introduction of the contract soldier, greater allowances are made for failure than when military service was mandatory and the selection criteria more restrictive.

Previously, assignment to a *spetsnaz* unit was kept a closely-guarded secret. Membership in such an elite unit was kept from friends, family members and even other military personnel. Since the *spetsnazovtsi* wore the uniform of airborne or signal troops, it was generally quite simple to explain to others that they were assigned to an army airborne unit. There was nothing special to distinguish them from other airborne soldiers and this explanation suited their needs.

With the introduction of *glasnost* (openness) and a need to recruit volunteers subsequent to the dissolution of mandatory conscription, the Russian MOD launched a propaganda campaign designed to bring new blood into the special combat units of the army and navy. With the introduction of new uniforms and the associated unit insignia, being a member of *spetsnaz* was no longer considered a state secret. As a result, Russian *spetsnaz* competition is shown on television and the exploits of *spetsnaz*ovtsi are described in journals and magazines. As mentioned earlier, there is even a special journal dedicated to the special forces of the world called *spetsnaz.*

Spetsnaz training largely mirrors the special forces training in other countries with the addition of specialized training geared toward prisoner interrogation and assassination techniques. While the U.S. special forces (green berets) have the primary function of training local indigenous personnel in the art of guerrilla warfare and resistance, the *spetsnaz*ovets has the responsibility of conducting his own mission of assault, surveillance, sabotage, diversion and reconnaissance. Perhaps *spetsnazovets* training can best be described as incorporating all the skills used by the U.S. special forces, rangers, delta force, and in the case of naval *spetsnaz*, the navy seals.

Techniques specific to *spetsnaz* training also include tracking and patrol techniques. *Spetsnazovtsi* are trained to follow their prey by walking, single file, in each other's footsteps, so the size and nature of the unit cannot be easily determined. One *spetsnazovets* even admitted that a special boot had been developed with reversed soles so as to disguise the direction of the patrol. On occasion, soles that mimic the boots of other (read NATO) countries have also been used to disguise the nature of the unit operating behind enemy lines.

Readers will no doubt recall the Willie Sanger battalion in East Germany that reportedly was to don U.S. uniforms and equipment in time of war so as to confuse the enemy. This was undoubtedly a direct descendent of Operation Greif. Under the command of Lieutenant Colonel Otto Skorzeny, operation Greif achieved limited success in World War II when specially trained German soldiers, disguised as U.S. military police, parachuted behind American lines and wreaked havoc with U.S. forces. Whether or not such a unit existed or still exists in Russia is a matter for speculation. Such a unit would almost certainly undergo the same type of training as *spetsnaz* and would undoubtedly be subordinate to the GRU.

Spetsnaz troops undergo rigorous physical training with an emphasis on endurance and strength. The majority of *spetsnaz*ovtsi must qualify for the master sportsman badge, a designation few in the regular army are able to achieve. It can be said that the candidate master sportsman and master sportsman badges are good indicators of *spetsnaz* affiliation.

According to Suvorov, and others, *spetsnaz* physical training includes running for speed and distance, endurance swimming, negotiating obstacle courses, and throwing entrenching tools and knives. *Spetsnaz*ovtsi must also be able to rappel from buildings and cliffs, air assault out of helicopters, and parachute from fixed wing and rotary wing aircraft.

The GRU recently formed special *spetsnaz* winter assault and mountain assault troops. While little is know about these units, insignia worn by *spetsnaz* units have identified them as the El'brus (Elbrus) and Edel'veis (Edelweiss) Mountain Diversionary Groups, and the Arktika northern diversionary group as well as other quick reaction units. The creation of these units has led to increased training in both mountain and winter operations. As a result, *spetsnaz* training requires that soldiers be able to employ skis for reconnaissance in mountainous areas and assaults against enemy troops entrenched in alpine settings. Operating deep in enemy territory, it stands to reason *spetsnaz* troops operating in Finland, Norway and Sweden, must be able to negotiate mountainous areas on skis complete with survival gear and rations for one to two week periods.

Of course, weapons training and hand-to-hand combat are of primary importance of *spetsnaz* training. *Spetsnaz*ovtsi learn to fire special weapons at their maximum range as well as up close and personal. Specially silenced (*bezshumnii*) 9mm pistols, automatics and in the case of naval *spetsnaz*, underwater rifles and pistols, are provided to the *spetsnaz* troops for operational use and it is up to each recruit to learn how to fire, field strip, maintain and repair their assigned weapons and the weapons of their teammates.

Typically a *spetsnaz* soldier must be able to engage and hit a stationary target at 1,600 feet with a rifle, 130 feet with a submachine gun, and between 80 and 100 feet with a pistol. Snipers reportedly must be able to engage stationary targets at 1,800 feet, and moving targets (two to ten feet per second) at 1,600 feet. As with infantry soldiers, *spetsnaz*ovtsi should be able to throw a hand grenade accurately from 80 to 160 feet when standing still or when running.

The use of bladed weapons has always been a source of fascination with western observers. The practice of silent killing is an important skill to the *spetsnaz*ovets. During the Soviet period, the entrenching tool was commonly seen as the usual weapon of choice for killing an opponent from a distance. The shovel could be thrown or, if close enough, swung, to kill an opponent quickly. Penetration by a sharp entrenching tool spade was usually sufficient to cause severe internal injuries and immediate death.

This technique was well demonstrated by airborne troops in Georgia and the Baltics during ethnic disturbances in which airborne forces were deployed to restore the peace. While MVD troops relied heavily on Cheremukha riot gas and suppressive fire from their automatics, airborne troops resorted to their time-honored tradition of using entrenching tools against the armed and unarmed opponents (or civilians according to most news reports).

In the early 1990s, elite troops gradually turned away from the entrenching tool and began to rely more heavily on various specially-designed knives and bayonets. Knife throwing became an important part of the soldier's training in his basic course. Since the AKM and AK-74 bayonets were suitable for cutting wire or cutting throats, the bayonet began to take on greater importance as a close-in weapon. The typical orange handled, bakelite AKM bayonet was the most commonly issued bayonet to airborne and *spetsnaz* troops and so it became the standard edged-weapon.

Later, the black bakelite "6x5" AK-74 bayonet with knurled grip became more widely distributed and it soon took its place among the edged arsenal. By the end of 1992, these two bayonets were supplemented by the less common NRS-1, NRS-2, *spetsnozh* and other, more specialized, airborne and special operations blades.

The NRS-2 folding reconnaissance knife, has a two-edged blade and is capable of firing a single 7.62 mm bullet. The projectile weighs 300 grams and is effective up to 60 feet. The green bakelite scabbard and handle of the knife attach to form a reasonably accurate single-shot weapon with which to aim and fire a rifle round. It is assumed that this is purely for defensive purposes as its range and accuracy are extremely doubtful. This is considered a silenced weapon and so may be useful for close in work.

Since the main reason for using edged weapons is silent killing, soldiers are taught to throw the bayonet from a distance of 20 to 26 feet striking the target and rendering the target defenseless. Additionally, knife throwing must be learned by the *spetsnaz*ovets while rappelling, low crawling, and as a defensive move against an oncoming attacker.

Rukopashni boi, or hand to hand combat, is an important facet of *spetsnaz* training. Fighting unarmed against an armed attacker is one of the fundamental skills learned by both airborne forces and special operations troops. Several versions of *Rukopashni boi* exist, including SAMBO, unarmed combat, and "The system," but all stress a combination of Eastern meditation and focusing and channeling one's strength against an opponent. *Spetsnaz*ovtsi learn one of several Russian versions of hand to hand combat and may adopt other, similar forms of unarmed combat as well.

Skills which *spetsnaz*ovtsi must also learn include language training, demolitions and improvised munitions training, wilderness survival, and the art of *maskirovka*, that is, camouflage employment and detection. While the *spetsnazovtsi* do not become experts in any of these areas, they must at least become proficient enough so as to be able to maximize their survival in order to carry out their missions. However, one area in which survival is absolutely dependent on is proficiency in parachuting.

Like airborne soldiers, *spetsnaz*ovtsi are trained in static-line jump techniques from low- flying aircraft. During their initial training, soldiers become familiar with the mock-ups, swing landing trainers, and towers familiar to most American and western paratroopers.

What is amazing to most Americans, however, are the numbers of jumps Russian airborne troops undergo as compared to most American paratroopers. It is typical for Americans soldiers to leave Fort Benning with five jumps to their credit and then, however many additional jumps while at their duty station. Russian *spetsnaz*ovtsi may jump one, two, three or more hundred times in their service. Some may make additional jumps in the hundreds as part of off-duty training or while training youngsters who are members of DOSAAF.

While U.S. special forces undoubtedly rack up as many jumps during their careers, Russian special operations units seem to be able to accrue more parachute training as part of their regular service. Whether this will change due to budget constraints remains to be seen.

Like their counterparts in Delta and the Navy's "teams", Russian *spetsnaz* also train in various forms of parachute assaults: high altitude low-opening (HALO) insertions, low altitude heavy equipment drops (similar to using low-altitude parachute extraction systems – LAPES), and airmobile and air assault techniques from helicopters into combat areas.

Since the goal of the *spetsnaz* troop is to be delivered unseen into the enemy's rear echelon and support area, the parachute assault from fixed wing aircraft is the preferred method of infiltration. Moreover, there are sufficient numbers of combined arms forces trained in air assault and air mobile insertions to make helicopter assaults by *spetsnaz* unnecessary.

Most of the *spetsnaz* officers are trained at the Ryazan Higher Airborne Assault School (RVVDKU) or are recruited out of the army and specially trained. While political reliability is a must, physical prowess and a successful military career are a must. In the case of Suvorov, he claims he was specifically recruited to join the GRU and underwent long-term, specialized training to perform his duties. Another similarly recruited *spetsnaz* soldier told me political reliability was important, but his physical capabilities and intelligence were of utmost importance.

A recommendation by a friend in the *spetsnaz* or from a relative is an important avenue to the elite forces; but, as mentioned previously, contract recruitment and application in response to an advertisement has become a routine avenue for joining the *spetsnazovtsi*.

Missions

Whereas *spetsnazovtsi* of the *spetssluzhbi* are operational in times of both peace and war, military *spetsnazovtsi* perform their functions only during periods of full scale war and low intensity conflict (that is, during operations other than war (OOTW)). While the special service *spetsnaz* forces have primarily peacetime missions of law enforcement, anti-terrorism, crowd control, and security operations, military *spetsnazovtsi* perform vital strategic missions of long- range reconnaissance, destruction of important weapons and command facilities, the elimination of key bridges and transportation routes, and the kidnaping and assassination of important military and political leaders.

Although military *spetsnazovtsi* may train and conduct strategic reconnaissance missions during peacetime, they do not become completely operational until a conflict is in its developmental stages or erupts into a full scale war. Prior to the collapse of the Soviet Union, all reconnaissance and *spetsnaz* units were maintained at full strength. Subsequent to the collapse, most *spetsnaz* units are now maintained at 50% or better of full strength. As a result, the typical military *spetsgruppa*, the smallest basic operational unit, will not be at full strength until deployed.

Because of the types of missions conducted by military *spetsnaz*: deep reconnaissance missions, diversionary tactics, sabotage and kidnapping/assassination of military and political leaders, their very deployment would constitute and act of war. If successful, the *spetsgruppa* would accomplish its missions before the enemy could react.

Historically, it can be reasonably assumed that spetsnazovtsi have been employed in various regions to perform training and operational missions against U.S. and western-trained forces. Reconnaissance and combat operations by Soviet *spetsnazovtsi* in Vietnam, Africa, and the Middle East were as common as employing Soviet pilots against American pilots during the Korean and Vietnam conflicts.

More recently, *spetsnaz* units have deployed to various hot spots to perform a variety of functions. While in Afghanistan, *spetsnaz* units performed deep reconnaissance and sabotage missions against the Mujahadeen supply and communications networks, and so-called pacification missions against villages reputed to have supported Afghani rebels.

There are also reports that *spetsnaz* troops have been used in riot suppression roles in Armenia, Georgia and the Baltic States. It is difficult to know precisely what units were active in these areas since both MVD and army airborne units were observed and reported to have engaged in operational activities during ethnic unrest in these locales.

Most recently it was reported that both army and naval *spetsnaz* units took part in hostilities during the Chechen crisis. While it is certain that MVD *spetsnaz* and *osnaz* units participated in military operations in the region, it is difficult to ascertain the extent to which military special operations units (other than the botched raid perpetrated by FSK units at the outset) participated in the war in Chechnia.

Equipment

As a strategic-level theater asset, *spetsnaz* brigades typically received greater funding and better equipment than their security counterparts. More often than not, military spets units were/are at the cutting edge of military doctrine.

The armament of *spetsnazovtsi* assigned to the special services up until recently has been equivalent to the regular forces of the MVD or former KGB. In contrast, GRU *spetsnaz* units were typically better armed owing to their combat-oriented missions. Fortunately for the special services, this situation has begun to change.

In addition to the previously mentioned bladed weapons, the AK-74 "6x5", NRS-1, and NRS-2, and the special *spetsnozh* or special operations knife, *spetsnaz*ovtsi might also be issued a shroud cutter knife, a ballistic knife (made famous by U.S. dealers selling poor copies), and a compact switchblade.

A *spetsnaz* team will normally be issued the standard AKS-74 (rifle); the AKSU-5.45 and PBS automatics; the RPG-7d, RPG-18d or RPG-26 antitank weapons; and the BG-15 40 mm grenade launcher (*Tishina*). Additionally, the designated sniper(s) will receive either the standard SVD sniper rifle or the silenced VSS sniper system.

One platoon in each brigade is trained to use 'Ptur' antitank guided missiles (nicknamed fagot, or 'bassoon'), and will be equipped with four of them. Each team is also equipped with anti-personnel mines (PP), MON-100 directional fragmentation mines, and explosives kits. For special missions, a commander might receive several specially silenced weapons to issue to his team.

Naval *spetsnaz* teams may receive similar weapons if their mission is land-based. However, underwater missions call for underwater weapons and explosives. Recently a series of specially-designed weapons that fire darts under water have been developed specifically for such special missions. The 5.66mm underwater APS can fire a dart to a range of 90 feet at a depth of 15 feet, or 33 feet at a depth of 120 feet. The rifle holds 26 darts. There is also a dart-firing pistol called a SPP-1 that can fire a dart up to 150 feet out of water or up to 51 feet at 15 feet of water.

Since each *spetsnaz*ovets is trained in radio communications, *spetsnaz* team members carry a R255-PP set that picks up the signal emitted by the R354M burst-transmission portable radio (one per team). The receivers are used for both mission instructions and for air drop coordination. The signals, since they are used in the burst-transmission mode, are difficult to identify and even harder to intercept, making them ideal for special operations usage.

Due to the difficulty in hiding standard analog radio transmissions, it is assumed the Russian military is switching out analog radio equipment for more advanced digital communications sets available off the shelf in the United States and Europe. As with U.S. special operations units, it does not seem unlikely that Russian *spetsgruppi* could incorporate currently available encryption technology with digital communications and laptop technology to create virtually undetectable ground-satellite-ground communications capabilities.

Uniforms of *Spetsnaz*

Spetsnaz, like other elite units, typically receive the latest equipment and uniforms; in this case, this means camouflage. However, because *spetsnaz* units have long been shrouded in secrecy, it was important to "camouflage" their actual identity by mimicking other units.

In most cases, *spetsnaz* troops simply adopted the uniforms of the unit to which they were assigned. For garrison troops, wearing the collar tabs, branch insignia and uniform piping of their hosts was usually sufficient to hide their actual assignment. Of course, the host unit soldiers were normally fully aware of the identity of the special troops assigned to the unit.

During World War II, the only troops to be issued camouflage uniforms were airborne troops, reconnaissance troops, snipers and engineer-sappers. According to Suvorov, *spetsnaz* units were called "minelaying" or "reconnaissance" units, while the remainder were simply described as airborne troops. During their infancy in World War II, NKVD *spetsnazovtsi* assigned to *otriadi* and *brigadi* wore camouflage uniforms of the period; as a result, many of the photographs showing the aforementioned units from World War II may actually be photos of *spetsnazovtsi*.

In the post World War II era, spetsnazovtsi donned the uniforms and insignia of airborne, signals, and reconnaissance troops assigned to airborne divisions. Within combined arms armies, they generally wore the combined arms collar tabs (red) and insignia (star and wreath) of their hosts.

GRU *spetsnaz* personnel assigned to diplomatic establishments, wore either airborne combined arms insignia on their uniforms. Regardless, the GRU spetsnaz personnel generally wore the mark of the airborne forces in the form of jump insignia (a parachute) or an academy badge from the RVVDKU. GRU *spetsnaz* personnel would likely as not wear the guard's badge since their current assignment as diplomatic personnel would preclude them from wearing the insignia. This brings up an interesting question first raised by Suvorov.

Carey Schofield and Suvorov each make contradictory claims concerning airborne soldiers not bearing the Guards badge; according to Suvorov, they can be assumed to be *spetsnaz*.

Suvorov's claim that there were no active military *spetsnaz* troops during World War II is the basis for his claim that real *spetsnaz* troops cannot wear guard's badges. However, according to Lieutenant-General D. M. Gerasimov, in his article *SPETSNAZ! History, Do we need them today?*,[1] *spetsnaz* (SpN) operated under the Fourth Directorate of the NKVD as subunits and operational groups and performed reconnaissance and counter-insurgency missions. The lineage of the NKVD as written about by Michael J. Parrish, and the discussion of the NKVD Special Purpose Motorized Brigade under the Special Tasks department of the NKVD bear out this assertion.[2]

It is highly unlikely that the military would not employ *spetsnaz* troops during the Second World War in support of combat operations against Germany. In fact, Suvorov states plainly that several special purpose units were operational during the war although they may not have been so designated.

Whereas Schofield makes the point that units can earn the Guard's designation only through participation in combat and earning the distinction through heroism, Suvorov states that a Guard's unit can receive the distinction upon its creation. Again, this seemingly contradictory argument actually adds little to identification.

There are several independent airborne brigades that do not share the Guard's designation. The same can be said for the independent airborne regiments stationed in Russia. While it is true that most of the airborne divisions are Guards units, the members of the airborne training unit in Fergana do not have this distinction. Due to the deactivation of the 105th Guards Airborne Division, formerly stationed in Fergana, a follow-on airborne unit was created to fill this vacancy. Since the new unit did not engage in combat activities or receive the Guard's designation, none of its members are entitled to wear the Guard's badge.

By the same token, there are also reportedly *spetsnaz* detachments and battalions with the Guard's designation that have not seen combat.[3] This occurs primarily when a new unit is created that is formed in honor of a previously active unit. The new unit can therefore trace its lineage back to an historical unit active during a war and therefore, carry the honorific, colors, and combat decorations received by the earlier unit.

It is a well-known fact that *spetsnaz* troops are known to have participated in the Olympic games trials for the purpose of intelligence collection just as they drove trucks throughout much of Western Europe to survey bridges, highways and airfields. However, it does not seem logical that if the GRU went to all the trouble of hiding the existence of *spetsnaz* troops, that it would make identification of *spetsnaz* soldiers so easy by the application of a simple Guard's badge.

If, after all, *spetsnaz* soldiers wore the uniforms of the unit to which they were assigned, isn't it also logical that the GRU would also simply pin on a Guard's badge in order to protect the identity of its elite forces? This seems especially poignant in light of Russia's steadfast refusal to order its soldiers in West Berlin to wear name tags (thus causing U.S. troops traveling to East Berlin to remove their name tags) or issue unit-distinctive insignia to its guard, airborne or elite units until the 1990s?

The other part of this argument about Guard's badges has dealt with female paratroopers and *spetsnaz*. Suvorov claimed that any female paratrooper not wearing a Guards badge was also *spetsnaz* since there were no female airborne troops.

Suvorov made this claim in response to a photo of four female Soviet airborne soldiers slated to attend the 1984 Olympics. Suvorov commented that the females must be *spetsnaz* because they were such fine athletes, had numerous jumps to their credit, and were not wearing Guard's badges.

Like their male counterparts, female soldiers wear the insignia and patches of the unit to which they are assigned. For instance, in the Soviet period, female soldiers assigned to the support units in a combined arms army, wore the specific branch insignia on red collar tabs and shoulderboards. Those soldiers assigned to the Independent air assault battalions of combined arms armies would be virtually indistinguishable from *spetsnaz* soldiers assigned to the battalion of the same combined arms army. Similarly, airborne soldiers assigned to such armies would wear the airborne insignia of their branch on the red background of the combined arms armies.

Most of this argument is now moot. In January of 1993, a *spetsnaz* brigade, redeployed from Georgia, inducted 26 female *spetsnaz*ovtsi on contract. Assigned to a special section within the brigade, they are nevertheless subject to the same high standards as their male counterparts. These female *spetsnaz*ovtsi wear the airborne berets, insignia, and camouflage uniforms associated with male *spetsnaz* troops.

During the 1970s and 1980s, *spetsnaz* troops were difficult to identify based solely on their uniforms. During this period, the majority of army and special service *spetsnaz* and *osnaz* units were virtually indistinguishable from regular combat and security units. While camouflaged uniforms and airborne insignia were generally key indicators of airborne and possibly, *spetsnaz* affiliation, there were no real key items that separated the two groups.

Then in 1979, the invasion of Afghanistan began to provide greater insight to the special operations forces and how they trained and fought. Slowly as equipment and uniforms made their way out of the embattled region, collectors and intelligence analysts were able to positively identify uniform components affiliated with *spetsnazovtsi*.

What was learned was *spetsnazovtsi* wore camouflage uniforms such as the KLMK overalls (1960s through 1980s) and woodland uniforms (1980s and 1990s) with airborne insignia on the latter and the characteristic blue-white striped *tel'niashkas* and airborne berets. These troops also received newly developed combat vests and load bearing equipment as well as the infamous entrenching tool.

A typical *spetsnaz* uniform identified in the late 1980s consisted of a one or two-piece khaki jumpsuit with extra cargo pockets on the legs in the front, above the knees. The uniforms were very similar to the six-pocket khaki uniforms issued to ground troops but had some styling differences making them unusual. Camouflage versions of these uniforms have yet to be identified.

By the early 1990s *Krasnaia zvezda* and *Orientir* began to show photos of *spetsnazovtsi* and describe their equipment and weapons. One *spetsnaz*ovets was shown wearing an unusual five-color camouflage uniform consisting of pastel greens, creams and blues. No other identification was present on the uniform and its identification remained a mystery. Soon, one of the uniforms was brought back by an East Coast dealer and sold to a collector. The dealer identified the uniform as a reconnaissance uniform. Still, its use and origins remained unclear. At present, only two or three other photos of the uniform have come to light and little else has been said concerning its development.

Of course today, the situation has changed considerably. Currently, several units have adopted patches that specifically identify their unit as *spetsnaz* units and articles describing *spetsnaz* troops and weapons are a relatively common occurrence – what a strange turn of events!

What we can now say is that the typical *spetsnaz* troop wears a camouflage uniform as his or her training and operational field uniform. Previously the KLMK (misnamed the computer pattern by American collectors) one-piece and two-piece uniform had been used for training by both *spetsnaz* and reconnaissance troops. It is still used by the majority of GRU and MVD special purpose troops for training.

Woodland uniforms largely replaced the KLMK as the operational uniform in the late 1980s, and VSR camouflage uniforms have subsequently replaced the woodland variants in the Russian republic. VSR uniforms are now generally used as operational field uniforms with the matching headgear; that is, berets or field caps. Full color patches and airborne insignia are generally only worn in garrison while stripped (unmarked) uniforms are used in the field.

Special load bearing equipment harnesses and combat assault vests in the same camouflage pattern or in a leather or khaki version accompany the camouflage uniform. Pouches, edged weapons, and helmet covers are also routinely issued to *spetsnaz* soldiers. Still, it is not necessarily an easy task to identify the *spetsnaz* soldier in the field.

Conclusion

While a great deal is now known about the Russian special operations forces or *spetsnaz*, there remains much more to be told about their historical development and deployment. The *spetsnaz* soldier of the 21st century faces numerous challenges. Budget shortfalls, equipment shortages, and heavy reliance on contract soldiers will greatly affect the Russian MOD's ability to prepare for peacekeeping operations and operations other than war. Nevertheless, the *spetsnaz*ovets remains a valuable tool for use by the Russian military as a response to low intensity operations and full scale conflicts of the future.

ENDNOTES CHAPTER 10

[1] *Spetsnaz*, 4/96, pp.1-3.

[2] Pavel Sudoplatov, *Special Tasks*, (NY: Little, Brown, 1994) pp. 126-127.

[3] *Spetsnaz*, A History of the Soviet Special Forces, Viktor Suvorov, p. 24.

ILLUSTRATION SECTION

World War II Camouflage Uniforms

WORLD WAR II CAMOUFLAGE AMOEBA PATTERN SUIT – MKK

YEAR ISSUED: 1937-1938

DESCRIPTION: This *maskirovochnyi kamuflirovannyi kostium* (MKK) two-piece uniform consists of an oversized pullover smock and pants designed to be worn over a standard field uniform. On some versions the jacket is equipped with attached mittens that tie at the wrists, a large sewn-on hood, and a green face veil made of a thin netting.

Early suits were issued with large jackets that possessed a smaller hood with cotton drawstrings that secured at the top of the hood and at the base of the neck. Later models included a larger hood buttoned in front with three large buttons; this design was retained on subsequent issues such as the leaf pattern suit Both versions have two slash openings permitting access to chest pockets.

Large, baggy pants designed to be worn over field pants include cotton drawstrings at the waist and cuffs; there are no pocket openings or buttons.

The lightweight cotton material construction makes the uniform comfortable, but not very sturdy.

The pattern consists of large, chocolate brown or black blobs on a green or tan background; thus giving it the suitable label of "amoeba pattern."

UNITS: Engineers, snipers, airborne forces and NKVD reconnaissance units were the most common recipients of this pattern. Snipers of the 106th border regiment[1] also wore this uniform during the Second World War. Although more common during the 1930s and 1940s, it is still issued to trainees and reservists of the MVD from existing war stocks. There is also a one-piece *maskirovochnyi kombinezon* (MK) which was issued to snipers, forward artillery observers, minelayers (probably spetsnaz troops) and communications specialists.

TOP: Typical configuration for Russian soldier with 1936 pattern helmet and Mosin-Nagant rifle with cartridge pouches. Photo by Brad Jacobs

BOTTOM: Close-up of early type smock showing the oversized hood, attached at the sides and closing the front with oversized buttons added at a later time.

WORLD WAR II CAMOUFLAGE LEAF PATTERN SUIT – MKK

YEAR ISSUED: 1941-1942

DESCRIPTION: A departure from the 1930s issue in camouflage design, the leaf pattern suit represents a slight modification over the early amoeba pattern suit. Although some existing stocks of the early two-piece uniform were used and the camouflage pattern changed, later models of the leaf pattern MKK incorporated slight modifications to the uniform design.

The hood is significantly larger as in the second model amoeba pattern, is sewn on three sides, and attaches to the front of the smock with metal or Bakelite buttons. The loose-weave face veil has been retained and is issued in green or sand color. The slash pockets are also present at about chest level.

The pants are of the standard pullover variety and secure with a cotton drawstring at the waist.

On some models the material is slightly heavier than in the early amoeba pattern models thus making the uniform more durable. This uniform does not appear to be reversible.[2]

For the first time an imitative camouflage pattern was employed as part of a field uniform. A complex design of cream and green leaves intermixed with grass outlines both breaks up the wearer's outline and allows the wearer to blend in with surrounding foliage.

UNITS: Like the previous model, the leaf pattern suit was issued to snipers, engineers, and reconnaissance troops. It remained in use through the 1950s although it can also be seen in photos of Romanian troops through the 1960s and 1970s.

TOP: Configuration for reconnaissance soldier of motorized rifle unit; note SVT 40 rifle.

BOTTOM: Close up of hood of leaf pattern suit showing the face veil and drawstring.

**WORLD WAR II CAMOUFLAGE
LEAF PATTERN COVERALLS – MK**

YEAR ISSUED: 1941-1942

DESCRIPTION: This is the coverall version of the Leaf pattern uniform (*masksirovochyi kombinezon*). The construction of this non-reversible uniform is identical to other one piece uniforms of the period.

This is a one-piece coverall with a button-up front (covered by a flap), an attached hood with cloth ties, and a collar which fastens at the wearer's right. The hood is smaller than earlier models and yet is able to cover the model SSh-40 helmet; it possesses vertical slash openings on each side and at the rear. As in other coveralls, a mask is issued in lieu of a face veil.

Buttons were made of simple tin or Bakelite although subsequent issues can be found with hammer and sickle marked buttons, plastic buttons, and civilian made fasteners. The pants portion close with a button-up flap on the seat. A right hip pocket has been provided in which the mask is usually stored, and slash pockets permit access to the field uniform worn underneath.

Nashivki (scrim tabs) are present on each side of the hood, chest, shoulders, upper arms, back and legs. The cuffs close with buttons as do the sleeves. There are large cloth slots for a field belt located in the rear and front.

The pattern is composed of complex design of cream and green leaves intermixed with grass outlines. This imitative camouflage design is intended to break up the wearer's outline yet permit him to blend in with surrounding foliage. There is reportedly a reversible version with the pattern resembling a sandy background with the leaf design presenting a lighter appearance.

Construction of the one-piece uniform was retained well through the 1950s and became a standard design for Soviet and client state uniforms.

UNITS: This uniform was issued to engineer, reconnaissance and engineer troops during the mid 1940s. It has also been issued to naval infantry soldiers as late as the 1960s and in Romania in the 1960s and 1970s.

TOP: Configuration for combat engineer (sapper) of the 1940s.

BOTTOM: Location of markings inside uniform jacket showing an issue date of 1950, color designation number 2, and a size marking of 2 (medium).

WORLD WAR II CAMOUFLAGE TRICOLOR SUIT-TTsMKK

YEAR ISSUED: 1944-1945

DESCRIPTION: The *tritsvetnyi kamuflirovannyi maskirovochnyi kostium* or tricolor camouflaged suit shown is the first of the stair-stepped pattern camouflage uniforms. The construction of the uniform is based on the cut of the two-piece 1940s leaf pattern while the design clearly represents a new trend in camouflage coloration and composition.

Like other uniforms of the period, this garment is oversized and made to be worn over field uniforms. The pullover smock possesses a button-up front and non-detachable hood. The veil is retained from earlier models and has not been significantly altered. Drawstrings are located on the hood's facing, waist and sleeves of the jacket. Two slits at waist level allow easy access to pockets and equipment. Buttons are of the open-face type and are made of tin alloy.

As in previous models, large, baggy pants allow for ease of movement. There a slash opening on each side which permits quick pocket access and a drawstring at the waist adjusts the fit.

Yellow, bright-green and forest-green geometric shapes cover the entire uniform in an overlapping stair-step pattern. The intent of the pattern here is disruptive rather than imitative and represents a prime example of dazzle camouflage. The colors are not colorfast and on several examples there appeared to be both die bleeding and fading.

The date and manufacturer's information is typically located inside the left pant leg.

UNITS: This uniform was issued to reconnaissance and border forces[3] under the control of the NKVD and later the MGB.[4]

TOP: Close-up showing arrangement of pattern of the TTsMKK.

BOTTOM: Smock with hood and face veil extended.

WORLD WAR II CAMOUFLAGE TRICOLOR TTsMK COVERALLS

YEAR ISSUED: 1940s

DESCRIPTION: The construction of the *tritsvetnyi maskombinezon* is ostensibly identical to the one-piece coveralls issued throughout the 1940s. This design was retained well throughout the 1950s, 1960s and 1970s.

This is an oversized one-piece coverall made to be worn over field uniforms. Except for the two exposed buttons on the collar, all of the buttons have been covered and reduced in size. A collar separates the hood and smock and closes in front with two small metal buttons. The collar has been added to the smock ostensibly to protect the wearer in heavy brush. A visor in front is sewn directly to the reduced-sized hood, and, like previous coveralls, the face veil has been replaced by a mask.

The sleeves and leg cuffs have buttons with cloth loops to adjust the fit. Scrim tabs are sewn to the uniform in the same camouflage material to provide slots for twigs and grasses and are located on the chest, back, hood, pant legs and sleeves.

UNITS: This uniform was issued to border guards and reconnaissance troops. Today it can be seen on reservists and MVD *spetsnaz* trainees. Recent films of unrest in Albania showed Albanian rebels wearing one-piece and two-piece versions of the TTsMK uniforms.

TOP: This shows a reconnaissance troop for the mid-1950s. The uniform is comprised of a model SSh-1940 helmet, standard issue field belt, and Soviet SKS rifle with folding blade bayonet.

BOTTOM: Close up of coveralls showing hood attachment and pattern.

WORLD WAR II CAMOUFLAGE
TRIAL CAMOUFLAGE SUIT

YEAR ISSUED: Late 1945 through 1950.

DESCRIPTION: The camouflage pattern shown here is a cross between the 1940s TTsMKK issue and the amoeba pattern. Although the cut shown is different, the camouflage design derives from the three-color uniform being overprinted with the amoeba pattern. This uniform represent either a transition pattern or trial uniform.

The suit is constructed simply: a smock with a small hood attached directly to the neck, a drawstring at the front of the hood to secure it, and large plastic buttons which close the jacket front. The material is medium weight cotton and appears fairly sturdy. One piece (MK) and two piece (MKK) versions were issued for a short period of time near the end of the Second World War and then through the 1950s.

The chocolate brown amoebae of the 1938 version are painted over the yellow, green, and forest-green geometric stair-stepped blotches from the 1940s pattern. The color, while unusual, serves to create an effective disruptive effect.

UNITS: This uniform was issued to border guards and reconnaissance forces in the late 1940s through the 1950s.

TOP: Unusual smock showing oversized buttons and open neck.

BOTTOM: View of traditional two-piece camouflage uniform. Note large hood with green face veil.

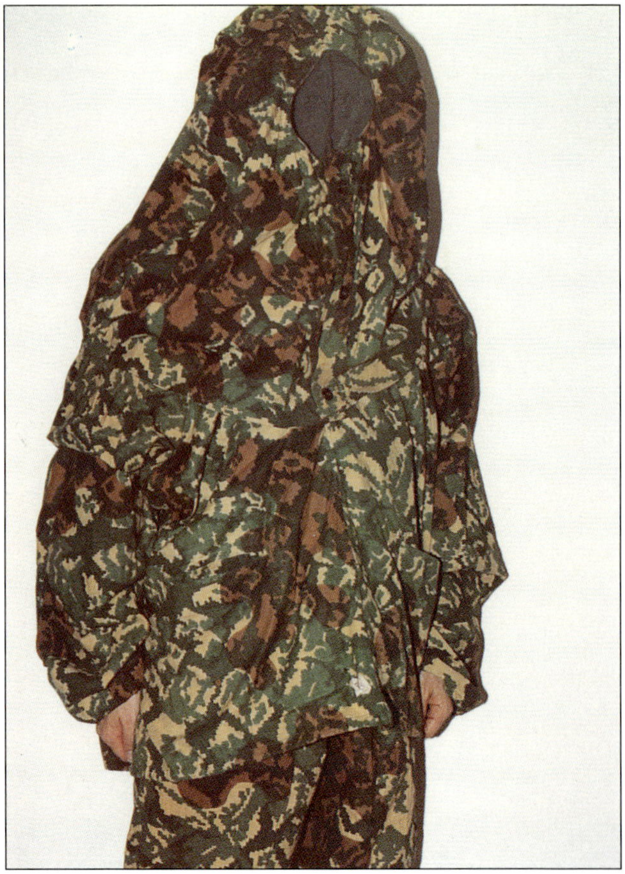

CAMOUFLAGE COMPARISON – WORLD WAR II UNIFORMS

WWII AMOEBA PATTERN

WWII LEAF PATTERN

TTsMKK TRI-COLOR PATTERN

TTsMKK TRIAL PATTERN

Cold War
Camouflage Uniforms

COLD WAR CAMOUFLAGE
TYPE II LEAF PATTERN COVERALLS – MK

YEAR ISSUED: 1948

DESCRIPTION: While the pattern of this uniform is unique in its design, the construction of this *maskombinezon* is identical to issues of the mid 1940s. However, because of a scarcity of open source information and lack of further examples, little is known about this uniform and it may represent a limited issue pattern piece. Furthermore, the manufacturer's mark inside the uniform has the word *"obrazets"* meaning sample or example and the date 1948. The uniform examined was new and unused.

The cut of the one-piece coverall consists of a button-up front (covered by a flap), an attached hood with cloth ties, and a collar which fastens at the wearer's right. The hood, although smaller than some previous issues, is still capable of covering the model SSh-40 helmet. To the front of the hood is sewn a small visor which extends slightly forward.

The trousers possess a button-up flap on the seat closed with three small black, plastic buttons. There is a right hip pocket which provides storage space for the face mask.

Large green leaves on a tan/yellowish background make up the pattern. Arrangement of the leaves is haphazard and far less detailed than the first leaf pattern uniform issued in the early 1940s. Moreover, this uniform has an internal light yellow grid-like pattern with the leaves faintly visible. The reverse side grid pattern was retained through to the 1980s in later KLMK versions. This provides a reversible capability for the uniform for use at night or in desert environs.

UNITS: This uniform may not have been issued. Judging by its construction and pattern, however, it would seem logical that it was designed for airborne, reconnaissance, and engineer troops in forest and field environments. Perhaps more information on its fielding will become available in the future.

TOP: Possible configuration for a reconnaissance troop, circa late 1940s. The standard issue enlisted field belt is worn as part of the uniform.

BOTTOM: Close up of interior of uniform showing markings and the grid pattern.

COLD WAR CAMOUFLAGE PARATROOPER KLMK COVERALLS

YEAR ISSUED: 1960-1961

DESCRIPTION: This issue of the *KLMK* (Camouflage Summer Deceptive Coveralls), while retaining the cut of the earlier *trekhtsvet* model, marks a shift from the more complex tricolor designs to a simpler bicolor pattern. Whereas earlier issues incorporated both a one-piece (MK) and a two-piece (MKK) version, this uniform appears to have been issued only in a coverall, a further departure from earlier designs.

This one-piece coverall incorporates a button-up front (covered by a flap), an attached hood with cloth ties, and a collar which fastens at the wearer's right. The hood is capable of covering the model SSh-40 helmet. An innovation in this uniform is the inclusion of a matching camouflage face mask which has replaced the sewn in green face veil.

The pants possess a button-up flap on the seat. A right hip pocket has been provided in which the mask is usually stored.

The pattern consists of intricate, rounded-edged, blobs (looking like paint splatters) on a forest-green background. The design is similar to the 1938 pattern with the blobs being narrower and more numerous.

UNITS: This uniform was issued to paratroopers, and reconnaissance troops during the 1960s on a limited basis and may have been issued to members of the GRU's *spetsnaz* units. The uniform was in use at least through the mid-1970s[5] and according to one source, was issued as late as the mid-1980s to airborne units in the former Soviet Union.

TOP: Reconnaissance troop, circa 1960s. Standard enlisted field belt is worn as part of the field uniform.

BOTTOM: Airborne Officer circa 1960s. The red/maroon beret is the early style worn by airborne forces during the 1960s to include reconnaissance troops. The flash is attached to the right side as is worn in parades.

COLD WAR CAMOUFLAGE KLMK ONE-PIECE COVERALL

YEAR ISSUED: 1968-1969

DESCRIPTION: The *KLMK* (*kamuflirovannyi letnyi maskirovochnyi kombinezon*) was among the last of the one piece coveralls to be fielded. Several improvements were made over earlier *KLMK* models.

The non-detachable hood easily covers model 40 helmets (SSh-40) and possesses a reduced neck piece which buttons in the front. Cloth ties are located on the inside of the hood at the front. A face-mask, issued with the uniform, eliminates facial glare and permits the wearer to blend in more easily with the surroundings. The number and location of scrim tabs remains unchanged from earlier models.

As in previous models buttons secure the front of the uniform. However, the middle button is uncovered and the cover flap is lacking. Sleeves and pants cuffs are secured by drawstrings or elastic. The large button up seat allows the wearer to quickly take care of personal matters.

Designed to be worn over regular field uniforms, it served as both summer and winter coveralls. The pattern resembles the leaves of zebra plants: single, light-colored (white, cream or yellow) splotches in a stair-step pattern on a green background. Splotch density varies considerably. The Russian slang term for this uniform means "sun-ray" pattern, denoting its similarity to sunlight coming through a forest canopy. The reverse side of the uniform shows the previously design grid pattern with the stair-step pattern clearly visible and can be worn in a snowy or sandy setting.

Although there is no place for rank to be worn, occasionally field modified versions are found where rank stars or field boards have been attached to the shoulders

Date and maker's stamps are typically located on the inside of the left pants leg.

UNITS: The *KLMK* was issued to KGB border,[6] airborne, GRU *spetsnaz*, reconnaissance, and sapper/minelaying units. At present, the uniform is issued to engineers,[7] Cossack units fighting in Moldova, trainees and reservists.

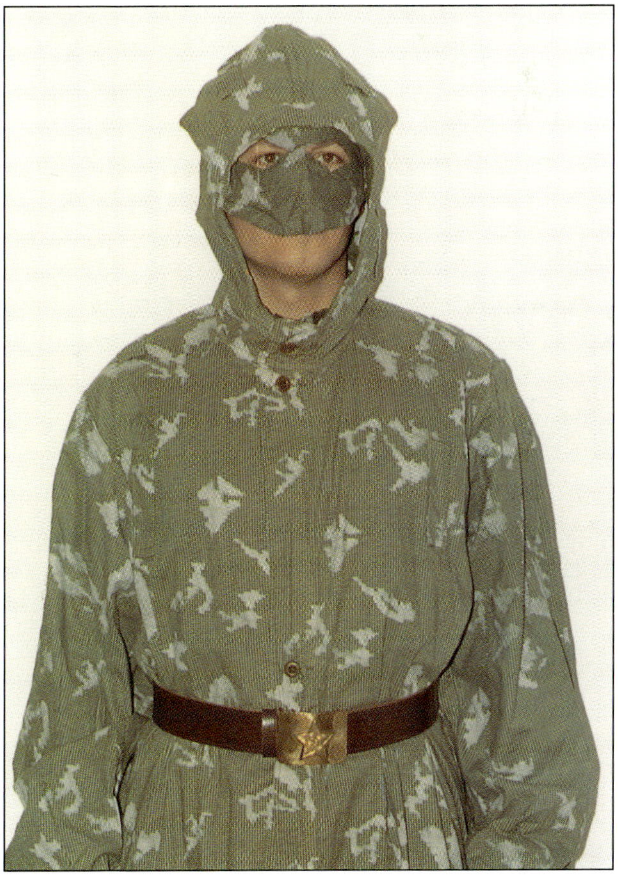

TOP: This photo shows a field-modified version with shoulder boards and a non-standard issue cap. Normally a helmet or beret is worn as standard headgear.

BOTTOM: Reversed uniform worn in winter.

COLD WAR CAMOUFLAGE KLMK TWO-PIECE UNIFORM

YEAR ISSUED: 1975-1976

DESCRIPTION: Constructed of lightweight cotton, the two-piece *kamuflirovanyi komplekt* has a much more tailored appearance and is designed to be worn as both a overgarment and a stand alone uniform. Several variations and modifications of this uniform exist.

Five metal buttons secure the front of the jacket and are covered by a flap. Three buttons secure the hood to the neck of the jacket and are covered by the collar. Two patch-pockets are located on the chest and two cargo patch-pockets are located at hip level; each pocket closes with a single metal button and a cloth loop. A simple flap covers the pocket opening. One button-through patch pocket is located on the right sleeve.

The pants have four (two pair) pockets located just below hip level; each measures seven inches by two inches and are secured by metal buttons. The function of the pockets is unknown. Although AK-74 magazines fit snugly into the pockets, they are not easily removed. There is a button-up fly covered by a flap instead of the rear drop seat as in the one-piece models. Two elastic loops, attached at the pants leg cuffs, prevent the trouser legs from creeping up and allow the pants to be worn bloused inside or worn over the boots.

The number of scrim tabs on the front and back of the jacket have been increased and permit the wearer to insert branches and grass for better camouflage. A face mask and matching beret come standard issue with the uniform.

UNITS: Airborne (VDV) soldiers, GRU *spetsnaz* and reconnaissance forces have worn this uniform at different times since its fielding. Troops of the Shock Assault Maneuver Groups (DShMG) of the federal border service (FPS – formerly KGB) fighting on the border of Tadzhikistan wear this as their summer field uniform. The KGB's 11th and 12th border detachments (*zastava*) wore this and the *spetsodezhda* while stationed in the region.[8]

TOP: Configuration for enlisted soldier of the KGB's 103rd airborne division, reconnaissance platoon, 1988.

BOTTOM: Member of OMON, Vilnius, Lithuania, circa 1990 through 1991. Winter configuration. Photo: Brad Jacobs.

COLD WAR CAMOUFLAGE
DESERT PMK COVERALLS

YEAR ISSUED: 1970-1971

DESCRIPTION: This is a color variation of the *KLMK* produced for desert operations during the 1970s. The cut is identical to the *KLMK* coverall developed in the late 1960s but possesses a more complex camouflage design. I have designated this uniform PMK for *pustinoi maskirovochnyi kombinezon* – desert camouflage coveralls.

As in earlier issues, the jacket, trousers and hood are sewn into a one-piece coverall with a button-up front. There is an attached hood with cloth ties, and a collar which fastens at the wearer's right; a matching face mask is standard issue and is stored in the rear pocket.

The pattern consists of light brown or reddish-brown stair stepped splotches against a tan or khaki background. The splotches seem to run vertically and diagonally, connecting at points to leave open areas of the tan or khaki field. Evergreen colored leaves and spots appear randomly in the design and measure from three eighths of an inch to approximately one half inch by two inches. The uniform is reversible but lacks the grid pattern present in earlier styles.

UNITS: The exact use of this uniform remains uncertain. According to some sources, it was issued to special purpose forces in Afghanistan in 1979 and may also have been issued to troops serving in Africa. While it is referenced in Soviet writings, only one example has become available for research and its origins are unclear. The pattern is undoubtedly desert, and inasmuch as camouflage was usually issued to *spetsnaz* and reconnaissance units, it may be considered to have been used accordingly.

TOP: Front of desert camouflage coveralls showing buttons and hood attachment.

BOTTOM: Coveralls showing concealment of buttons.

PHOTOS: Chris Smith

COLD WAR CAMOUFLAGE KLMK UNIFORM ACCESSORIES

YEAR ISSUED: 1975-1990

DESCRIPTION: These photos show the items typically associated with the KLMK two piece uniform; that is, the mask (*maska*) beret (*beret*) and panama style sun cap. The mask was included as part of the uniform during its initial issue and changed little from previous styles. The beret entered service around the late 1970s, and the panama cap began to appear in the mid 1980s.

These items are made from a lightweight cotton material and are easily stored in the rear pocket.

RIGHT: Beret and mask of the Two piece KLMK.

BELOW LEFT: Panama sun cap.

BELOW RIGHT: Field furazhka, custom made.

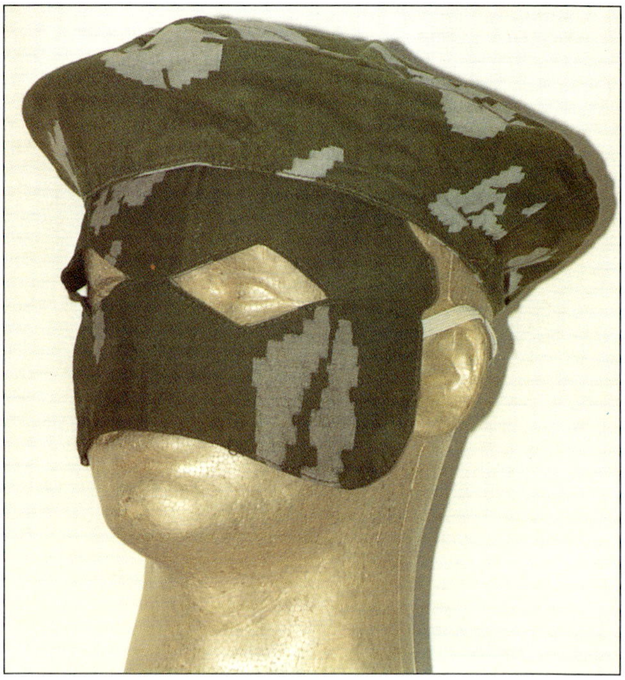

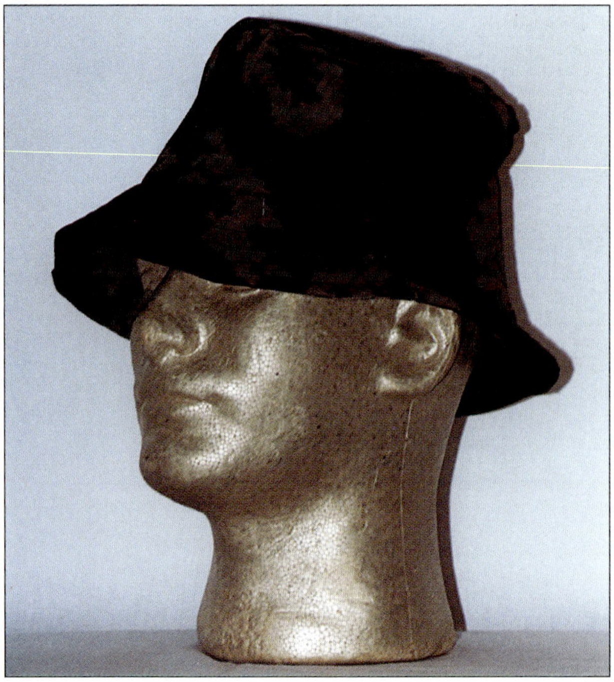

CAMOUFLAGE COMPARISONS – COLD WAR CAMOUFLAGE UNIFORMS

TYPE II LEAF PATTERN

POSTWAR KLMK PARATROOPER COVERALLS

ONE AND TWO-PIECE KLMK UNIFORM

DESERT PMK KLMK

Spetsodezhda
Camouflage Uniforms

SPETSODEZHDA
KGB BORDER GUARD *SPETSODEZHDA* - TYPE 1

YEAR ISSUED: 1981-1982

DESCRIPTION: Designated "*spetsodezhda*" (or special purpose clothing), this uniform is the KGB border guard version of the earlier lightweight two-piece outfit. Identified by its heavier construction and button-through pockets, it also possesses many of the same characteristics of the 1981 six-pocket uniform from which it was no doubt developed.

The material is a heavy cotton and serves as a sturdier field uniform than the lightweight *KLMK*. Two patch-style chest, cargo, and sleeve pockets are located on the jacket. Buttons on the chest and cargo pockets and those on up the front of the jacket are marked with a hammer & sickle and are exposed. Velcro closures secure the sleeve pockets. A small pocket is present on the inside left of the jacket which is held closed by a small button. A drawstring allows for adjustment of the jacket.

The pants are equipped with two special pouches for holding extra magazines and close with small, unmarked, plastic buttons.

The pattern is the standard stair-step design with coloration being highly variable: ranging from faded yellowish-green blotches on an olive drab background to bright-yellow on a bright green field.

UNITS: In the past, camouflage uniforms were issued simultaneously to several army and special service units. This uniform marks the first time a specific uniform was designed and issued solely to border and special operations units.

The border *spetsodezhda* was worn with or without the blue striped T-shirt depending on the unit of assignment. The 103rd Airborne Division (Guards), subordinate to the KGB Border Forces reportedly wore airborne insignia and a green striped *tel'niashka* (although the airborne *tel'niashka* was usually substituted for the former) as their standard uniform.[9] KGB special purpose units also wore this uniform on a limited basis.

TOP: Standard configuration for border officer, circa 1981. The camouflaged furazhka or panama was worn as the standard headgear.

BOTTOM: Enlisted border guard, circa 1986, in Tadzhikistan.

SPETSODEZHDA
KGB/MVD *SPETSODEZHDA* – TYPE II

YEAR ISSUED: 1983-1984

DESCRIPTION: This uniform is an updated version of the KGB *Spetsodezhda* and is based on the 1981 khaki airborne uniform.

Several tailoring differences separate this uniform from the border guard style of 1981. These differences include: chest and cargo patch pockets which are closed by smaller, open-faced, plastic buttons and covered by a protective flap; shoulder loops (epaulets) added for rank; and cargo pockets which have replaced magazine pouches on the pants.

The pattern is that of the *KLMK* stair-step style with yellowish or green markings on a green or olive background. There is much less variation in color than in the *KLMK* or *KZS* uniforms.

Subdued officer's rank stars or enlisted cloth stripes may be worn in lieu of full color shoulder boards. Accessories such as full-color collar tabs, awards and belts may be highly variable and depends on the environment in which the soldier is serving.

UNITS: This uniform is worn mainly by border troops, MVD units of special designation (RSN, Osnaz and ChON), and internal troops (VV MVD) of the Dzerzhinsky Division. Soldiers under the control of the Main Guard's Administration (formerly under the control of the KGB's 7th Guard's Administration) assigned to the *Al'fa* and *Vympel'* special purpose units also wear the *spetsodezhda* as their field uniform.

Branch patches may or may not be present making unit identification difficult. Headgear includes the branch specific berets (with associated insignia), riot helmets, or field caps.

This uniform is worn with the summer (*tel'niashka*) or winter (*fufaika*) T-shirt. Certain MVD units wear a maroon-striped T-shirt as part of their uniform while border units may wear a green version.

TOP: Configuration for enlisted soldier of the MVD's Dzerzhinsky Division (pre-1992).[10]

BOTTOM: KGB Border guard cadet, Leningrad, 1991.

SPETSODEZHDA
KGB/MVD *SPETSODEZHDA* – TYPE II UNIT UNIFORM CONFIGURATION

YEAR ISSUED: 1981-1991

DESCRIPTION: These photos show the configuration for various security units who employ the *spetsodezhda* as part of their field or operational uniform.

UNITS: Since the early 1980s various units, detachments, and companies of the MVD and KGB have used the *spetsodezhda* as their primary operational uniform. In the post Soviet era, field units of the successors to the KGB issued this uniform to most of its units.

In order to keep the identity of the unit secret, or reduce its public visibility, members of the security services seldom wore sleeve patches. The exceptions to this were border guards and the Kremlin guards. More often, airborne, motorized, or branch-specific (e.g. transport) insignia were used. Recently, special operational units *(Opnaz)* and KGB counterterrorist units (*Al'fa, Omega,* and *Vympel*) have adopted unit-specific patches and are occasionally seen sporting them on *spetsodezhda* clothing.[11]

The MVD is less secretive; Dzerzhinsky and *spetsnaz* and *osnaz* subunits frequently use the unit specific patches as unit identification. Although MVD soldiers occasionally wear the *spetsodezhda* during training at Balashikha, the majority of detachments and MVD *spetsnaz* units have adopted the woodland, SMK or MVD KKO uniforms as their primary field or operational uniform. MVD Internal troops have largely switched to the VSR pattern as their primary camouflage field uniform.

TOP: This photo represents the separate training company of the KGB's 27th guard's separate motorized brigade of special designation. The patch was developed from the U.S. Army's 101st Airborne division and was adopted in 1991 (see text for more details).

BOTTOM: This photo represents a member of the 11th outpost (zastava) stationed on the Tadzhik/Afghan border in 1993.[12] *The soldier is assigned to the Federal Border Service DShMG – motorized assault group. Note the rare camouflaged panama cap.*

SPETSODEZHDA
MOTORIZED CREWMAN'S UNIFORM

YEAR ISSUED: UNKNOWN

DESCRIPTION: This is a one-piece smock based on the *KLMK* but of the heavier KGB/MVD material. The construction is very simple: a one-piece overgarment with attached hood, open belt loops, and two pockets: one on the left sleeve (open) and one at the right hip (button-through with flap). The front of the uniform is closed with oversize plastic buttons.

The sleeve and leg cuffs are elasticized as is the waist. Knees and elbows have reinforcing material sewn over them. The uniform is unlined and lacks any internal pockets or holsters.

The pattern is that of the typical MVD s*petsodezhda*: yellowish green stair-step splotches on an olive background.

UNITS: I have examined only three such uniforms, all of which came from Poland. None of the uniforms were marked and their origin and use remains unknown. They may have been manufactured from existing stocks of textiles for resale or use by non military personnel.

TOP: One-piece crewman's uniform with polevaia furazhka (field cap).

BOTTOM: Reverse of uniform showing hood, button-up right hip pocket, and cinch waist.

SPETSODEZHDA HEADGEAR

YEAR ISSUED: 1981-1991

DESCRIPTION: During the last decade the border forces have used several types of headgear. Camouflaged variants typically worn under field conditions are shown here. The items match the *Spetsodezhda* patterned uniform issued to KGB border and security forces. The field furazhka is the most commonly seen since border, Kremlin guard, and KGB cadets wore this as their standard headgear with field uniforms.

RIGHT: Polevaia furazhka – field cap.

BELOW LEFT: Kamuflirovannaia furazhka – peaked cap.

BELOW RIGHT: Kamuflirovannyi beret.

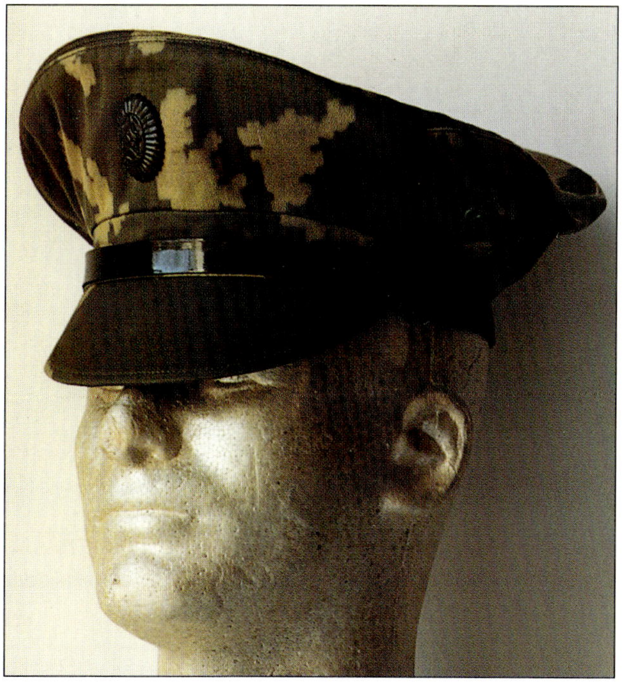

SPETSODEZHDA
KZS UNIFORM

YEAR ISSUED: 1975

DESCRIPTION: This disposable uniform is referred to as the *Kostium zashchitnoi seti* (*KZS*) or camouflaged net outfit. It appears to have served as an inexpensive alternative to the widely used *KLMK* uniforms of the period.

Constructed from a loose weave, cotton fabric, the *KZS* is often referred to as the "burlap" uniform. It possesses exceptionally long sleeves which may be rolled back and secured with buttons and cloth loops. There is an attached hood with a cloth tie which fastens to either side permitting adjustment for improved cover and protection. There are no pockets but slits located on the sides of the pants at hip level permit access to the field uniform worn underneath.

The uniform is not color-fast and experiences dye bleeding and fading when wet. Although there are a great many color variations ranging from light-yellow to orange and mustard, the uniform typically fades to yellow blotches on a light-green background.

Examples exist with and without shoulder loops for rank boards.

UNITS: During the Afghanistan conflict, the *KZS* burlap uniform was most often worn by sapper engineers and reconnaissance forces. Currently, this uniform is worn by the Airmobile Detachment of the Quick Reaction Force of Civil Defense,[13] paramilitary groups and training units of the Russian armed forces.

TOP: Configuration for enlisted soldier serving in Afghanistan, 1982-1989. (Rita Vaughn Desmond)

BOTTOM: Mountain troop configuration. (Brad Jacobs)

SPETSODEZHDA
KZS UNIFORM VARIATIONS

TOP: Color variations of KZS uniforms

BOTTOM: Mismatched KZS trousers

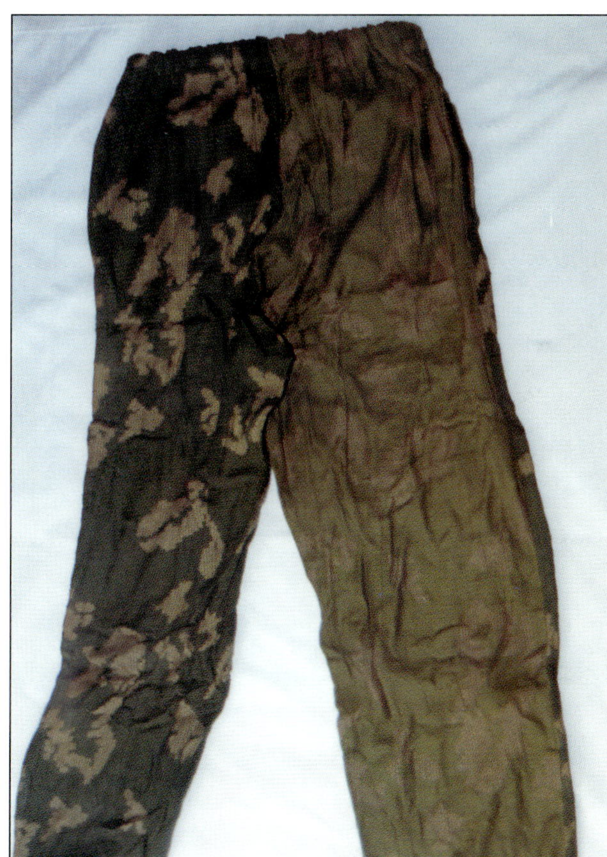

CAMOUFLAGE COMPARISONS – *SPETSODEZHDA*

KGB *SPETSODEZHDA*

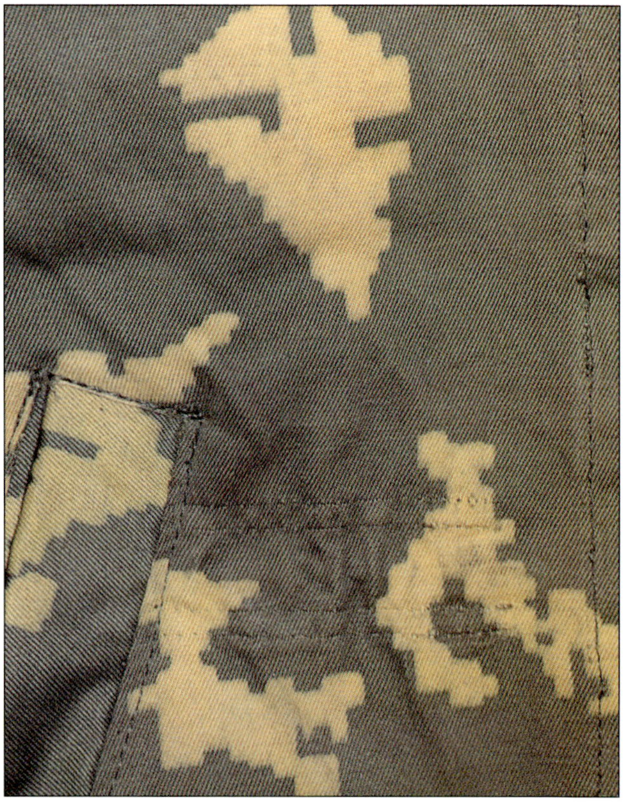

KGB/MVD *SPETSODEZHDA*

KZS OVERGARMENT

KZS OVERGARMENT

Soviet Woodland Camouflage Uniforms

SOVIET WOODLAND CAMOUFLAGE
TYPE I VARIATIONS
ARMY SUMMER CAMOUFLAGE

YEAR ISSUED: 1981-1982

DESCRIPTION: This is the initial version of the Woodland version and I have designated it Type I. Sometimes referred to as the tricolor camouflaged uniform (*tritsvetnaia kamuflirovannaia odezhda*), this uniform earned the nickname "Mabutu" by Soviet security forces serving in Africa. It is also referred to as a *maskkombinezon* in some articles.[14]

It is constructed of a medium-weight, 100% cotton. Army versions possess an internal holster with lanyard, two chest pockets (button closure), and two sleeve pockets (velcro closure). Type I Army uniforms have slots for suspenders which are located on the front (two) and back of the jacket (one). Inasmuch as there are no epaulets, camouflaged shoulder boards are sewn on to the shirt's shoulders. The shirt is worn tucked into the pants with a standard issue belt. The elbows and knees are reinforced.

Pants have open slash pockets at hip level and cargo pockets on each side with button closures covered by a flap. There is also a cotton strap sewn on the bottom of the trouser cuffs to secure the pant legs inside or outside of the boots.

The primary colors of this pattern are brown and dark-green whorls intermixed on an olive-green background. Generally the brown blotches are thinner, giving the appearance of fingers surrounding the dark-green blobs. Neither color of whorl obscures the background. Single green dots of varying sizes appear in the olive-green background and brown fingers. This pattern also comes in a greener tinge in the Type I varieties (see also Type II patterns).

UNITS: Soviet Army airborne, GRU *spetsnaz* units, and ground forces have worn this uniform since 1985. KGB and MVD security forces adopted this pattern in various colors beginning in 1987 and 1988.[15] Other versions have been worn by various paramilitary and security forces since its creation.

TOP: Airborne (VDV) officer assigned to one of the main divisions. Occasionally full color insignia and distinctive service awards are worn on the uniform.

BOTTOM: St. Petersburg OMON troop. Although pictured here with the grey beret, a black beret or camouflaged field cap may also be worn.

SOVIET WOODLAND CAMOUFLAGE
TYPE I VARIATIONS
NAVAL SUMMER CAMOUFLAGE

YEAR ISSUED: 1982

DESCRIPTION: Similar to the Type I Army/Airborne style, this camouflage field uniform is the camouflaged version of the 1981 khaki field uniform.

The Naval infantry issue is in many respects, simply a camouflage version of the 1981 khaki airborne uniform. The naval uniforms lack an internal holster but have added cargo pockets at waist level and shoulder epaulets. There are usually two internal open pockets with a single button to secure them. Since the jacket is worn untucked, there are no slots for suspenders and the belt is worn around the waist instead of the pants.[16] A drawstring is usually present on the jacket to adjust the fit.

Pants differ from the army cut only in that they lack the AK magazine pocket and, instead, possess a cargo pocket on each side secured by two buttons. There are no metallic loops to attach suspenders; rather, the pants use a standard belt to secure the waist.

The pattern is the same Woodland tricolor as the Army pattern; also with a brown or green background. Variations in color are the result of two types of issue: a Forest pattern (green) and a Desert-Mountain pattern (brown) as with the later VSR (Schofield) pattern.

Most are issued with naval infantry patches sewn on the uniforms (either from the factory or from the unit). A beret or camouflaged field *furazhka* is the standard headgear for this uniform.

UNITS: This uniform has been worn almost exclusively by naval Infantry and naval *spetsnaz* units.

TOP: Naval infantry officer: a naval infantry officer's cap device and officer's belt are worn as standard components of the officer's field uniform.

BOTTOM: Naval infantry enlisted soldier. Enlisted cap device and belt are standard issue.

SOVIET WOODLAND CAMOUFLAGE
TYPE I VARIATIONS
CREWMAN'S WINTER CAMOUFLAGE

YEAR ISSUED: 1982

DESCRIPTION: This is yet another version of the 1981 Woodland camouflage pattern.

The jacket possesses a pair of open slash-pockets at waist level and no other pockets. The front of the jacket closes with a set of large plastic buttons. A second set of buttons (three) is set to the right of the main set and allows the jacket to be closed tighter. The buttons are covered by a flap when buttoned.

At waist level is a 3 cm wide belt which can be used to tighten the coat. A metal loop at one end fastens to a metal hook at the other.

The inside is of the jacket has a removable quilted liner, similar to those produced during the mid 1960s. There is a large fake-fur collar which can be removed and provides added comfort and warmth. Behind the collar can be attached a camouflaged hood. Although similar to the hoods of the Type I winter jackets, this one cannot be tucked into the rear of the jacket's collar. The hood attaches to the collar with four plastic buttons.

UNITS: This uniform was probably issued to armored and motorized rifle crewman. It is so similar to the general officer's version that it may have also served this purpose through the addition of a higher quality collar.

TOP: Standard configuration for winter wear by enlisted armored crewman. (Brad Jacobs).

BOTTOM: Jacket showing hood.

SOVIET WOODLAND CAMOUFLAGE TYPE I VARIATIONS WINTER CAMOUFLAGE

YEAR ISSUED: 1982

DESCRIPTION: This winter version of the 1981 Woodland camouflage pattern possesses only minor tailoring differences which distinguishes it from both the Type I summer versions and Type II uniforms, the primary difference being the attachment of the liner to the jacket.

The pattern is the same woodland tricolor with a brown or green base color. An internal holster is present and is lined with a water resistant nylon fabric; an attached cord with clip prevents the loss of the pistol. Cargo and chest pockets are secured with open-faced buttons that are covered by a flap. A drawstring cinch cord allows the wearer to adjust the fit at the waist. A concealable khaki hood tucks neatly into the base of the collar (the hood is more likely to be camouflage in Type II models). The collar has a small strap which permits the collar to be fastened in front in cold weather.

Two open slash pockets, two back hip pockets, one cargo pocket on the right side, plus a pair of magazine (AK) pouches on the left side at thigh level provide adequate storage space on the pants. Both the knees and seat are covered with reinforcing material. Cloth ties attached to the cuffs secure the trouser legs. A pair of suspenders can be buttoned into the rear of the pants at the waist and secure in front the same way.

There is a detachable liner for the pants and jacket; the jacket liner has a detachable blue, fake-fur collar. In the Type I, the jacket liner buttons through the front flap thus giving the impression of there being two rows of front closure buttons. The liner for the pants and jacket is made of a heavy, cotton-flannel material. The uniform, when liners are added, is extremely heavy and makes movement difficult.

In the winter, the *fufaika* sweater is worn in either the blue striped or turtleneck version.[17]

UNITS: This uniform was issued to Army, Airborne and Naval Infantry units,[18] MVD OMON, GRU *spetsnaz* troops and to members of the KGB's *spetsgruppa "A"* group.[19]

TOP: Airborne officer winter camouflage. This photo represents a female spetsnaz officer recently recruited for contract service.

BOTTOM: Pants showing high waist and suspenders.

SOVIET WOODLAND CAMOUFLAGE AVIATION SUMMER FLIGHT SUIT

YEAR ISSUED: 1984-1985

DESCRIPTION: This is the summer version of the 1984 Woodland camouflage pattern for pilots.

The jacket possesses a pair of slash-pockets with zippered closures at chest level and a pair of vertical open-slash pockets at the sides. A metal zipper closes the front of the jacket while two metal snaps secure the bottom of the jacket. Two metal loops with cloth straps, allow the wearer to adjust the fit at the waist.

The pants are of the bib-overall style. The front is zippered as are the sides. Two patch-pockets, one on each leg at knee level, permit storage and easy retrieval of records or flight rations. There is a small survival knife pocket on the right pant leg next to the patch pocket. Elastic bands attached to the cuffs keep the trouser legs while non-detachable, elasticized suspenders and a cinched waist prevent hold up the pants.

UNITS: Helicopter pilots and air technicians wear these uniforms during flight operations in tropical and arid regions.

TOP: This particular uniform shows a color variation probably used in Central Asia and Africa. Shown here is a close up of the uniform showing the jacket and Zsh-7M flight helmet.

BOTTOM: Full length photo showing jacket and trousers.

PHOTOS: Alan Wise

SOVIET WOODLAND CAMOUFLAGE AVIATION WINTER FLIGHT SUIT

YEAR ISSUED: 1984

DESCRIPTION: This is the winter version of the 1984 Woodland camouflage pattern for pilots.

The jacket possesses a pair of slash-pockets with zippered closures at chest level and a pair of vertical open-slash pockets at the sides. A heavy zipper closes the front of the jacket while two metal snaps secure the bottom of the coat. Two metal loops with cloth straps permit sizing. The inside is lined with a high-quality fabric making it more comfortable than standard winter uniforms. A large fake-fur collar in brown, black of grey provides added comfort and warmth.

The pants are of the bib-overall style and are heavily lined for winter operations. The front is zippered as are the sides. Two patch-pockets, one on each leg at knee level, permit storage and easy retrieval of records or flight rations. There is a small survival knife pocket on the right pant leg next to the patch pocket. Elastic bands attached to the cuffs keep the trouser legs while non-detachable, elasticized suspenders and a cinched waist prevent hold up the pants.

UNITS: Helicopter pilots and air technicians wear these uniforms during cold weather operations.

TOP: Configuration for wear by a Mi-24 Hind pilot with communications helmet (ShZ).

BOTTOM: Jacket lining and bib overalls.

SOVIET WOODLAND CAMOUFLAGE
TYPE II VARIATIONS
ARMY GREEN VARIATION

YEAR ISSUED: 1991

DESCRIPTION: This photo shows the improved version of the standard 1985 Woodland camouflage uniform in a green variant.

The Type II army camouflage has certain characteristics of both the Type I naval and army varieties – namely: the Type II possesses an internal holster and epaulets, yet lacks both cargo pockets and openings for suspenders.

On the left side of the pants are double magazine pouches which lack the center button. The right side cargo patch pocket is retained as is the center button.

Although the pattern has remained unchanged, the color varieties have increased substantially. Base colors of brown, green, pink, blue, yellow, and white have replaced the standard two-color varieties.

Two primary colors of light and dark whorls join on a lighter background color with the background remaining larger than the whorls. As before, one of the dark whorls appears as thin fingers surrounding the darker blobs. Neither color of whorl obscures the background. Single dark dots of varying sizes appear both in the lighter background and fingers.

UNITS: As of 1993, Russian Army ground and airborne forces wore this uniform; however, it appears that the VSR pattern is rapidly taking its place. It is also issued to MVD special operations detachments and Internal Troops.

TOP: The photo is representative of an enlisted soldier of the Dzerzhinsky Division (ODON) of Internal Troops, assigned to the 14th Army in northern Ossetia.[20]

BOTTOM: Internal holster location. This uniform is dated 1991 and was purchased in Saint Petersburg in 1993.

SOVIET WOODLAND CAMOUFLAGE TYPE II VARIATIONS ARMY PINK VARIATION

YEAR ISSUED: 1991

DESCRIPTION: This is the pink color variation of the Type II woodland Army camouflage. The uniform has an internal holster with cord, epaulets for rank yet lacks both cargo pockets and suspender openings.

There are double magazine pouches on the left pant's leg held secure by two buttons, and a single cargo pocket on the right side. The pants have reinforcing material sewn directly over the knees.

The color scheme of this pattern combines dark-green and reddish-brown whorls intermixed on a pink background. The reddish brown fingers surround the dark-green blobs. The pink background is very prevalent. Single dark-green dots of varying sizes appear in the pink background and fingers.

The pink variation first appeared in articles in *Raids* (6/92) and *Voenniy vestnik* (12/92). These publications associated this uniform with the GRU's *spetsnaz* and Airborne forces respectively.

UNITS: This uniform was initially issued to airborne units of the Tula Division and those stationed at Riazan. It is typically seen worn by Russian peacemakers in the former Yugoslavia,[21] and in hot spots of the former Soviet Union.

TOP: Standard configuration for peacemakers stationed in republics of the former Soviet Union. Airborne patch is located on wearer's right shoulder, РОССИЯ (Russia) patch is worn on the left. Airborne Forces (VDV) tape is worn over the right breast pocket while Blood Group and Rh factor are found on the left. The white letters MC stand for mirotvorcheskii sili (peacemakers).

BOTTOM: This is the standard configuration for the UN Peacekeeper units stationed in the former Yugoslavia.[22] Note the UN beret and tel'niashka. This configuration differs from the above only in that the UN patch substitutes for the airborne patch and RUSSIA in English replaces the Airborne Forces patch. Unit-specific insignia is also rapidly being added to the uniforms.

SOVIET WOODLAND CAMOUFLAGE
TYPE II VARIATIONS
NAVY COLOR VARIATIONS

YEAR ISSUED: 1993

DESCRIPTION: This is a naval variation of the Type II Camouflage uniform introduced in 1993. It does not differ substantially from the Type I naval uniform.

The Type II naval variant possesses two chest and two cargo patch pockets secured by two plastic buttons and two sleeve pockets secured by velcro. Epaulets and a waist level drawstring are present. The jacket lacks the internal holster as in Type I variations.

The pants are identical to the Type I variants with two cargo pockets, one on each side.

Some Type II variants have button-down sleeve pockets instead of velcro and the naval infantry patch may not be sewn at the factory as with Type I variants. Furthermore, more color varieties are available rather than just the Desert-Mountain (summer) and the Forest (spring) varieties.

On the blue green version, dark-green and light-green whorls are present on a blue background. Here the light-green fingers surround the dark-green blobs. As with other Type II patterns, dark-green dots of varying sizes appear in the blue background and fingers.

UNITS: This uniform, since it is also sold in retail outlets, is worn mostly by paramilitary units in major cities and possibly the southern republics. However, there is the possibility that these variants, in a military form, may also be issued to naval and naval infantry units of the former Soviet republics.

TOP: This photo shows a Type II camouflage variation purchased in Saint Petersburg in June of 1993.

BOTTOM: Off-brown variant in a naval infantry configuration.

SOVIET WOODLAND CAMOUFLAGE
TYPE II VARIATIONS
WINTER CAMOUFLAGE

YEAR ISSUED: 1991

DESCRIPTION: This version of the Woodland Type II camouflage uniform has minor tailoring differences that distinguish it from the Type I.

The pattern is the same as the standard Woodland pattern and has been observed in shades of both green and brown. There is an internal makarov holster which is lined with a waterproof fabric and an internal cord with a metal clip which prevents loss of the pistol during use. Cargo and chest patch pockets are secured with two open faced buttons covered by a flap. A drawstring cinch cord adjusts the fit at the waist. The front of the uniform is closed with a single row of buttons. There is a detachable liner with attached blue, fake-fur collar for the jacket. The front of the jacket closes with a single row of large plastic buttons. As in the Type I, there are two qualities of collar: a plush officer's version and a coarser enlisted style. The internal hood may be either a dull olive drab color or camouflage although the latter are considerably less common. The liner buttons into the jacket and is made of a medium weight flannel and cotton material. The weight of the uniform has not been substantially reduced from the Type I issue.

The pants possess two standard open slash pockets, two hip back pockets, one cargo pocket on the right side, plus a pair of AK magazine pouches on the left side at thigh level. Both the knees and the seat are covered with reinforcing material. Cloth ties attached to the cuffs secure the pant legs. Suspenders button into the rear of the pants at the waist and secure in the front above the belt line. There is a removable padded liner which buttons into the pants.

UNITS: Members of the Airborne, Naval Infantry, MVD's OMON, *Spetsnaz* units, and counterterrorist *Al'fa* and *Vympel'* units wear this uniform as their standard field uniforms.

TOP: Airborne Officer from Pskov Division – brown variant with winter fufaika.

BOTTOM: Comparison of enlisted (left) and officer (right) quality collars and shapka ushankas.

SOVIET WOODLAND CAMOUFLAGE
TYPE I AND TYPE II VARIATIONS
OMON CAMOUFLAGE

YEAR ISSUED: 1984 (1988)

DESCRIPTION: These photographs show the two versions of Woodland camouflage worn in special purpose *militsiia* detachments (OMON). Both the Type I (above) and Type II (below) variations are shown.

UNITS: This was the primary uniform for the OMON detachments which served throughout the USSR during the 1980s. Headgear is highly variable and includes berets, field *furazhkas*, or *militsiia* caps.

TOP: The Type I is the standard Army/Airborne Woodland version with four patch pockets (two chest and two sleeve), an internal holster, openings for suspenders, and an internal drawstring. There are no epaulets; instead, rank stars or stripes are attached to matching camouflage boards.

Pants are equipped with open slash pockets and cargo patch pockets. Belt loops are present on the pants which use the standard issue army belt for officers; the shirt is worn tucked in. Here the early black beret is worn with red flash and militsiia insignia. (Brad Jacobs)

BOTTOM: Type II uniforms retain the chest pockets and two sleeve pockets but lack the suspender openings. Epaulets have been added for rank. The internal holster and drawstring also remain.

No major modifications have been made to the trousers.

The grey beret with OMON cutout flash is standard for omonovtsi stationed in Saint Petersburg.

The tel'niashka or fufaika are worn as part of the field service uniform; both light blue (airborne) and dark blue (navy) varieties can be observed.

SOVIET WOODLAND CAMOUFLAGE BICOLOR VARIATION

YEAR ISSUED: 1989-1990

DESCRIPTION: This is the special operations two-color version of the 1981 Woodland camouflage pattern. The summer version is identical to the Type I while the winter uniform differs from both the Type I and Type II winter uniforms in the location and configuration of its pants pockets.

The pattern consists of green splotches, similar to those present on woodland tricolors, on a khaki base color. On the left inside of the jacket there is an unlined internal holster; there is an attached cord with a clip which prevents the loss of the pistol. There are two chest and two cargo pockets, each secured with two open-faced buttons that are covered by a flap. Single pockets on each sleeve are secured with velcro squares. A drawstring cinch cord at the waist allows the wearer to adjust the fit. There is a concealable khaki hood which tucks neatly into the base of the collar. The liner cuffs are elasticized.

The pants possess two open-slash and two side cargo pockets, yet lack both the two back hip pockets and magazine (AK) pouches. Both the knees and seat are covered with reinforcing material. Cloth ties attached to the cuffs secure the trouser legs. A pair of detachable suspenders can be buttoned at the rear of the pants at the waist and secured in front with metal loops.

There is a detachable liner for the pants and jacket; the jacket liner possessing a detachable blue, fake-fur collar. The liners button into the jacket and pants and are made of a heavy, cotton-flannel material.

In the winter, the *fufaika* sweater is worn in either the blue striped or turtleneck version.[23]

There are also lightweight longsleeve and shortsleeve shirts made in the same pattern.

UNITS: This uniform was issued only to Army airborne and special operations (spetsnaz) units.

TOP: Summer version worn by individual in Moscow, 1991. Subject is wearing the bicolor jacket over a woodland camouflage shirt.

BOTTOM: Winter enlisted version configured for a soldier of the 16th spetsnaz brigade.

SOVIET WOODLAND CAMOUFLAGE RECONNAISSANCE UNIFORM

YEAR ISSUED: 1985-1988

DESCRIPTION: This uniform represents either a trial pattern or one which saw limited use. The design is based on the 1981 khaki airborne uniform and is identical in construction.

The material is medium weight cotton and is unlined except for beneath the arms. This six-pocket uniform also has two internal pockets, but, like the navy version, the jacket lacks the typical internal holster of earlier uniforms. The pockets and front of the jacket are closed with dark-green, open-faced, plastic buttons.

This uniform was issued with a matching fabric belt which can be worn with the trousers or as an external waist belt. A large metallic open buckle with fasteners which permits better adjustment. The uniform is also issued with a matching field *furazhka* cap which is identical to the airborne khaki field cap.

The pattern consists of five pastel colors: dark-green, light green, blue-grey, olive and cream arranged in a vertical jagged design (superficially resembling the VSR pattern). Unlike most uniforms, however, there does not appear to be one color which dominates the background; rather, all five colors blend into and run over each other. The cream color is generally surrounded by olive providing some disruptive counter shading.

This particular uniform showed wear on the knees, seat and elbows indicating short term use. Holes were present in the epaulets showing officer's stars had at one time been used. Although the cap was dated 1988, overall the uniform was poorly marked thus making it impossible to determine at what location it had been produced or in what year.

UNITS: This uniform was issued to reconnaissance personnel of special purpose combat units. It may also have been issued to soldiers operating in the steppe regions of Central Asia beginning in the 1980s. Units currently associated with this uniform are those fighting in the Prednestrov region (Trans-Dniester) of Moldova,[24] and GRU *spetsnaz* personnel of the Russian army.

TOP: Reconnaissance uniform in possible service configuration for officer of reconnaissance platoon of motorized unit or long range spetsnaz reconnaissance unit. Pocket configuration and pattern are clearly visible in this photo.

BOTTOM: Photo showing matching cloth belt which may be worn on the trousers or around the waist outside the uniform jacket.

SOVIET WOODLAND CAMOUFLAGE
REPUBLIC UNIFORM VARIANTS
GEORGIAN UNIFORM

YEAR ISSUED: 1992

DESCRIPTION: One of several variants of the Woodland camouflage uniform, this uniform, manufactured in Ukraine is worn primarily by regular army and rebel forces from the Georgian Republic.

As with the VSR (Schofield) and Reconnaissance uniforms, the cut is based on the khaki six-pocket airborne uniform introduced around 1981. The fabric is medium weight cotton and very comfortable. The design differs from both the Type I and Type II Army Woodland styles in that it lacks both external openings for suspenders and an internal holster. It does possess epaulets and six patch-pockets (2 chest, 2 cargo, and 2 sleeve). Pockets on the sleeves close with velcro patches whereas the others button through a single flap and are covered by a top flap of the same camouflaged material.

The pattern is comprised of three basic colors: dark-green, brown and tan. The whorled pattern, common throughout the FSU, consists of large rounded edged whorls on a solid background; yet, unlike other republic camouflage, it lacks the small round dots in the whorls or in the background. A repeating whorl pattern resembling a large "3" seems consistent in this pattern and may be used as a distinguishing feature in photos. To distinguish it further from the Moldovan pattern, the whorls of one color seem to surround sections of the other whorl color.

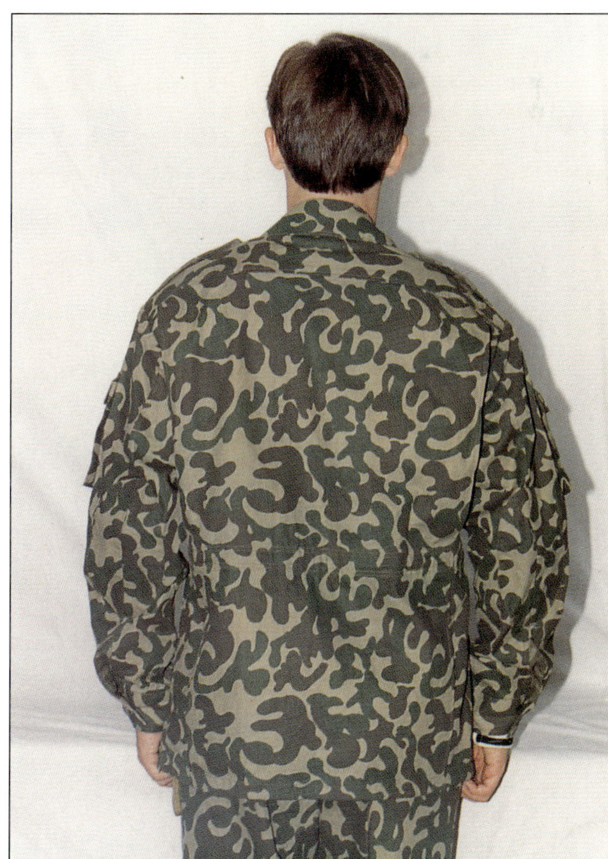

UNITS: This uniform is issued to paramilitary and military units fighting in Georgia, especially in the Nagorno-Karabakh region. Peacemakers in the region, probably fighters from the Chechen-Ingushetia regions, also appeared in this uniform during the siege of the parliament in October 1993; the most recent photo showed a peacemaker in a winter field jacket (*zimnaia kurtka*) over another camouflaged pattern.[25] Whether or not Ukraine will adopt this pattern as its own remains to be seen.

TOP: Front view of uniform showing pocket locations.

BOTTOM: View of the whorled camouflage pattern including the repeating "3's" evident in brown.

SOVIET WOODLAND CAMOUFLAGE REPUBLIC UNIFORM VARIANTS MOLDOVAN UNIFORM

YEAR ISSUED: 1991-1992

DESCRIPTION: This 100% cotton uniform is one of many that began to appear in late 1991 and early 1992 and is based on the six-pocket khaki uniform.

Like other uniforms of this style, it possesses six pockets, epaulets, and an internal drawstring. There are two internal pockets at chest level but no holster. The uniform material may be lightweight, medium-weight, a course twill, or a winter-weight with detachable liner. A light-weight vest is also issued.

Although similar to other uniforms in that the sleeve pockets may close with velcro, there are versions that button through the flap with one or two plastic buttons. The pants, like those of the Georgian, possess two open slash pockets and two simple cargo pockets.

Three colors combine in whorls to create a pattern similar to woodland, Georgian, and some Latvian patterns: dark-green (forest-green) and brown (reddish-brown) on a tan or khaki background. Whorls on the Moldovan pattern are more scalloped in appearance and may have straight edges which overlap each other rather than surround one another. There are also likely to be small angular blobs on the light background. Occasionally these lie within the opposite color whorls. As in other patterns, the Moldovan camouflage is issued in forest (green) and mountain (tan) variants.

UNITS: Most recently this uniform has been associated with combatants in the Predenstrov (Trans-Dniestr) region of the FSU. The newspaper *European*[26] showed Moldovan volunteers wearing this pattern in the form of a padded assault vest. Cossacks fighting in Moldova occasionally wear this pattern as well in the form of grenade vests and complete uniforms. Armenians are also frequently seen wearing this pattern in their struggle against Azerbaijanis in Nagorno Karabakh.[27] Some of the most commonly seen users, however, are members of paramilitary units in Moscow and St. Petersburg and most recently, the Chechen Republic.

TOP: Russian nationalist wearing medium-weight uniform in St. Petersburg, June 1993.

BOTTOM: Typical configuration for combatants in the Prednestrov region.

SOVIET WOODLAND CAMOUFLAGE – REPUBLIC UNIFORMS
MOLDOVAN ACCESSORIES

Field furazhkas. L-R: forest, desert medium-weight, desert light-weight.

Side View, Moldovan field furazhka

CAMOUFLAGE COMPARISON – WOODLAND CAMOUFLAGE UNIFORMS

SOVIET WOODLAND CAMOUFLAGE
BROWN (MOUNTAIN) COLORATION

SOVIET WOODLAND CAMOUFLAGE
GREEN (FOREST) COLORATION

SOVIET WOODLAND CAMOUFLAGE
PINK (AIRBORNE) COLORATION

SOVIET WOODLAND CAMOUFLAGE
DESERT/MOUNTAIN COLORATION

CAMOUFLAGE COMPARISON – WOODLAND CAMOUFLAGE UNIFORMS

SOVIET WOODLAND CAMOUFLAGE
FADED GREEN COLORATION

SOVIET WOODLAND CAMOUFLAGE
FADED BROWN COLORATION

SOVIET WOODLAND CAMOUFLAGE
BROWN AND OXBLOOD COLORATION

SOVIET WOODLAND CAMOUFLAGE
GREEN AND BLUE COLORATION

CAMOUFLAGE COMPARISON – WOODLAND CAMOUFLAGE UNIFORMS

SOVIET WOODLAND CAMOUFLAGE
GREEN, RED-BROWN ON OLIVE COLORATION

SOVIET WOODLAND CAMOUFLAGE
BICOLOR COLORATION

CAMOUFLAGE COMPARISON – WOODLAND CAMOUFLAGE UNIFORMS

SOVIET WOODLAND CAMOUFLAGE
RECONNAISSANCE UNIFORM

SOVIET WOODLAND CAMOUFLAGE
LATVIAN UNIFORM (FOR COMPARISON)

SOVIET WOODLAND CAMOUFLAGE
MOLDOVAN UNIFORM

SOVIET WOODLAND CAMOUFLAGE
GEORGIAN UNIFORM

VSR
Camouflage Uniforms

RUSSIAN ARMED FORCES – VSR "SCHOFIELD" CAMOUFLAGE PATTERN DESERT/MOUNTAIN VERSION

YEAR ISSUED: 1991

DESCRIPTION: This is the officially adopted field uniform for the *Vooruzhennye sili Rossii* (Armed Forces of Russia – VSR) which was fielded in 1992.

Construction is based on the 1981 khaki airborne uniform and is issued in lightweight and medium weight styles. The uniform is of the six pocket style with two breast and two cargo patch pockets (button closure) and two sleeve patch-style pockets (with velcro squares on the flaps). Epaulets are present for rank stars or stripes. An internal drawstring permits size adjustment and slits are present under the arms for ventilation. Although no holsters were present on the ground forces versions I examined, they were on both the flight and winter versions. Holsters may be included on later ground force issues as well. Jackets exist with and without hoods.

Pants possess standard open-slash pockets at hip level and cargo pockets on the thighs secure with two buttons covered by a flap. There are no magazine pouch pockets on ground forces versions (see winter issue).

The pattern consists of jagged green and reddish elongate splotches on backgrounds of tan, khaki, green, or olive. The green splotches are larger and surround the smaller reddish or brown streaks. Two official color variations exist: Forest (darker green) and Desert/Mountain (tan or khaki).[28]

UNITS: The Russian Armed Forces officially adopted this uniform as their field uniform in March of 1993. As of this writing this uniform has been noted on peacemaker battalion in Sarajevo,[29] the Taman and Kantemir Divisions[30] located near Moscow, the 35th Division fighting in Georgia[31] the MVD's guard's directorate (UVO MVD),[32] and various MVD and former KGB units. The uniform is also available commercially (unmarked) and is frequently worn by civilians.

TOP: Configuration for officer of the VSR. Shirt is worn untucked and belt is worn outside above the cargo pockets. Full color patch is worn on left side.

BOTTOM: Bright variation in Saint Petersburg, September 1994. Individual is a member of the Saint Petersburg OMON and is wearing the new Russian MVD cap device.

RUSSIAN ARMED FORCES – VSR
"SCHOFIELD" CAMOUFLAGE PATTERN
FOREST VERSION

YEAR ISSUED: 1991

DESCRIPTION: These photos show variations of the VSR pattern seen in Saint Petersburg, Russia.

Both patterns are in the forest camouflage pattern: deep, purplish/red and forest green splotches on an olive background.

UNITS: As with the other VSR issues, this is the official uniform for the Russian Armed Forces and other units within the Russian Federation and Commonwealth of Independent States.

TOP: Material of this uniform is medium weight serge-wool/cotton and is in the forest pattern camouflage.

Pocket arrangement and accoutrements are the same as the standard issue uniform: six pockets, no holster, and epaulets for rank on the shoulders (see basic description on preceding page).

Uniform is dated 1993 and was produced in the Mukhtoveskaia factory of special purpose clothing.

BOTTOM: Considerably different from the above uniform because of its lighter weight material and non-detachable hood. The jacket lacks the epaulets of the above and there is no apparent drawstring. This may be a civilian issue and not a military version. I was not able to examine the jacket for military markings.

RUSSIAN ARMED FORCES – VSR "SCHOFIELD" CAMOUFLAGE PATTERN FLIGHT UNIFORM

YEAR ISSUED: 1992

DESCRIPTION: This is the summer-weight flight uniform for the Russian Armed Forces. Material is a lightweight cotton and virtually identical to flight uniforms in the *spetsodezhda* and Woodland patterns.

Two slash zippered pockets are present on the front of the jacket at about chest level; the left pocket serves as an internal holster for a small 9mm or revolver (there is an internal cord to prevent loss). The right pocket has a small slot for pens. There are no other pockets on the exterior of the jacket; however, there is an internal (open) pocket on the inside wearer's right. The jacket closes with a zippered front and there are short cloth straps with metal loops to tighten the waist.

Pants have two patch-pockets with zippered closures at thigh level on the front of the trouser legs, an open slash pocket on each side at hip level, and a knife pocket on the right side with attachment cord. There is a pair of suspenders which button to the waist in the rear and secure with metal loops in the front.

A light fatigue cap is standard issue which matches in color and pattern. It has a small band in front to which a cap badge can be secured. Flaps and ventilation holes are absent unlike standard field *furazhkas*.

UNITS: This uniform is issued to helicopter, naval, and flight personnel of the Russian Armed Forces. Although not verified, it may also be worn by aviation technician personnel and civilian pilots during reservist activations (formerly Aeroflot personnel).

TOP: Standard configuration for VSR pilot.

BOTTOM: Photo shows the full flight uniform with headgear and pants.

RUSSIAN ARMED FORCES – VSR "SCHOFIELD" CAMOUFLAGE PATTERN WINTER UNIFORM

YEAR ISSUED: 1991

DESCRIPTION: This winter variant is made of a heavy, padded, cotton material and is based on the winter khaki airborne uniform of 1981.

The jacket has two breast and two cargo patch-pockets (button closure) and two sleeve pockets (velcro). Two internal pockets are located on the liner and another is located inside the coat; these may be of a nylon or camouflaged cotton material. Epaulets are present for rank stars or stripes. A drawstring permits the wearer to adjust the jacket's fit. An internal holster which may/may not be lined is located on the inside right. A concealable hood in either khaki or camouflaged material tucks neatly into the jacket behind the collar.

The liner, made of a heavy dark or khaki cotton material, has an attached fake-fur collar which, like the liner, can be unbuttoned from the jacket. Seven open-faced, plastic buttons secure the front of the jacket.

The trousers have standard open-slash pockets on each side at hip level and cargo pockets on the thighs closed with flaps and secured by plastic buttons. On some variants the left side pocket is configured for AK magazines. Like the jacket, the pants have a detachable liner. Suspenders affix to the waist of the trousers with buttons and fasten in front with metal loops at the waist. Belt loops are large enough for the field belt to be worn although civilian-style leather belts seem to be more common.

The pattern is of the standard VSR type: jagged green and reddish/brown splotches on a tan, khaki, or olive background.

UNITS: As with other VSR uniforms, this version is issued to the security, ground and naval infantry forces of the Russian Armed Forces.[33] During the siege of the Russian parliament in October of 1993, Soldiers of the Taman, Kantemir and Tula divisions were shown wearing these uniforms.[34]

TOP: Saint Petersburg OMON troop wearing a dark jacket with officer's quality fake-fur collar, and light-colored, summer-weight pants.

BOTTOM: Photo portrays an enlisted soldier of Tula airborne division wearing a bright version of the VSR pattern. Both the collar and the shapka-ushanka are of enlisted quality.

RUSSIAN ARMED FORCES – VSR "SCHOFIELD" CAMOUFLAGE PATTERN ASSAULT VEST

YEAR ISSUED: 1991

DESCRIPTION: One of many assault vests issued in the VSR pattern. It is designed for extra ammunition and combat equipment storage and does not protect the wearer from ballistic projectiles.

The sleeveless vest is made of a lightweight cotton with padding in the shoulders to support load bearing equipment and to protect the wearer's neck and shoulders. At the outer edge of each shoulder is a raised, padded strip which is purportedly designed to prevent load bearing equipment harnesses from slipping.

Early vests (Type I) possess either two or four AK-74 magazine pouches which close with button-through flaps. Two small pockets in back at waist level provide storage for personal items. These are covered by button-through flaps. On Type I vests there is no provision for tightening the vest; the front is secured by a row of buttons covered by a flap and velcro patches at the top.

The metal buttons are the same as those found on the SMK uniforms indicating a possible relationship with either the manufacture or supplier. The belt appearance is also similar and is inconsistent with previous Russian or Soviet production. These characteristics may indicate the vest is manufactured from largely imported parts. Moreover, none of the vests are issued with production marks which indicates a possible source outside Russia or civilian contract production.

Type II vests are more simple in their design but provide better storage and retrieval of ammunition. Unlike Type I vests, Type II vests possess a black nylon belt which runs through belt loops behind the magazine pouches. Type II vests use a button-through flap to close the front which lacks any cover. In both the Type I and Type II vests a high collar, secured with velcro squares

UNITS: This vest has heretofore only been observed on paramilitary units fighting in Ossetia and the Nagorno-Karabakh autonomous oblast' (NKAO) in Georgia. During the conflict in Chechnia, some combat units of the Russian army were observe wearing both Type I and Type II vests.

TOP: Front of assault vest showing pocket arrangement and belt.

BOTTOM: Rear of vest showing rear pockets and cinched waist.

RUSSIAN ARMED FORCES – VSR
"SCHOFIELD" CAMOUFLAGE PATTERN
VARIATIONS IN HEADGEAR

L-R: Desert (garrison), Bright Desert (UVO MVD), Forest (Field)

VSR COLOR VARIATIONS

VSR CAMOUFLAGE HEADGEAR

YEAR ISSUED: 1991-1994

DESCRIPTION: The VSR camouflage uniform differed from woodland camouflage issues due to the creation of the system concept of uniform issue. Early woodland camouflage uniforms were issued only with field caps as accessories. The VSR "system" concept allowed for the production of berets, helmet covers, field caps, vests, and other accouterments. Later woodland issues were retrofitted with these items but it was the VSR and MVD issues that established the precedent.

RIGHT: Polevaia furazhka – field cap with mismatched brim (woodland/VSR mix).

BELOW LEFT: Titanium helmet with VSR cover.

BELOW RIGHT: Kamuflirovannyi beret – camouflage beret.

CAMOUFLAGE COMPARISON – VSR CAMOUFLAGE UNIFORMS

VSR (SCHOFIELD) CAMOUFLAGE
DESERT/MOUNTAIN COLORATION

VSR (SCHOFIELD) CAMOUFLAGE
FOREST COLORATION

VSR (SCHOFIELD) CAMOUFLAGE
BRIGHT COLORATION

VSR (SCHOFIELD) CAMOUFLAGE
BRIGHT COLORATION

MVD
Camouflage Uniforms

MVD CAMOUFLAGE UNIFORMS
SPETSNAZ KLMK CAMOUFLAGE VARIETIES

YEAR ISSUED: 1992-1993

DESCRIPTION: This uniform is issued in four color variations for use under diverse field environments.

This uniform is virtually identical to later versions of the two-piece *KLMK* uniforms in construction. Each jacket has four pockets on the front: two breast and two cargo pockets held closed by one and two buttons respectively – each of which is covered by a flap. Each sleeve has a single button-through pocket; the right side pocket being considerably narrower (possibly for pens). Several scrim tabs are present on the jacket in which can be inserted twigs or branches; four on the right breast, two on the left, and two each on the left and right side of the upper back.

The pants have smaller belt loops than on the two-piece *KLMK* which are too small for the standard Army field belt. Although cargo and magazine pockets are lacking, there is one right hip pocket, the type one would expect for carrying identification papers.

Despite the thinness of the material these appear to be stand alone uniforms and are worn with the blue striped *tel'niashka* T-shirt. The 23 July *Krasnaia zvezda* (Red Star) shows an officer assigned to the Brigade of Special Designation (BONVV) wearing the European-style pattern with a Woodland pattern field cap. Each uniform comes with a matching beret, large face mask, and hood which is fastened by two buttons on the collar of the jacket.

UNITS: These uniforms are used by the MVD's Brigades of Special Designation (BONVV).

TOP: Tropical Pattern.

BOTTOM: Factory markings from Saint Petersburg.

MVD CAMOUFLAGE UNIFORMS
SPECIAL CAMOUFLAGE UNIFORM – SMK

YEAR ISSUED: 1992

DESCRIPTION: Issued in both winter and summer versions, this *spetsial'nyi maskirovochnyi komplekt* (Special camouflage outfit – SMK) consists of a jacket with sewn-on hood and matching bib overalls. The uniform is constructed of nylon and lined with a cotton fabric.

Versions exist with and without large reflective patches on the uniform. When present, they are located on the sleeves, chest, back and hood; ostensibly they are for quick identification at night. Initially the interior of the uniform was lined with a white cotton material; in recent versions, however, this has been changed to black. There is also a matching field cap with a frontispiece for a cap device.

The summer version lacks the heavier lining and padding of the "sneg" or winter version. It retains the pocket locations and military markings (see section on civilian issues). The jacket possesses two chest and two cargo patch pockets, there may also be two open slash pockets at waist level. The bib overalls have a zippered front, two slash pockets, and are held up with suspenders using interlocking plastic connectors.

Three color schemes are produced for the military version: Forest, with olive, black, slightly edged with white, yellowish-green and dark green; Urban, with black, light grey, dark grey and white streaks, and Light Urban, with dark blue, light blue, grey and white streaks. The patterning in the latter is much more open and is significantly lighter than the other two patterns. MVD *Militsiia* and *spetsnaz* wear all three patterns operationally and are situationally dependent.[35]

UNITS: The sole users of this uniform are MVD *spetsnaz* units (*Vitiaz*), detachments of the Internal Troops assigned to the Dzerzhinsky division,[36] OMON detachments of the economic and organized crime units,[37] and counter-terrorist units of the Internal Troops directorate (GUKVV).[38] During the parliament standoff in October of 1993, several subunits of the Dzerzhinsky Division could be seen in both green and urban versions with matching assault vests and titanium riot helmets.[39]

TOP: Vew of nighttime five-color forest pattern with reflective patches and white lining.

BOTTOM: Front view of five-color forest pattern with dark lining. Worn as optional headgear with the SMK is the kolpak defensive helmet with visor in matching pattern.

**MVD CAMOUFLAGE UNIFORMS
KOLPAK SPECIAL OPERATIONS
DEFENSIVE HELMET**

YEAR ISSUED: 1992-1993

DESCRIPTION: *Kolpak* defensive helmets are made to accompany SMK special operations uniforms and are produced in three models: *Kolpak 1, Kolpak 1M* and *Kolpak 2.*

The *Kolpak 1*, and *Kolpak 1M* are made from high-impact plastic to withstand blows of a non ballistic type whereas the *Kolpak 2* is made of *Vinivlon* (ballistic kevlar) to resist small caliber bullet penetration. A matching camouflaged helmet cover is produced in the forest and urban versions for each helmet type.

The helmet has a foam interior that provides comfort to the wearer and reduces the chance of head injury from attacks. An adjustable, clear plastic visor permits wide vision yet affords limited eye protection from frontal assaults.

During assaults involving the use of CS gas or smoke, it is assumed that a protective mask would preclude the use of the visor. This is an obvious disadvantage of the helmet in riot situations.

UNITS: This helmet is issued to members of the Internal Troops Directorate of the MVD including OMON and *militsiia.*

Helmet Type	Weight (Kg) not considering lining	Level of Defense
Kolpak 1	0.8	Typical strikes
Kolpak 1M	1.0	Thrusts-stabbing strikes with non firing weapons
Kolpak 2	1.5	Dynamic influences of projectiles 9.2x18mmPM, traveling at 320 m/s.

Translation of data sheet accompanying helmet.

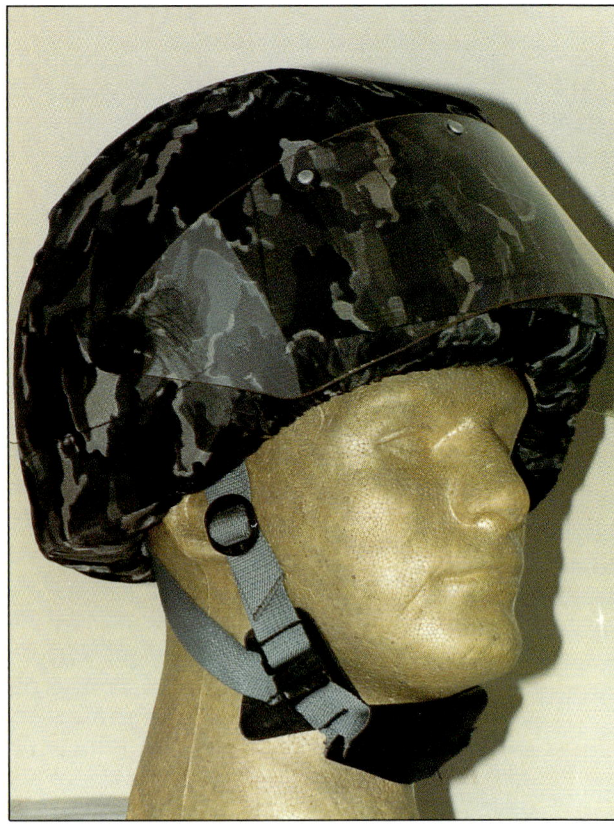

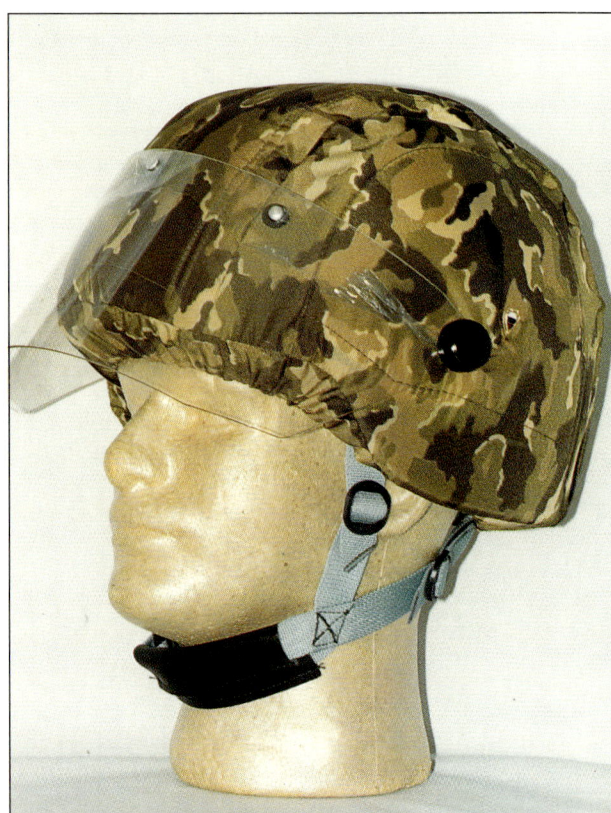

SMK CHARACTERISTICS

CHARACTERISTICS OF SMK JACKETS

ATTRIBUTES	TYPE I MVD SMK UNIFORM	TYPE II MVD SMK UNIFORM
LINING	white cotton	black cotton
WAIST	cinched waist, elastic	not cinched
FRONT CLOSURE	zippered with cover flap closed with velcro	plastic buttons w/covered flap closed by velcro top two and bottom buttons stamped metal
REFLECTIVE PATCHES	located on hood, sleeves, chest, and back	no reflective patches
CHEST POCKETS	large pocket on left side with cover flap, slot for pens attached to pocket front	two large pockets with button-through flaps, smali pocket attached to left front, velcro closure
CARGO POCKETS	two pockets with non-securing cover flaps	two double pockets: large pocket with button-through flaps, attached open slash pocket
SLEEVE POCKETS	none	small pocket on left side with button-through flap
ADDIT'L POCKETS	none	inside left of jacket with velcro closure

CHARACTERISTICS OF SMK TROUSERS

ATTRIBUTES	TYPE I MVD SMK UNIFORM	TYPE II MVD SMK UNIFORM
LINING	white	black
BACK POCKETS	two open back pockets (no flaps)	none
FRONT POCKETS	two slash open pockets at hip level	two open -slash pockets at hip level; two button-through w/velcro beneath slash pockets.
SIDE POCKETS	none	two button through pockets at hip level knife pocket right. side beneath; small pocket left side beneath with velcro closure
SUSPENDERS	secured with 2 piece interlocking connectors; slip through adjustment	tightened with one-piece open ring; slip through adjustment
WAIST	elastic	no waist adjustment
FRONT CLOSURE	zippered front without cover flap	button without cover flap

MVD CAMOUFLAGE UNIFORMS CIVILIAN VERSION

YEAR ISSUED: 1992-1993

DESCRIPTION: Issued in both winter and summer versions, this is the civilian version of the *SMK*.

The jacket is made of lightweight nylon and is lined with a colored plaid flannel material (winter) or is unlined (summer). There are two open slash pockets at chest level and two cargo patch pockets with covered flaps secured with velcro at about hip level. There are no sleeve pockets. A blue, black, red or green drawstring adjusts the waist fit of the jacket. There is an attached hood which can be tucked into the rear of the collar and secured with velcro. There is a high collar which also can be tightened with a colored drawstring. There is a zippered front covered by a flap and secured with velcro.

Inside the jacket are sewn swatches of nylon camo and flannel material, ostensibly for repair purposes. The size of the jacket is marked, in English, in sizes ranging from S to XL.

The pants are actually bib overalls with attached suspenders. The suspenders are padded and attach in the rear and secure in the front with two plastic, imported fasteners. The fasteners are marked in English with the word "Apri." Patch cargo pockets are present on the sides at thigh level. A larger front pocket is present on the bib and can be secured with a velcro strip. There is an elastic waistband and two nylon straps to tighten the overalls. They secure with the same imported plastic fasteners.

Three color schemes are produced: Forest, consisting of black edged with white, yellowish-green, olive and dark-green jagged streaks; Desert with brown, white, black and tan streaks; and Urban, with black, light grey, dark grey and white streaks.

UNITS: These are strictly civilian produced and are sold in Russian hunting stores to hunters and fishermen. However, it is possible for military personnel to purchase the uniforms to augment their uniform issue. See text for more details.

TOP: Green SMK showing hood.

BOTTOM: Urban SMK showing field cap.

MVD CAMOUFLAGE UNIFORMS
SMK CIVILIAN ACCESSORIES

Since the civilian SMK sets are designed for use in hunting and fishing, it seems logical that various accessories would be produced for the sportsman.

The shotgun vest is a lightweight nylon vest with numerous slots for shotgun shells and supplies. There is a large front pocket for storing game or food items as on the bib overalls of the hunting sets.

I photographed the brown field jacket in Saint Petersburg near Nevsky Prospekt in June of 1993. A two piece suit is also available in this color. Rucksacks and backpacks are available in all three colors and numerous styles.

RIGHT: SHOTGUN VEST

BELOW LEFT: SMALL RUCKSACK

BELOW RIGHT: BROWN FIELD JACKET

MVD CAMOUFLAGE UNIFORMS
SMK MILITARY ACCESSORIES

Military accessories are fewer but are better made and much more useful for tactical situations. These items are generally not available to the public.

The riot vest is a medium weight nylon vest with pouches for flares, grenades, rifle magazines and tactical supplies. Protective coverings on the shoulders are resistant to strikes with batons and incorporate metal plates. Several pouches and equipment slots are present for ammunition, flares, and a baton in the rear.

The assault vest is a lightweight tactical vest for carrying extra ammunition and supplies; several of the pouches possessing elastic loops for ammunition storage. On the left front of the vest is a holster pouch with strap for a makarov pistol. The rear of the vest has three large pouches for gear storage. Inside the vest is black cotton lining. The vest closes in front with a zipper.

RIGHT: RIOT VEST

BELOW LEFT: TACTICAL ASSAULT VEST

BELOW RIGHT: FIELD CAP

MVD CAMOUFLAGE UNIFORMS
MVD KKO TYPE I UNIFORM

YEAR ISSUED: 1992

DESCRIPTION: This uniform is designated as "*Komplekt kamuflirovannogo obmundirovannogo*" or camouflage uniform suit. It represents the first variant of the MVD's four-color combat uniforms. This uniform is very simple in contrast to the later Type II KKO issues.

It consists of five pieces (shirt, pants, hood, face mask, and beret) plus an optional assault vest. Two weights of material are available: a heavy cotton and a lightweight cotton mix depending on the region in which the uniform is used. As with most of the new uniform styles, this four-color pattern is based on the airborne khaki six-pocket uniform of Afghanistan. The uniform jacket, pants fly, and vest are closed with green or reddish-colored plastic buttons. Sleeve pockets are secured with velcro.

The Jacket and pants have elasticized cuffs. Furthermore, elastic bands attached to the cuffs help keep the pant legs tucked in the field boots.

The pattern consists of black "fingers" covering a green and oxblood background with cream-colored splotches. The black "fingers" are very similar in design to those found on American battle dress uniforms (BDU's); in fact, both designs could be confused with each other although the effect of the Russian uniform has a much tighter grouping of whorls.

On versions I've examined, the jacket, pants and vest were marked with "MVD" and the uniform size in black ink (the three group numbered size was used). The beret was marked only with "OTK" and a two digit size indicator. Civilian versions (usually lighter in weight and lacking all but the chest pockets) are unmarked.

UNITS: MVD internal BONVV[40] troops, MVD *spetsnaz* troops of the OSN ("Vitiaz"),[41] Saint Petersburg's organized crime unit,[42] and internal troops of the Moscow region (MOVV),[43] wear this uniform as their operational field camouflage.

TOP: Operational uniform with assault vest configured for members of MVD's OSN unit.

BOTTOM: Close up showing patch and tab worn by members of an MVD spetsnaz detachment (OSN).

MVD CAMOUFLAGE UNIFORMS
MVD KKO TYPE I ACCESSORIES

The accessories for the MVD KKO Type 1 uniform include an assault vest (above and below left) and beret (below right). The vest has several pockets on the front designed to hold grenades, magazines, flares, and radios. On the back of the vest at waist level are three large pouches which are secured by subdued (black) metal buttons. The vest can be tightened with cinch flaps (three on each side).

The beret is made of medium weight cotton, lacks a liner and a headband but has a small elastic band to provide a more secure fit.

MVD CAMOUFLAGE UNIFORMS
MVD KKO TYPE II UNIFORM – WOODLAND

YEAR ISSUED: 1992

DESCRIPTION: This is the second issue KKO camouflage uniform and is identical in construction to the MVD's PFO Tiger camouflage uniform.

This uniform can be found in summer and winter versions with a variety of accessories to include field caps and berets. Unlike other uniforms, this four-color pattern is not based on the airborne khaki six-pocket; rather, it is a variation of the grey and black *militsiia* uniforms currently in service.

The Jacket is unusual in its construction in that it lacks internal pockets and does not possess an internal holster. There are two breast pockets and a pocket on each sleeve; the pockets close with velcro squares. The front of the jacket closes with six oval, black plastic buttons with a cover flap over the button holes. On some variants there are two additional buttons on the neck at the base of the collar; these buttons may be used to attach a hood. The jacket's waist has an elastic band sewn into it with a short cloth strap which can be used to further tighten the jacket.

The pants are variable but generally are equipped with two open slash pockets at hip level, and two patch pockets sewn to the front at thigh level. There is one patch pocket on the rear left hip with a cover flap and velcro square. A magazine pouch pocket is located on the left side at thigh level. Buttons secure the fly and are of the same black plastic style. The belt loops are larger than standard types and appear to fit the military issue belts. There is a wide, elasticized waist band with double reinforcing. The seat and knees are also reinforced. The pants cuffs are elasticized. Jackets and pants are both marked with "MVD" and the uniform size in red ink

There are several color variations of this uniform: urban, with dark grey, and black "fingers" on a blue-grey and cream background; subdued forest with dark brown and chocolate brown "fingers" on a green and khaki background; and forest with reddish brown and black "fingers" on a forest green and yellow-green background. There are also be urban versions where the cream is replaced with olive green.

UNITS: This uniform is most commonly worn by combat units of the MVD's internal troops divisions.

TOP: Member of the MVD's spetsnaz unit (Vitiaz') of Internal Troops Division.

BOTTOM: Member of Main Guard's Administration, Saint Petersburg, Russia.

MVD CAMOUFLAGE UNIFORMS
MVD KKO TYPE II UNIFORM – WOODLAND VARIANTS

YEAR ISSUED: 1992

DESCRIPTION: These are the woodland variants of the KKO Type II uniforms issued in 1994 for use by the MVD's special operations forces. The pattern is identical to that of the MVD Woodland uniform but in two different colors.

As in the PFO tiger uniform, this uniform differs from the Army woodland patterns in both construction and camouflage pattern. However, as with the PFO, this uniform is issued as a four piece set: shirt, pants, field cap and assault vest. It is strictly an MVD issue item.

The pattern consists of three-color swirls on a light background. The forest version is comprised of green, purple/brown, and black swirls on a yellow-green background. The urban version consists of dark grey, blue-grey, and black on a light-grey background.

Each uniform is issued with a matching vest and field cap. Except for internal reinforcement and the presence of an extra AK magazine pouch on the upper right chest area, the vests are identical to those associated with MVD KKO Type I versions.

UNITS: The MVD appears to be the sole user of this uniform. Typically members of the Main Guard' Administration of the MVD and private security units such as Grom wear this as part of their standard issue uniform.

TOP: Forest coloration showing two-piece uniform and cap. Although used by several units of the MVD, this particular photo illustrates the standard configured for a member of the MVD's spetsnaz unit of Internal troops – OSN.

BOTTOM: Urban coloration with assault vest. While the cap is standard issue, regional OMON units and spetsnaz units may opt to use the standard issue grey beret or a matching camouflage beret. This photo shows the configuration for a member of the MVD's Main Administration Counter-Organized crime unit – RUOP.

MVD CAMOUFLAGE UNIFORMS
VITIAZ' PFO TIGER PATTERN

YEAR ISSUED: 1993-1994

DESCRIPTION: The tiger pattern was referred to in a recent article in *Stolitsa* as a "...spotted violet uniform" (*Piatnisto-fioletovoe obmundirovanie*).[44] Therefore, until a more concrete designation is found, the above descriptive title will be used.

The PFO tiger pattern represents a departure from other heavy weight uniforms in both construction and pattern. The uniform is issued as a four piece set: shirt, pants, field cap and assault vest.

The jacket consists of four pockets: two chest, and two sleeve, all secured with velcro patches. There is an internal, nylon pocket on the left side, secured with a button-through flap. On most shirts a swatch of cloth with an attached button, is sewn to the inside of the jacket. The jacket can be tightened with an elasticized cinch strap which buttons internally at the waist. Six plastic buttons, buttoning through the front and covered by a flap, secure the front of the jacket.

Durable cotton pants are designed for combat operations. Patch pockets, secured by velcro, are located one each on the front thighs, one on the right seat, and a specially designed twin-pocket on the left hip. The narrow width of the pockets indicate use for flares, narrow flashlights, or truncheons. Additionally, there is a special knife pocket, secured with a flap and metal snaps, located on the right hip. Two slash pockets, one on each hip, complete the pocket arrangement. The waist has a 7 cm thick elasticized waistband, with belt loops configured for the army belt. Reinforced knees with protective lining provide limited protection; the reinforcing can be removed by opening velcro closures. A heavy lining sewn into each pants leg tucks into the combat boots, allowing the cuffs to be bloused and tied.

The pattern consists of tri-color jagged, horizontal splotches on a light background. Both forest and urban variations exist: green, purple/brown, and black on a yellow-green background; and dark grey, blue-grey, and black on a light-grey background, respectively.

UNITS: The sole user of this uniform is the OSN (*otriad spetsial'nogo naznacheniia*) of ODON of the MVD, also known *as Vitiaz'*.

TOP: Forest coloration with assault vest and cap.

BOTTOM: Urban coloration with assault vest and issue mask.

MVD CAMOUFLAGE UNIFORMS
MVD KKO TYPE II UNIFORM – ASSAULT VEST

TOP: This photo shows the standard non-ballistic assault vest issued as part of the MVD PFO tiger pattern uniform. It is constructed of 100%, heavy weight cotton with full color patterning on both sides.

Pocket arrangement includes three AK-74 magazine pockets: one on the upper right chest, and one each on the left and right side at waist level. Between the two right side AK pouches are two grenade pouches. On the upper left side is a small pouch (closed by velcro only). Immediately beneath this pouch is an oblong pouch, suitable for flares or truncheons; it secures with velcro. A pistol holster, suitable for a makarov 9mm is located just below this pouch on the left side; this pouch closes with a strap which wraps around the trigger and closes with a metal snap and velcro. Just below the pistol pouch is a medium sized grenade pouch, also closed by velcro. The left side AK pouch is located under the grenade pouch. All pouches, except those specifically noted, close using subdued metal snaps.

BOTTOM: On the rear of the vest are located three rather large equipment pouches, each of which closes with metal snaps. The center pouch is the largest of the three (8 1/2 x 7 inches). The bottom of the vest secures with a black nylon strap with a metal slip fastener.

MVD CAMOUFLAGE UNIFORMS
MVD KKO TYPE II UNIFORM
HEADGEAR

YEAR ISSUED: 1993-1994

DESCRIPTION: These photos show various types of headgear adopted for use with the MVD combat and KKO special operations uniforms. Although most uniforms are issued with the field *furazhka* as standard, berets may also be issued or purchased separately. Cap devices vary with Soviet, Russian military, and MVD and OMON cap devices being issued depending on the unit. On some later berets, a metal or cloth beret flash representing the Russian tricolor are sewn on the wearer's left side (standard) or on the right for parades.

RIGHT: Green PFO pattern field furazhka issued to Vitiaz' members.

BELOW LEFT: OMON field furazhka in urban woodland coloration.

BELOW RIGHT: Camouflaged beret in urban variant.

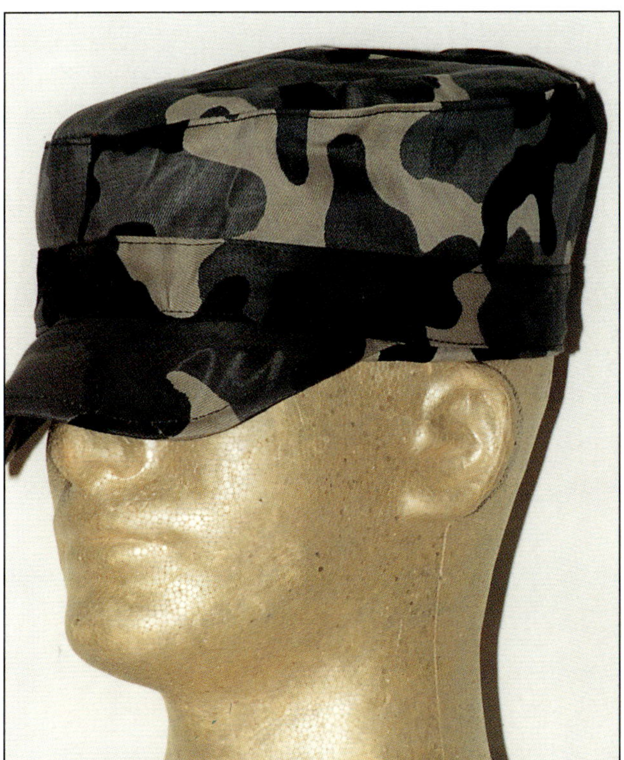

MVD CAMOUFLAGE UNIFORMS
REED PATTERN UNIFORM

YEAR ISSUED: 1995-1996

DESCRIPTION: Newest of the MVD issues, the *kamyshovy risunok* or reed pattern uniform, is a tropical uniform issued to MVD combat units fighting in the Chechen conflict.

The weight of the shirt and pants are very light, affording limited protection, but being significantly more comfortable in warmer climates. The shirt has two patch pockets located at chest level, and the front closes with seven buttons, much like the older mundir shirts where there are five buttons up the front and two closer together at the neck. The back of the shirt is pleated and is made to be tucked into the pants.

All of the buttons are clearly marked with the letters MVD in Cyrillic and bear the manufacturers marks of the LSMT factory in Saint Petersburg, Russia.

The pants are made of the same lightweight cotton material. There are two slash pockets in front and two patch pockets in the rear. The front closes with a single button and zippered front. Belt loops are present which facilitate a standard army-type belt. There are no cuff straps or buttons and it appears the trouser legs may be worn in either a bloused or un-bloused fashion.

This uniform is issued in both forest and urban versions. The forest version consists of green splotches on a light-yellow or tan background with sharper, narrower brown reeds running diagonally and vertically throughout. The urban version consists of dark grey blotches on a light grey background with black reeding.

UNITS: This uniform, while designed for and worn by MVD combat units, has also seen duty with various infantry and support units of the Russian Army. Commander of the combined forces in Chechnia can also be seen wearing this pattern on the cover of the December, 1996 issue of *Orientir*. This has become a standard issue uniform for the RUOP and *Opnaz* forces of the MVD.

TOP: Standard configuration for a MVD combat troop in Chechnia.

BOTTOM: Member of RUOP assigned to the Moscow district, headgear type is unit-dependent.

MVD CAMOUFLAGE UNIFORMS
REED PATTERN ACCESSORIES

YEAR ISSUED: 1995-1996

These are two of the optional accessories issued with the MVD reed pattern uniform – a tactical assault vest with backpack, and a sniper cap.

TOP: The tactical assault vest is far more advanced in design than previous issues, incorporating black webbing and double-stack magazine pouches. Constructed as a harness type of assault vest, it is well suited for hot climates and provides greater mobility. Four double-stack magazine pouches (one in front and one immediately behind), allows the wearer to carry considerable amounts of extra ammunition. Each pouch is held closed with a large velcro patch attached to a wide web strap.

Attached to the rear of the vest, set at mid-back level, is a water-resistant knapsack. Secured with a zipper top, the knapsack is suitable for carrying small items and an additional uniform. It has a smaller compartment readily accessible through a flap secured with velcro.

The entire vest is adjustable through a series of wide web straps with cinches and buckles. Due to the open, lightweight construction of the vest, it is very suitable for both temperate and tropical climates.

BOTTOM: The sniper cap is made of a water resistant material and provides the wearer with both protection from the sun and added concealment in tactical situations.

Similar in construction to "panama" style caps of previous years, the reed pattern sniper cap has several improvements. A band around the cap secures the face netting which attaches via button-through slots in the band. These same buttons also serve to secure the netting in a up and away from the face when not needed. The netting is simply rolled up and buttoned down through the flap.

The interior of the cap is lined with nylon fabric which apparently serves to wick away moisture from the wearer's head, providing an additional measure of cooling through the vest holes around the crown of the cap.

The material of the cap may also undergo some chemical treatment to reduce the infrared and reflected light signatures.

CAMOUFLAGE COMPARISON – MVD CAMOUFLAGE UNIFORMS

MVD SPETSNAZ CAMOUFLAGE
TROPICAL COLORATION

MVD SPETSNAZ CAMOUFLAGE
MOUNTAIN COLORATION

MVD SPETSNAZ CAMOUFLAGE
DESERT COLORATION

MVD SPETSNAZ CAMOUFLAGE
EUROPEAN COLORATION

CAMOUFLAGE COMPARISON – MVD CAMOUFLAGE UNIFORMS

MVD CAMOUFLAGE
GREEN SMK COLORATION

MVD CAMOUFLAGE
DARK URBAN SMK COLORATION

MVD CAMOUFLAGE
LIGHT URBAN SMK COLORATION

CAMOUFLAGE COMPARISON – MVD CAMOUFLAGE UNIFORMS

MVD KKO CAMOUFLAGE
TYPE I FOREST COLORATION

MVD KKO CAMOUFLAGE
TYPE II URBAN COLORATION

MVD KKO CAMOUFLAGE
TY II SUBDUED FOREST COLORATION

MVD KKO CAMOUFLAGE
TY II FOREST COLORATION

CAMOUFLAGE COMPARISON – MVD CAMOUFLAGE UNIFORMS

MVD PFO TIGER CAMOUFLAGE
FOREST COLORATION

MVD PFO TIGER CAMOUFLAGE
URBAN COLORATION

MVD PFO TIGER CAMOUFLAGE
COLOR VARIATION

MVD CAMOUFLAGE
LT GRAY, BLUE GRAY, OLIVE AND BLACK

CAMOUFLAGE COMPARISON – U.S. AND FOREIGN UNIFORMS

UNITED STATES CAMOUFLAGE
BATTLE DRESS UNIFORM (BDU)

UNITED STATES CAMOUFLAGE
DESERT "CHOCOLATE CHIP" PATTERN

UNITED STATES
URBAN BDU PATTERN

UNITED KINGDOM
DISRUPTIVE PATTERN, MILITARY (DPM)

ENDNOTES ILLUSTRATION SECTION

[1] *Krasnoznamennyi pribaltiiskii pogranichnyi* (Red Banner Pribaltic Border guards),

[2] Despite claims by D. J. Borsarello in *Camouflaged Uniforms of the Warsaw Pact & Non Aligned Forces*, (Kent: Galago Publishing Ltd., 1989), p. 14, this uniform does not appear to be reversible. Rather, dye penetration and bleeding indicate the fabric is screen dyed on a tan/yellow colored material; true reversible uniforms are usually dyed on both sides. Additionally, this uniform's button placement and stitching seem to prohibit reverse wear.

[3] *Granitsa rozhdaet geroev* (The border spawns heroes), Moscow, 1976.

[4] Ministry of State Security until 1953, later, the KGB.

[5] V. Sukhodol'skii. *Soldaty rodiny moei* (Soldiers of my motherland). (Moscow: DOSAAF USSR, 1982.)

[6] *Granitsa na zamke*, edited by V. Taborko and M. Lavrik, TsK VLKSM Molodaia Gvardiia, Moscow 1969, p. 141.

[7] Schofield, p. 94-95.

[8] Krasnaia zvezda (Red Star), Wednesday, 18 August 1993, p187,

[9] Schofield, p. 181.

[10] *Na boevom postu*, cover, 5/91.

[11] N. Timofeev, "Operatsiia nabat", (Operation alarm), *Sluzhba bezopasnosti* (Security service), 3/93, pp. 8- 9.

[12] Aleshin, Andrei. "Kto streliaet v spinu?" (Who shoots people in the back?). *Sluzhba bezopasnosti*. 2/93, inside cover.

[13] *Voenniye znaniia*, cover, 9-10/92.

[14] *Na boevom postu*, January 1993, p. 9.

[15] V. Bezrukov. "Sluzhba s riskom dlia zhizni" (Service with a risk for life), *Voennye znaniia* (Military knowledge). Number 11, 1989, pp. 12-13.

[16] Prikhno, I. I., Colonel and Captain A. V. Nekrakha, Pravila nosheniia voennoi formy odezhdy (Regulations for the wearing of military uniforms), (Moscow: Voennoe Izdatel'stvo, 1989), p.173.

[17] Artyom Borovik. *The Hidden War*. (New York: Atlantic Monthly Press, 1990). Opposite p 179; Mark Buser and Gail Broadhead, translators, *Afghanistan weighs heavy on my heart*.(New Dehli: Progress Publishers, 1992), 6th photo plate.

[18] N.V. Danilenkov, ed. Pravila nosheniia voennoi formy odezhdy (Regulations for the wear of military service uniforms). (Moscow: Military Press, 1989). pp. 145, 173.

[19] Vladimir Svartsevich. "White House Model Remains Undiscovered: How musketeers of the Speaker of the Parliament searched for a secret training base of President's guards." *Nezavisimaia gazeta* (Independent Gazette), 6-7 September 1993, p. 10.

[20] Vladimir, Zhitarenko, Colonel. "Tsveta beretov 14-i armii" (Color of the berets of the 14th Army). *Krasnaia zvezda* (Red Star). 16 January 1993, pp. 1-2.

[21] J.F.O. Mc Allister, "Next, friendly persuasion," *Time*, 7 March 1994.

[22] Cover photo, *Jane's Defence Weekly*. Volume 18, Number 15, 10 October 1992; "Risking only themselves,"*Krasnaia zvezda*, (Red Star) 13 July 1993, p. 1.

[23] Artyom Borovik. *The Hidden War*. (New York: Atlantic Monthly Press, 1990). Opposite p 179; Mark Buser and Gail Broadhead, translators, *Afghanistan weighs heavy on my heart*.(New Dehli: Progress Publishers, 1992), 6th photo plate.

[24] Oleg Matiatin, "Nas lishaiut budushchego," (We are deprived of our future), *Pravda*, May 30, 1992, p. 1.

[25] Serge Schmemann, "Army ousts Yeltsin foes from Parliament; president takes steps to solidify power," New York Times, 5 October 1993, p1.

[26] August 6-9, 1992, p. 3.

[27] Raymond Bonner, "War in Caucasus Shows Ethnic Hate's Front Line," *The New York Times International*, August 2, 1993, p. (A) 4.

[28] Ivan Ivaniuk. O novoi veonnoi forme bez slovesnogo "kamufliazha." (About the new military uniform without verbal camouflage), *Krasnaia zvezda* (Red star), 27 July 1993, p. 2.

[29] Fred Coleman, "For the Russian bear, one last hurrah," U.S. News and World Report, 7 March 1994, p. 10-11.

[30] *Novosti*, 7 October 1994.

[31] Ibid.

[32] Personal observation, June 1993.

[33] Ibid.

[34] CNN coverage showed many units wearing this particular camouflage. In Anthony Suau's "Red October," (Time, October 18, 1993, pp62-63) the uniform is shown alongside Woodland patterns indicating complete fielding of the uniform has yet to be achieved.

[35] J.F.O. Mc Allister and William Mader, "Now who rules Russia?" *Time*, 4 October 1993, p. 45.

[36] "Krapovyi berety-vruchaiut ne kazhdomy" (Mottled berets-they're not entrusted to just anyone). *Krasnaia zvezda*, September 15, 1993, cover.

[37] Polkovnik Vladimir Zhitarenko, "Trinadtsat' zhivyk vliuchaia rasstreliannykh" (Thirteen survivors including those executed). *Krasnaia zvezda* (Red Star), 19 January 1993, p. 2.

[38] *Krasnaia zvezda* (Red Star), 5 June 1993, p. 1.

[39] *Na boevom postu*, January 1993, p. 9.

[40] Na boevom postu (At the combat post), 11-12, 1992, inside front cover.

[41] Krasnaia Zvezda (Red Star), 9 October 1993, p. 1; *Novosti*, September 24, 1993.

[42] Personal observation, June 1993, Saint Petersburg, Russia.

[43] Krasnaia Zvezda (Red Star), 5 June, 1993, p. 1.

[44] Vladimir Voronov, "Strana Spetsnaza" [A country of Spetsnaz], *Stolitsa*, Number 8 (170), 1994, pp. 9-12.

GLOSSARY

RUSSIAN	TRANSLITERATION	TRANSLATION
берет	beret	Beret
белье теплое	bel'e teploe	Winter underwear
ботинки	botinki	Boots - lace up[4]
-парадно-выходние	-paradno-vykhodnie	-parade/walking out
-юфтевые повседневные	-iuftevye povsednevnye	-leather everyday wear
брюки	briuki	Pants
галстук	galstuk	Tie
эмблема	emblema	Emblem
камуфлированный летный маскировочный комбинезон	kamuflirovannyi letnyi maskirovochnyi kombinezon	Camouflage summer deceptive overalls
камуфлированный комплект	kamuflirovannyi komplekt	Camouflage outfit/set
канти	kanti	Edging/piping
китель	kitel'	Tunic
кокарда	kokarda	Cockade/Cap device
комплект защитного цвета	komplekt zashchitnogo tsveta	Protective uniform (set)[5]
комплект камуфлированного обмундированного	komplekt kamuflirovannogo obmundirovannogo	Camouflage uniform set
костюм рабочий	kostium rabochii	Work suit
-чёрного цвета	-chernogo tsveta	-dark colored
-защитного цвета	-zashchitnogo tsveta	-protective colored
котелок	kotelok	Mess tin
куртка	kurtka	Jacket
лампасы	kampasy	Stripes
майка	maika	T-shirt (underwear)
мешок вещевой	meshok veshevoi	Ditty bag[6]
мундир	mundir	uniform dress coat
нашивка	nashivka	Chevron or scrim tab
нарукавный знак	narukavnyi znak	Shoulder patch
носки	noski	Socks
панама	panama	Panama hat/Boonie hat[7]
перчатки	perchatki	Gloves
петлицы	petlitsy	Collar tabs
пилотка	pilotka	Side cap/Overseas cap
платки - носовые	platki-nosovye	Nose handkerchief
плащ палатка	plashch palatka	Shelter half/Raincoat
плащ пальто	plashch pal'to	Shelter half/Overcoat
погоны	pogony	Shoulderboards
подворотнички	podvorotnichki	Detachable collar lining
полевое снаряжение	polevoe snariazhenie	Field equipment
полушубок	polushubok	Short sheepskin coat
портянки летние	portianki letnie	Summer foot wraps
ремень	remen'	Belt
-брючный	-briuchnyi	-pants
-поясной	-poiasnoi	-waist belt
-поясной, бел. цвета	-poiasnoi, bel. tsveta	-waist belt, white
рубахи верхние к мундиру	rubakhi verkhine k mundiry	Outer shirts for the Dress Coat
рукавицы меховые	rukavitsi mekhovye	Fur mittens
сапоги	sapogi	Boots - no laces/slipover
специальный маскировочный комплект	spetsial'nyi maskirovochnyi komplekt	Special deceptive/camouflage suit
специальная одежда (спецодежда)	spetsial'naia odezhda (spetsodezhda)	special-purpose uniform (*spetsnaz* uniform)
сумка полевая	sumka polevaia	Field bag
тельняшка	tel'niashka	T-shirt, usu. airborne[8]
телогрейка	telogreika	Field jacket - padded
тужирка	tuzhirka	Double-breasted jacket
трицветний комклект	tritsvetnii komplekt	Three color uniform set
-трёхцвет комплект	-trekhtsvet komplekt	-tricolor set
фляга с чехлом	fliaga s chekhlom	Water bottle/Canteen
форма одежды	forma odezhda	Order of Dress
-вне строя	-vne stroia	-out of formation
-для строя	-dlia stroia	-for formation
-полевая	-polevaia	-field
-камуфлированного цвета	-kamuflirovannogo tsveta	-camouflage color
фуражка	furazhka	Peaked/Visor cap
-полевая	-polevaia	-field
-парадная	-paradnaia	-parade
-рабочая	-rabochaia	-work, fatigue dress
фуфайка	fufaika	Sweater[9]
шаровары	sharovary	Pants, usu. loose fitting
шапка ушанка	shapka ushanka	Winter cap[10]
шинель	shinel'	Heavy overcoat
шлем	shlem	Helmet
-стальный	-stal'nyi	-Steel helmet

BIBLIOGRAPHY

Akhromeev, S. F. ed. *Voennyi entsiklopedicheskii slovar'* [Military Enclyclopedic Dictionary]. Moscow: Military Press, 1986.

Aksenov, Oleg and Valerii Kulik, "Riskovie liudi" (Risky people), *Sovetskaiia Militsiia*, January 1991: 1-6.

Andreyev, I. Interview with Victor Pugo, Minister of Internal Affairs, *Izvestiia*, January 23, 1991, as reported by *FBIS-SOV-91-015*. January 23, 1991.

Ardashev, Aleksei and Liudmila Shchekotova. "Snariazhenie Britanskikh Spetschastei," *Tekhnika Molodezhi*. Moscow: Argumenty i fakty, 1994.

Bakatin, Vadim V. Interview with KGB Chief V. V. Bakatin by V. Filin in *Komsomolskaia Pravda* as translated by *FBIS-SOV-91-206* on October 24, 1991.

Viktor Barranikov. Interview with Internal Affairs Minister Viktor Barranikov by Vladimir Gondusov of *TASS*, as translated by *FBIS-SOV-91-215*, November 6, 1991: 17.

Beaumont, Roger. *Maskirovka: Soviet Camouflage, Concealment and Deception.* College Station, TX: Center for Strategic Technology, the Texas Engineering Experiment Station of The Texas A&M University, 1982.

Behrens, Roy. *Art and Camouflage.* Cedar Falls, IA: North American Review, UNI.

Beketov, A. A., Belokon', A. P. and S. G. Chermashentsev, *Maskirovka, deistvii podrazdelenii sukhoputnikh voisk* [Camouflage of actions of ground force subunits]. Moscow: Order of Labor of the Red Banner Military Press of the Ministry of Defense USSR, 1976.

Bellamy, Christopher "Troops and Parliament in Showdown; Yeltsin orders disarming of guards in Parliament as Russia and eight other CIS States form an economic union," *The Independent*, September 25, 1993.

Belikov, I. G., I. K. Boiko and M. S. Logunov. *Imeni Dzerzhinskogo,* [In the Name of Dzerzhinsky], Moscow: 1976.

Belykh, Vadim. Crime continues to rise in Russia, but a little more slowly. *Izvestiia*. July 21, 1993, p. 2. Condensed text translated by *The Current Digest*, vol 45, No. 29, August 18, 1993, p. 25.

Oleg Byurov. Interview with Head of Department for Combatting Organized Crime, Oleg Byurov by Lev Fisher of *Sovetskaia Militsiia*, March 1991, pp. 2-5.

Conquest, Robert. *The Soviet Police System.* London: The Bodley Head, 1968.

Department of the Army, *FM 100-2-3, The Soviet Army.* Washington, D.C.: U.S. Government Printing Office, 1991.

Deriabin, Peter. *Watchdogs of Terror.* University Publications of America, 1984.

—. and T. H. Bagley. *KGB, Masters of the Soviet Union,* New York: Hippocrene Books, 1990.

Dorenko, Sergei "Bakatin interviewed on reorganization of KGB," Russian Television, August 29, 1991. Translated and reported by The British Broadcasting Corporation, September 2, 1991.

Dunayev, Andrey. Report from *INTERFAX* as translated by *FBIS-SOV-91-188,* September 27, 1991.

Dziak, John J. *Chekisty: A History of the KGB,* New York: Ivy Books, 1988.

V. D. Egorov. Interview with Commander GUVD V. D. Egorov by unknown interviewer in *Na Boevom Postu,* [At the Combat Post] July 1990.

Fedorova, Sergei. "*spetsnaz*: There will not be a new Karabakh in Northern Ossetia."*Krasnaia Zvezda,* [Red Star], June23, 1992 [in Russian].

Fuller,William C. *The Internal Troops of the MVD SSSR.* College Station, TX: 1983.

Galustian, Oksian. "The Defenseless Militiaman: the State is not Protecting the Lives, Health, Honor and Dignity of the Staff Members of the Internal Affairs Organs." *Nezavisimaia Gazeta*, May 6, 1993, p. 2. Text translated by *FBIS-USR-93-071*, June 9, 1993, p. 28-29.

Glinka, V. M. *Russki voennyi kostium, 18 – nachala 20 veka* [The Russian military uniform, the 18th to the beginning of the 20th century]. Leningrad: Khudozhnik RSFSR, 1988.

Golov, Aleksandr. All Russian Center for the Study of Public Opinion: "Crime and Security in the Mass Consciousness." *Izvestiia*, July 23, 1993, First Ed., p. 4. Text translated by *FBIS-USR-93-104*, August 9, 1993, p. 19.

Gorbunova, Nataliia. "Nad chem smeemsia," [At what are we laughing]. *Sputnik – Digest of the Soviet Press.* June 1991.

Gorlov, A. *V karaule bessonnom*, [On Guard Without Sleep]. Moscow: Molodaiia gvardia, 1984.

Grienko, Aleksandr. Interview with Head of Political Directorate of the MVD USSR Major General Aleksandr Grienko by Igor Aramov of *TASS,* as translated by *FBIS-SOV-90-114,* June 13, 1990.

A. Gurov. Television report by Aleksandr Gurov, Head of the 6th Administration of the MVD USSR as translated by *FBIS-SOV 91-136,* July 16, 1991, p. 68.

Guzhvin, P.F. The Development of Economic Reforms in the Russian Federation [January-March 1993], pp. 1-

91. Text translated by *FBIS-USR-93-103,* August 11, 1993, pp. 1- 13.

Gwertzman, Bernard and Michael Kaufman, eds. *The Decline and Fall of the Soviet Empire.* New York: New York Times Company, 1992.

Hartcup, Guy. *Camouflage, A History of Concealment and Deception in War.* New York: Charles Scribner and Sons, 1980.

Hiatt, Fred. "Moscow: a Judicial System That Doesn't Work," *The Washington Post,* November 15-21, 1993, p. 7.

Hill, Elizabeth. *Russian-English Military Dictionary.* [London: Her Majesty's Stationary Office].

Hingley, Ronald *The Russian Secret Police.* New York: Dorset Press, 1970.

ITAR-TASS news agency, "Stepashin made deputy head of new counterintelligence service," Moscow, December 21, 1993. Translated by The British Broadcasting Corporation, December 23, 1993.

Ivan Ivaniuk, "*O novoi voennoi forme bez slovesnogo kamufliazha,*" [About the Military Uniform Without the Verbal Camouflage], *Krasnaia zvezda,* July 27, 1993.

Karpov, B. "Kavkaztsi," [Caucasians]. *Na boevom postu, Zhurnal vnutrennikh voisk,* May-June 1993.

Karpov, B. "You Can't Get ALong Without Internal Troops." *Krasnaia zvezda,* June 30, 1992, p. 2.

G. Kazimir. Interview with Director of special sections of the KGB G. Kazimir by unknown correspondent. *Na Boevom Postu,* Auggust 1990.

Klebnikov, Peter. "Visitors' corruption driving up Russian crime rate." *We/My,* April 5- 18, 1993, p. 3.

Knight, Amy W. *The KGB.* Boston: Unwin Hyman, 1990.

Kositsyn, A. P. *Sovetskaia Militsiia: Istoriia i sovremennost' 1917/1987.* [Soviet Militsiia: History and Contemporary 1917/1987] Moscow: Iuridicheskaia Literatura, 1987.

Lenisov, V. V., L. P. Mikhailyuk, S. S. Pylev, and E. I. Spiridonov. *Sovetskaia Militsiia 1917-1987.* Moscow: Planeta 1987.

John Lepingwell, "Russian Army on the Offensive," *RFE/RL Daily Report,* October 4, 1993.

L. M. "*spetsnaz* save us form our Misfortune."*Voennye znaniia,* [Military Knowledge]. January 1992.

Lodder, Christina. *Russian Constructivism.* New Haven, CT: Yale University Press, 1983.

Marnie, Sheila and Albert Motivans, "Rising Crime Rates: Perceptions and Reality," *RFE/RL Research Report,* vol. 2, no. 20., May 14, 1993.

Matsulenko, V. A. *Operational Camouflage of the Troops.* Moscow: Order of Labor of the Red Banner Military Press of the Ministry of Defense, USSR, 1975.

Mollo, Andrew. *The Armed Forces of World War II.* New York: Crown Publishers, 1981.

—. *Red Army Uniforms of World War II.* London: Winrow & Greene, 1993.

Mollo, McGregor, Smith and Chappell. *World Army Uniforms Since 1939.* Poole, England: Blandford Press, 1981.

F. I. Myshak. *Maskirovka soldata, oruzhiia, i boevoi tekhniki* [Camouflage of soldiers, weapons and combat equipment]. Moscow: Voennoe izdatel'stvo, Ministerstvo oborony, 1954.

Neliubin, L. L. *Illustranyi voenno-tekhnicheskii slovar',* [Illustrated Military-Technical Dictionary]. Moscow: Order of Labor of the Red Banner Military Press of the Ministry of Defense of the USSR, 1968.

Orenstein, Harold S. *Crime and Punishment: Old Problems and New Dilemmas for an Emerging Eastern and Central Europe.* Fort Leavenworth, KS: European Military Studies Office 1992.

Parrish, Michael. *Soviet Security and Intelligence Organizations 1917 – 1990.* New York: Greenwood Press, 1992.

Petrov, Aleksei. " 'Zaslon-93' ChP ne zastanet vrasplokh," [Barrier '93 – the Emergency Situation Will Not Catch Them Unawares]. *Krasnaia zvezda,* June 4, 1993.

Polubinskiy, V. Znakom'tes': MUR. *Dokumental'naia povest' o liudiakh i deliax moskovskogo ugolovnogo pozyska.* [Get acquainted with MUR. Documentary story about the people and activities of the Moscow Criminal Investigation]. Moscow: Moskva izdatel'stvo DOSAAF, 1988.

Podgotovka snaiperov, [Training of Snipers]. Moscow: Voennoe izdatel'stvo, 1987.

Pravila nosheniia formy odezhdy militsii [Correct wear of the duty uniform of the *militsiia*], Moscow, 1978.

Riasanovsky, Nicholas V. *A History of Russia.* New York: Oxford University Press, 1977.

Raymond E. Zickel, ed. *The Soviet Union, a Country Study,* DA PAM 550-95. Wash. D.C.: Library of Congress, 1989.

Rottman, Gordon L. *Warsaw Pact Ground Forces.* London: Osprey Publishing, 1987.

Schofield, Carey. *Inside the Soviet Military.* New York: Abbeville Press, 1991.

—. *The Russian Elite: Inside Spetsnaz and the Airborne Forces.* London: Greenhill Books, 1993.